T0190433

Advanced Arduino Techniques in Science

Refine Your Skills and Projects with PCs or Python-Tkinter

Richard J. Smythe

Apress®

Advanced Arduino Techniques in Science: Refine Your Skills and Projects with PCs or Python-Tkinter

Richard J. Smythe
Wainfleet, ON, Canada

ISBN-13 (pbk): 978-1-4842-6786-8   ISBN-13 (electronic): 978-1-4842-6784-4
https://doi.org/10.1007/978-1-4842-6784-4

Copyright © 2021 by Richard J. Smythe

This work is subject to copyright. All rights are reserved by the publisher, whether the whole or part of the material is concerned, specifically the rights of translation, reprinting, reuse of illustrations, recitation, broadcasting, reproduction on microfilms or in any other physical way, and transmission or information storage and retrieval, electronic adaptation, computer software, or by similar or dissimilar methodology now known or hereafter developed.

Trademarked names, logos, and images may appear in this book. Rather than use a trademark symbol with every occurrence of a trademarked name, logo, or image we use the names, logos, and images only in an editorial fashion and to the benefit of the trademark owner, with no intention of infringement of the trademark.

The use in this publication of trade names, trademarks, service marks, and similar terms, even if they are not identified as such, is not to be taken as an expression of opinion as to whether or not they are subject to proprietary rights.

While the advice and information in this book are believed to be true and accurate at the date of publication, neither the authors nor the editors nor the publisher can accept any legal responsibility for any errors or omissions that may be made. The publisher makes no warranty, express or implied, with respect to the material contained herein.

Managing Director, Apress Media LLC: Welmoed Spahr
Acquisitions Editor: Natalie Pao
Development Editor: James Markham
Coordinating Editor: Jessica Vakili

Distributed to the book trade worldwide by Springer Science + Business Media New York, 1 NY Plaza, New York, NY 10014. Phone 1-800-SPRINGER, fax (201) 348-4505, email orders-ny@ springer-sbm.com, or visit www.springeronline.com. Apress Media, LLC is a California LLC and the sole member (owner) is Springer Science + Business Media Finance Inc (SSBM Finance Inc). SSBM Finance Inc is a **Delaware** corporation.

For information on translations, please e-mail booktranslations@springernature.com; for reprint, paperback, or audio rights, please e-mail bookpermissions@springernature.com.

Apress titles may be purchased in bulk for academic, corporate, or promotional use. eBook versions and licenses are also available for most titles. For more information, reference our Print and eBook Bulk Sales web page at http://www.apress.com/bulk-sales.

Any source code or other supplementary material referenced by the author in this book is available to readers on GitHub via the book's product page, located at www.apress.com/ 978-1-4842-6786-8. For more detailed information, please visit http://www.apress.com/ source-code.

Printed on acid-free paper

Table of Contents

About the Author vii

About the Technical Reviewer ix

Acknowledgements xi

The Author's Preface to *Arduino Advanced Techniques in Science*...xiii

Roadmap to the Exercises in *Advanced Arduino
Techniques in Science* xxi

Chapter 1: Arduino and Raspberry Pi 1

    Arduino...1

    Raspberry Pi..5

    Raspberry Pi Arduino Combinations......................................14

    Interfacing Arduino – C with Python and the Matplotlib
    Plotting Programs 16

    Arduino Interrupts and Timing Applications 20

    Code Listings 26

    Summary..31

Chapter 2: Development of a Simplified Python Supervisory
Control and Data Acquisition System 33

    Program 1: Display Frame..36

    Program 2: Display of Changing Data in Realtime 38

    Program 3: Activation of Experimental Devices from Button
    Displays...45

        Program 4: A Sliding-Scale Implementation...........................49

Program 5: Radio Button Controls..53

Program 6: Graphical Data Display—A Realtime Strip-Chart Recording............59

Summary...69

Chapter 3: Experimental Work at High Temperatures and High Heats 71

Safety Considerations 72

Experimental 81

    Simple Measurement of Elevated Temperatures.................................81

    Dry Wells...82

    Resistance-Wire Heating...85

    Powering Heating Elements 89

    Solid-State Relays (SSR) 93

    Refractory Insulation 98

    Observations...103

    Failures Involving High Heat and Temperatures 106

    Discussion 110

High Temperature and High Heat with Fuel Gases....................................113

    Brazing 115

Discussion..115

Code Listings 117

Summary...131

Chapter 4: The PID Process Control Algorithm 133

Theory..133

Tuning and Practical Applications of the PID Controller 139

PID for Thermal Control...145

PID Control of Optical Brightness...148

Code Listings 152

Summary...158

Chapter 5: Realtime Data Plotting and Visualization.......................161

Summary...171

Chapter 6: Frequency Measurement...173

Experimental...176

Observations...179

Discussion..182

Summary...184

Chapter 7: Quality Assurance, Quality Control, and
Error Analysis...185

Quality Assurance and Control..185

Error Analysis...189

Calibration and Curve Fitting 197

Summary...198

Chapter 8: Power and Noise from the USB 199

Typical Baseline Noise and Large Signal Distortions 202

Commercially Available Noise-Reduction Devices............................205

Discussion..206

Summary...207

Chapter 9: Analytical Front Ends 209

IC-based Sensors..211

Microcontrollers...212

Operational Amplifiers..213

Calorimeter Testing, Validation, and Applications............................234

Code Listings 240

Summary...247

TABLE OF CONTENTS

Chapter 10: The Kalman Filter 249

The Single-Dimension Kalman Filter Process 250

Code Listings 254

Summary 257

Appendix 1: List of Abbreviations 259

Appendix 2: List of Suppliers 269

Index 271

About the Author

Richard J. Smythe attended Brock University in its initial years of operation in southern Ontario and graduated with a four-year honors degree in chemistry with minors in mathematics and physics. He then attended the University of Waterloo for a master's degree in analytical chemistry and computing science and a doctorate in analytical chemistry. After a post-doctoral fellowship at the State University of New York at Buffalo in electro-analytical chemistry, Richard went into business in 1974 as Peninsula Chemical Analysis Ltd. Introduced in 1966 to time-shared computing with paper tapes, punched cards, and BASIC prior to Fortran IV at Waterloo, as well as the PDP 11 mini-computers and finally the PC, Richard has maintained a currency in physical computing using several computer languages and scripting codes. Professionally, Richard has functioned as a commercial laboratory owner and is currently a consulting analytical chemist, a civil forensic scientist as PCA Ltd., a full partner in Walters Forensic Engineering in Toronto, Ontario, and senior scientist for contrast engineering in Halifax, Nova Scotia. A large portion of Richard's professional career consists of devising methods by which a problem that ultimately involves making one or more fundamental measurements can be solved by using the equipment at hand or using a readily available "off-the-shelf/out-of-the-box" facility to provide the data required.

About the Technical Reviewer

 **Roland Meisel** holds a B. Sc. in physics from the University of Windsor, a B. Ed. from Queen's University specializing in physics and mathematics, and an M. Sc. in physics from the University of Waterloo. He worked at Chalk River Nuclear Laboratories before entering the world of education. He spent twenty-eight years teaching physics, mathematics, and computer science in the Ontario secondary school system. After retiring from teaching as the head of mathematics at Ridgeway Crystal Beach High School, he entered the world of publishing, contributing to mathematics and physics texts from pre-algebra to calculus in various roles, including technology consultant, author, interactive web files (which he conceived, created, published and edited), and photography. He remains active in several organizations, including the Ontario Association of Physics Teachers, the Ontario Association of Mathematics Educators, the Canadian Owners and Pilots Association, and the Wainfleet Historical Society.

He has always had a strong interest in technology, mail-ordering his first personal computer, an Apple II with a 1 MHz CPU and 16 kB of memory, from California in 1979. At leisure, he can be found piloting small airplanes, riding his bicycle or motorcycle, woodworking, reading, or playing the piano, among other instruments.

Acknowledgments

Acknowledgements begin with the author's late parents, Richard H. Smythe and Margaret M. Smythe (nee Earle), who emigrated from the remains of London England after the war with their small family of three and eventually raised four children in Canada. Our parents instilled in us the need to be educated as much as possible in order for each of us to be self-sufficient and independent. That independence has led to the comfortable retirement of the middle two, the youngest continuing in her chosen occupation for close to a decade past retirement, and the oldest still actively engaged in the business of chemical analysis consulting and the practice of civil forensic science.

Along the way, numerous individuals have served as an inspiration while teaching and mentoring this author, imparting knowledge, the art of rational thinking, tenacity, and in most cases valuable wisdom: From Merritton High School in St. Catharines Ontario, Mrs. E. Glyn-Jones, mathematics, Mr. J. A. Smith, principal, and Mr. E. Umbrico, physics. From Brock University in St. Catharines Ontario, Prof. E. A. Cherniak, Prof. R. H. Hiatt, Prof. F. Koffyberg, and Prof. J. M. Miller. From the University of Waterloo in Waterloo Ontario, Prof. G. Atkinson. From The State University of New York at Buffalo, Prof. S. Bruckenstein.

It may also be said that the seeds for the growth and development of this work began when as a parent the author made sure that both his daughters—Wendy and Christie—could read at a very early age and devised graphic teaching aids for them to learn and understand binary digital arithmetic.

ACKNOWLEDGMENTS

Acknowledgements would not be complete without recognizing the person who has allowed me the time required to write, in spite of life's every day chaos in the country, my spouse Linda. She has suffered through many years of papers, notes, books, breadboards, wires, electronic components, and desktop experiments scattered everywhere in our home and when she wasn't looking, on the kitchen table! Thank You my love.

Although the author's career consists of solving essentially chemistry-based problems and writing reports explaining how the problem came into existence, how to correct its effects or avoid its recurrence, the author has never written a book. This work would not be possible without the help and guidance of editors at Apress—Ms. Natalie Pao, Ms. Jessica Vakili, and Mark Powers.

The Author's Preface to *Arduino Advanced Techniques in Science*

Arduino Advanced Techniques in Science is written to provide an introduction to the more advanced techniques used to aid in taking basic scientific measurements. Techniques are presented that can be used by individuals to engage in hopefully more advanced experimental science. It is hoped that the book can assist students, both those new to and those with limited backgrounds in electro-mechanical techniques or the physical sciences, to devise and conduct better experiments in order to further their research or education. It is also hoped that the book will be useful where there are limited financial resources available for the development of experimental designs and experimental or educational programs.

Migrating or foraging animals and insects use daylight, near infra-red light, polarized light, celestial indicators, chemical traces in water, the Earth's magnetic field, and other aids to navigate over the Earth's surface in search of food or to return home to their breeding grounds. Astronomy, biology, chemistry, geology/geography, mathematics, physics, and other subjects through to zoology are human concepts and classifications entirely unknown to the travelers of the animal world. There are parallels between the animal kingdom's usage of multiple scientific phenomena of which they have no knowledge and current scientific investigations. A significant amount of new scientific knowledge is being revealed by investigators educated in one classifiable discipline using the unfamiliar experimental techniques from another. Although written by an analytical chemist, this book is a compilation of introductory basic techniques applicable to any scientific discipline that requires the experimental measurements of basic physio-chemical parameters.

The author is an experimental analytical chemist who has worked with vacuum tubes, transistors, integrated circuits, mainframe, mini-computers, microcomputers, and microcontrollers, over a period during which computing technology transitioned from BASIC, Fortran, and variations of C into iterations of the open source systems such as Python, Processing (the basis of the Arduino microcontroller integrated development environment [IDE] language), and Linux operating systems used in the Raspberry Pi. New and revised versions of languages, IDEs, and operating systems are available free of charge from the internet and are constantly in a state of flux.

This book could be considered virtually obsolete as it is being written, but as with the science and technology that it describes, it is a starting point in an ever-changing subject. For the researcher and practicing scientist, the basic fundamentals of science are relatively constant and reasonably well understood, so a great deal of caution must be used when deciding that a concept or technique is "obsolete." The SCADA concept and its development significantly pre-date the PC. Some of the transistor and complementary metal oxide semiconductor integrated circuit(s) (CMOS ICs) and the 7400 series of integrated circuitry that are in heavy use today date from the 1970s. Many chemical analysis and physical measurement techniques, taught and in use today, date virtually from the Middle Ages.

SCADA is the acronym for Supervisory Control and Data Acquisition. SCADA software allows a computer to supervise an electro-mechanical process and do so by acquiring data from sensors that are monitoring the process being controlled. Many of the measurement techniques to be discussed can be considered as single-element components that are now a part of the developing technology being called the internet of things (IOT) with the Node-red connectivity open source software.

HMI is the acronym for human–machine interface. The HMI can be an electronic device or construct that provides an interface between a computer, an experimental setup, and a human operator. (A graphical user interface [GUI] may serve as an HMI).

USB is the acronym for universal serial bus, which is, in reality, a written standard of specifications to which electro-mechanical hardware systems are expected to conform. The USB is a subsystem that lets a personal computer communicate with devices that are plugged into the universal serial bus.

When a personal computer runs supervisory control and data acquisition software with a human–machine interface connected via the universal serial bus system, then investigative science experiments or other processes, experimental apparatus, or equipment setups, either "in the field" miles away or "on the bench" next to the computer/workstation/laptop, can be monitored and controlled in realtime.

Laptops, stand-alone desktops, and cabled or wireless networked workstations together with internet connections now allow unprecedented flexibility in laboratory or "in-field" monitoring of investigative science experiments. The options available to the experimentalist for implementing SCADA systems can essentially be divided into three categories based upon the amount of development work required to achieve a fully functional system.

Complete, finished, working software systems that are able to measure and control virtually any electro-optical-mechanical system are available from manufactures such as National Instruments and Foxboro. Commercially available fully functional, basic, software-only systems can be expected to cost in the range of several thousands of dollars.

The author chose to develop this manuscript on three much lower-cost options for SCADA implementation on experimental setups.

A moderate-cost implementation strategy involving the following list of resources has been used to develop the exercises in this manuscript. These resources should also be adequate for further experimental development of new applications:

1) A PC with SCADA software. Numerous systems are available; the DAQFactory Express and the base-level DAQFactory version of the system from Azeotech have both been used in this manuscript. (Cost for DAQFactory base-level software approx. $250 CDN in 2008.) There are on-line, advanced, freeware versions of SCADA systems available for those who are able to adapt the software and may require the extended flexibility.

2) A USB HMI; again, there are many devices available from many manufacturers, and the device chosen for this monolog is the model U12 from the LabJack Corporation. (U12 cost approx. $120, a U3 was added later, approx. cost $110 USD.) The LabJack devices are provided with software in the form of a working version of the DAQFactory program called Express. The LabJack-supplied software is excellent with respect to its graphical display capabilities, and for many applications in investigative sciences is more than adequate. The DAQFactory Express is, however, limited to ten lines of script code, five script sequences, and two display pages. For some of the topics discussed and project exercises described in this manuscript, the more extensive capabilities of a commercial version of the DAQFactory software may be required. If the software is to be purchased, the reader should start with the most basic program available and add upgrades as required.

3) The third option for experimentalists is the newest and lowest-cost approach to the implementation of a SCADA system, which consists of the Raspberry Pi, its Linux operating system, and the Python programming language with its Matplotlib library and Tkinter graphical user interface. The Linux operating system, Python, and its modules are all open source projects and hence free for download from the internet. The Raspberry Pi project has made available the Raspberry Pi board that can be purchased from many large electronics supply houses such as Digikey or Newark Element 14, to name only two, for $35 USD. The Raspberry Pi board requires an HDMI-compatible TV or computer monitor, mouse, and keyboard to form a fully functional computing system. In addition to the virtually no-cost software, the Raspberry Pi board contains its own general-purpose input–output bus as well as its USB input–output connection, and hence contains its own HMI, requiring no additional circuitry or expense to be interfaced to external electronics or experimental setups. The Raspberry Pi board is manufactured with an Ethernet connection and is thus network capable.

In 2008, an open source project called Arduino made available a series of USB-connected microcontroller boards that allowed designers, artists, hobbyists, and non-electronics specialists to interface optical-electro-mechanical devices to a computer. The basic Arduino Uno Revn. 3 board can be purchased from any of the major electronics supply houses for $25 USD. The software to program the microcontroller board is another open source project and is freeware that can be downloaded from the internet.

The Arduino board can be used with Windows or Linux-based operating systems and is fully supported with an online forum, many tutorials, and an extensive range of example programs and applications.

The costs to be expected for experimental investigations using SCADA-type implementations can thus take the form of a complete commercially available package, useable as received with no required development time, as opposed to a lesser-cost system requiring a moderate amount of programming using the DAQFactory program and commercial HMI devices such as the LabJack series of interfaces, or even an assemblage of very low-cost hardware and open source software freely available for download from the internet.

In addition to the software and hardware required to implement the monitoring and controlling system, additional ancillary equipment may be required in the form of the following list:

1) A solderless breadboard system, appropriate power sources such as battery- or electronic-regulated supplies, and access to various IC and passive electronic components is required.

2) For troubleshooting, a multimeter is required, and for more advanced work an oscilloscope— either standalone or an oscilloscope program for a PC—may be required.

It is suggested that the reader, new to this technology, work through the book in order of presentation so as to gain practice and confidence with software, wiring, and increasing project complexity. The basics of scripting software, hardware interfacing, electronics fundamentals, and IC usage will all progressively become more complex, and the basic knowledge and procedures established in the earlier exercises will not be repeated in the more advanced projects. All science is empirical in nature, and this book is no different than real-life scientific work; the investigator must progress from the simple to the more complicated facets of the project at hand, verifying and validating each intermediate step in a multi-stage measurement process.

The rate at which the individual can progress through the various topics presented will be dependent upon their knowledge of the basic physical sciences that form the core of the exercises. If difficulty is encountered, textbooks, online tutorials, and academic course outlines with exercises can be located to further aid in understanding the required base knowledge.

As the title states, this book deals essentially with monitoring and measuring physical–chemical parameters with integrated circuitry and physical computational systems. In this work, inexpensive "off-the-shelf" components are used to monitor and control experimental setups that are able to measure data in the form of basic physio-chemical parameters of interest to investigators in many of the classified sciences, in some cases astounding: sensitivity, flexibility, accuracy, and precision.

DISCLAIMER

1) 110 volt electricity can be lethal and will start fires.

2) Soldering irons are hot enough to cause serious burns.

3) This book is for educational purposes only and presents concepts that are demonstrated through experimental formats. These experimental setups have not been tested for robustness and are not designed or intended for any form of implementation in field service. These concepts are the basis for education only and are intended as

starting points for further R and D into instrumental methods of monitoring experimental scientific apparatus for the purposes of gathering data or making physical measurements.

4) The concept for this book came to the author in the mid-1960s, and in the interim years various portions of this book were developed with the technology available at the time, while other concepts were found to be unworkable. Although formal assembly of this book was begun in 2008 and 2009 using the integrated circuitry, physical computing, and internet information resources available at that time, the book continues to develop as it is being written using new integrated circuits, physical computing software, and online information sources. The continued availability of either software or electro-mechanical hardware can never be assured, and hence the practitioners of this or any science must learn the art of "a workaround."

Roadmap to the Exercises in *Advanced Arduino Techniques in Science*

As noted in the author's preface, this book is not intended to be a first-time or *ab initio* introduction to the use of microprocessors as smart peripherals in scientific experiments. This text is directed to those who have some experience in working with electronic hardware and computer software and are looking to expand the capabilities of their research or experimental setup. A basic familiarity with simple electronics as well as some elementary programming knowledge in a structured language such as Python or C++ will be required to complete some of the *Advanced Arduino Techniques in Science* chapter exercises.

New hardware or components introduced in the chapters should be evaluated from the manufacturer's literature to gain an appreciation or understanding of the advantages or capabilities to be realized from the implementation of the new techniques the device will enable. Online forums and application notes can also provide numerous practical applications of the hardware at hand.

This book is devoted to describing auxiliary techniques, methods, equipment, and precautions to be used in improving the application of Arduino microprocessors to scientific investigations. A large portion of the following text in this roadmap to the exercises reviews numerous topics, some of which include the terminology of specifications, suggested best practices in scientific methods, established or standardized methods for implementing SCADA unit operations, and the general precautions to be aware of while improving experimental setups. *Advanced Arduino Techniques in Science* is an attempt to gather together most of the additional techniques, modifications, and improvements using simple, relatively inexpensive components and materials to improve the quality and quantity of data obtained from the basic experimental setups used over the past years' various investigations.

Several of the chapters in *Advanced Arduino Techniques in Science* can be considered as "unit operations." Baking a cake is a process consisting of a number of individual steps that in chemical engineering are referred to as "unit operations." Measuring out and blending the cake ingredients, baking, and decorating can be considered as unit operations. A cake-baking process can thus be defined in terms of the individual unit operations required to completely describe the process. A series of electro-mechanical unit operations can be combined to measure or control more complex experimental investigations. Several of the chapters and exercises are unit operations that can be assembled into existing experimental setups to better control a process or to greatly extend the sensitivity or range of measurements being made by the system.

Project Management

When altering or adding to an experimental setup, the investigator should review as much up-to-date information as is available on the intended change. If an alteration involves the addition of a self-contained unit operation such as a PID controller, the controller should be assembled and tested on a simpler but representative system to both validate controller function and ensure the controller will not damage the in-service process or experimental setup.

Prior to any alterations to an in-service experimental setup, the investigator should thoroughly test and document system performance. The documentation should be of sufficient detail that in the event of failure the original experimental setup's configuration can be reproduced. Documentation may include noting response to a standard test, photographing circuit configuration, or recoding whatever is necessary to reestablish initial performance conditions.

For the modification of complex experimental setups, begin assembling the hardware/electronics and corresponding software from the simplest unit operations of the project, debugging the individual modules then verifying operational status until the entire project functions as designed.

In all scientific reports, the documentation must be complete to the point at which any other researchers can duplicate the original experimental work and confirm the reported observations or system performance. Newly developed or modified software code must be liberally commented for those attempting to duplicate the work being described and for the investigator to be able to modify the code as required for more efficient operation or changes made to the electro-mechanical system under development.

To duplicate the work of another, clear definitions of units must exist. Caution is required in reading schematic diagrams and attempting to duplicate their assembly as certain discrete components and integrated circuitry are constantly decreasing in physical size or are replaced with newer technology. The decrease in size means that identification markings on components are getting smaller also.

Resistance and capacitor markings may appear in several formats as combinations of numbers and letters with the magnitude symbol sometimes replacing the decimal point.

Resistors (Ω)

M is 10^6 or 1,000,000 ohms and typical identifications may be 1.5M or 1M5.

K is 10^3 or 1,000 ohms and typical identifications may be 1.2K or 1K2.

R is 10^0 or 1 or unity ohms and typical identifications may be 100R or just 100 as there is no decimal point to replace.

m is 1/1000 or 10^{-3} ohms and 0.052 Ω is written as 52 mΩ.

Capacitance units in older works were mainly limited to micro and pico Farad designations, and the range of nano was covered either by thousands of pico or thousandths of microFarads. Most current capacitor notation usage seems to adhere to the three main fractional designations listed below, but has recently been expanded to include the Farad to avoid using thousands and millions of the *micro* term when describing ultra- and super-capacitor devices.

Capacitors (F)

u is microFarad and is 10^{-6} Farads.

n is nanoFarad and is 10^{-9} Farads.

p is picoFarad and is 10^{-12} Farads.

When selecting the components or techniques intended to alter or augment an in-service experimental setup, a certain amount of caution must be exercised to ensure that the finished construct is suitable for the desired measurement. A case in point can be found in the creation of something as simple as a linearly changing voltage value. Modern electronics technology presents two simple methods for the creation of a "voltage ramp" in which the value of a voltage varies linearly with time between a lower and upper voltage value. In a linear system, the electrical potential can be deemed to "ramp up" or "ramp down." If a four-bit digital-to-analog converter is used, the values from 0 to 2^4 (0 to 15 or 16 digital values) can be created as incremental voltages. A 16-volt signal applied to the digital-to-analog converter (DAC) can thus provide a series of discreet steps between the values of 0 and 15 volts in approximately one-volt increments. The one-volt steps may be adequate for positioning a robot or mirror in any one of sixteen possible positions but may not be of use in an electrochemical application. If particular chemical reactions were to occur in which several metals were deposited from a solution at several different impressed non-integer voltage levels, it may be necessary to have a smooth voltage waveform whose voltage value continuously ramps between the desired levels. The smooth transition of continuously varying voltage values is of course an analog waveform and must be generated by special methods, one of which is using a constant current source to charge a capacitor in order to produce a linear voltage change across the capacitor plates.

Although calculus demonstrates that by selecting a sufficiently large number of tiny steps we are able to mimic an analog signal with a digital, the approximation is still a digital signal that may not have the exact desired value for the application at hand, and a continuously variable analog voltage signal from a constant current-based capacitor charging methodology may be necessary. The selection of which variation technique to use will depend upon the voltage resolution required and the availability of the electronic components at hand.

In the *Advanced Arduino Techniques in Science* chapters and exercises, very simple electrical circuits will be assembled on a breadboard and connected to the LabJack HMI, DAQFactory Express system, Arduino microcontroller DAQFactory combination, or directly to the Raspberry Pi or RPi Arduino systems, to provide an interface between the working electronic circuit and a computer-generated GUI. Each of these combinations allows the experimenter to exercise supervisory control, acquire data, or monitor a data-stream trend through a software, user-interface screen. The modification of an in-service electro-mechanical experimental setup should be done incrementally if possible.

Experimental modification actions should mechanically assemble circuits, test them, and establish their functioning before configuring software for new data acquisition or hardware-control operations. As a general rule, the hardware is assembled, tested, and validated before one moves on to interfacing and software development.

When working with electrical signals from a new sensor or experimental apparatus, ensure that the output voltage level does not exceed the input voltage capability of the electronic components being used to process the signal. Most discrete integrated circuitry is limited to 5 volts, some op-amps will operate at up to 18 volts, and most surface-mount technology operates at a nominal 3.3 volts.

As with all scientific endeavors, a logical progression should be made from the simplest to the more complex. When developing the software for the augmented project at hand, the experimenter should begin with the simplest code possible to establish communication and then consider additional software for DSP, error checking, or implementing any additional logic circuitry.

Advanced Arduino Techniques in Science uses three different programming languages: Arduino's form of C, Python, and DAQFactory's sequence and quick-sequence code. Follow the proper formal methodology built into the software at hand. In the DAQFactory software, creating the channels first allows DAQFactory to populate the pop-up intelligent listing of channels, variables, and constants to cut down on error-prone typing. The primary step in all troubleshooting procedures involving written coded systems that do not work is to check all spelling. Names are case sensitive.

As noted previously, when altering working experimental setups, keep detailed notes of what is being done, write down calculations, and sketch schematics and rough mechanical drawings. This is, after all, science. The formal drawing conventions for mechanical systems and electronic circuits can be found in several reference works[1, 2, 3] that the reader is encouraged to follow.

As an experimental setup is modified from software control of the HMI to wiring of the circuitry on the breadboard, test each segment of the process modification. Work neatly; lay out the wiring parallel to the lines and rows of pins on the breadboard socket. Cross wires at right angles and only bend small copper wires to right angles with your fingers in order to achieve a relatively large radius of curvature. Recall that copper, although very ductile, "work hardens," so use new wire where possible or make sure that a wire is re-bent to large radius, gentle curvatures no more than a half-dozen times at most.

As an example of the "unit operation" testing philosophy, it is inherently assumed that if all the component parts of a system work then the entire process will work. Remember, however, that the assumption is just that!

Isolation

Chapter 8, "Power and Noise from the USB," discusses the structure, design and briefly describes the desired functioning of, the communication bus. When modifying an in-service experiment and additional power is required, the investigator is reminded that the USB implementation is

---

[1]*Building Scientific Apparatus*, 4th Ed., J. H. Moore, C. C. Davis, and M. C. Coplan, Cambridge University Press, ISBN 978-0-521-87858-6.

[2]*The Art of Electronics*, 2nd Ed., P. Horowitz and W. Hill, Cambridge University Press, ISBN 978-0-521-37095-7.

[3]*Practical Electronics for Inventors*, 3rd Ed., P. Scherz and S. Monk, McGraw-Hill, ISBN 978-0-07-177133-7.

essentially a communications standard able to provide limited power to the essentially digital peripherals joining the bus. It is reported that USB 1 and 2 can supply 500 mA and USB 3 900 mA. For experimental modifications in which more than a half Ampere of current is required or the sensitivity of an in-service essentially analog-based experiment is being increased, it is good practice for an external power supply to be used to power the new system. This book is directed at investigators and researchers working on a bench or desktop with self-contained power supplies, such as those that will be encountered in many field or laboratory experimental setups. It is important to realize that in many experimental setups in either laboratory or field, larger currents, line voltage control, and wireless SCADA software will mandate the use of external power-source control for some experimental work.

Software Scripting

All new scripting developed should be fully documented. The name of the sequence, the date the code was written, and the purpose of the new sequence should all be placed at the head of the actual code in accordance with the details for naming and commenting, as given in the various software language references. The heading should also outline what the code does, describe the algorithm in text, and define the variables used. Recall also that a variable must be declared in a scripted sequence, plus the sequence must be running for the variable to exist and be useable. DAQFactory has an auto-start option for a sequence, which will start the sequence when the page is loaded, and if required the auto-start option can be used to automatically start a sequence that declares a set of variables for use in configuring a control screen or sequence.

The RPi and Arduino auto-start their operating system, and defined software variables are available on the application of system power.

Integrated Circuitry and Surface Mount Technology (SMT)

Traditionally, experimenters bought components for mounting on breadboards during testing and project development. The successful breadboard circuit could then be transformed into printed circuit boards with single- or double-sided etched patterns. The double-sided boards often used drilled holes to connect both sides of the board. However, as integrated circuits became significantly smaller they drew less current, became faster, became significantly more sensitive, and are now at the point at which many of these miniature ICs can neither be handled manually nor be electrically connected into circuits by the average researcher.

Smaller IC size has given rise to smaller component area and surface mount technology (SMT) that in turn has made circuit boards much smaller, easier to manufacture, and less expensive. The decrease in physical size and the development of SMT has added a layer of complexity for the experimentalist. Using the advantages gained by physically decreasing the size of the integrated circuits requires adapters to convert SMT components into compatible breadboarding formats.

Electronics exercises in *Advanced Arduino Techniques in Science* use ICs and SMT ICs that are compatible with the readily obtainable common breadboard systems.

SMT can be used by the experimentalist in development projects, through printed circuit board adapters that can be created from the data sheets published by the IC manufacturer. Adapters often called "breakout boards" are available from several commercial suppliers, and one of the more extensive selections is available from Proto-Advantage of Ancaster, Ontario. In addition to a large collection of adapters, the company also offers an assembly service and will use SMT techniques to mount the IC on the breakout board adapter for the researcher.

SMT-to-breadboard transitions are affected by mounting the microchip on a small, printed circuit adapter board that connects the IC to a series of header pins. The square or round header pins are then used with prototyping boards, sockets, or wire wrap to provide an electrical connection for power and I/O requirements between the IC and the experiment under development.

Many SMT components are available in several different mounting patterns that are usually defined and described in detailed drawings at the end of product data sheets. Some of the acronyms used in describing the SMT devices are as tabulated below:

Capacitors – SMT capacitors are specified by their four-digit size code of length and width in 1/10 in. (1210 is 0.12 long by 0.10 wide)

CQFP – Ceramic multilayer QFP

LCC – Leadless Chip Carriers are packages that are soldered directly onto circuit boards and have no leads.

PLCC – Plastic Leaded Chip Carriers

PQFP – Plastic Quad Flat Pack

QFP – Quad Flat Package; a rectangular IC with leads on all four sides. Resistors follow the convention of capacitors.

SOIC – Small Outline Integrated Circuit is often followed by the number of pins on the package and sometimes is even further abbreviated to SO-8, for example.

SOP – Small Outline Package has the variations Plastic Small Outline Package (PSOP), Thin Small Outline Package (TSOP), and Thin-shrink Small Outline Package (TSSOP)

TQFP – Thin QFP

More-detailed dimensions are always to be found in the product data sheets and should be reviewed carefully before deciding upon a component and the breakout board required for a given prototype or project. SMT is a rapidly changing field, and new production methods are making obsolescence a frequently encountered problem for the investigator. However, equivalent, more-powerful integrated circuits in newer and smaller packages are being brought to market virtually on a daily basis, and investigators must research the literature for the present form of the circuitry required for a given prototype.

Prototyping breadboards, jumper wires or cables, and integrated circuits are usually the format used to develop, test, modify, or validate a working experimental system. In several of the exercises and measurement techniques encountered in this book, the investigator/experimenter will find that the use of a printed circuit board will be required to enclose a working breadboard circuit in a shielded metal enclosure. Prepared printed circuit boards such as those depicted in Figure RM-1 are available for assembling circuitry into a fixed, secure, and compact format. The two boards to the extreme right are in fact the top and bottom of prototyping boards that mount directly onto the Arduino microprocessor boards to hold either test or permanently wired circuitry within the microcontroller footprint. All of the I/O and power pins are carried through from the microcontroller board underneath to the circuit board above. These boards are often referred to as "shields" and are available from several manufacturers; similar types of circuit boards are available for the RPi and are termed "HATs."

The etched "universal" boards displayed are available from electronics supply stores and online. The copper traces are 0.1 in., spacing that matches standard dual inline package pin spacing.

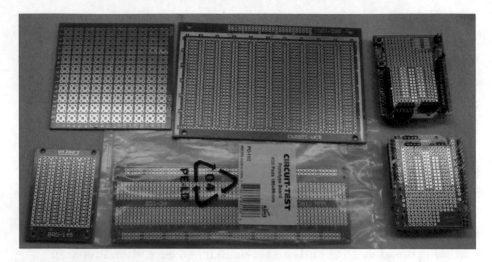

Figure RM-1. *Prototyping circuit boards*

There are several circuit board manufacturers that provide or are able to use standardized circuit board design software to manufacture a small or large number of complex circuit boards. Multiple-layer boards and those involving multi-leaded SMT components are best produced by automated systems of commercial manufacturers. Occasionally it may be necessary for the investigator to design and make one or perhaps two simple printed circuit boards for a special application such as the mounting of special components. Figure RM-2 depicts one of a pair of small 1 in. x 1 ½ in. (2.45 cm x 4 cm) hand-drawn PCBs used to mount a pair of 30 KΩ thermistors and 33 KΩ resistors for the measurement of the hot and cold sides of a thermo-electric cooling plate test cell.

Figure RM-2. *Hand-drawn PCB for mounting and wiring sensors*

The basic size of the board needed and the basic simple outline of the copper traces required to hold the components essentially define the size of the board to be fabricated. In the case of the PCB illustrated in Figure RM-2, a pair of boards was needed—one for each side of the test cell—and a single board with two copper tracings was etched, drilled, and then cut in half to facilitate handling during etching and drilling. As can be seen in Figure RM-2, there is a small, brass, round-head mounting screw that holds the PCB, wiring, and mounted thermistor sensor in place on the outside surface of the two-chamber test-cell walls.

A closer inspection of the copper tracing indicates coarseness in both the shape and surface texture of the etched copper patterns. The roughness is reflective of the hand drawing and the very thin nature of the marker-pen ink forming the etchant "resist" layer. A more even and dense copper pattern can be obtained by using either several coats of marker ink or using a much more dense resist, such as a colored cosmetic nail polish. A colored nail polish is easier to see and can be removed after etching with nail polish remover or acetone.

There are several formulations available for etching the excess copper off of the epoxy-clad blank on which the desired pattern is drawn, and the author has had consistent success with a ferric chloride solution. Commercial ferric chloride etchant in 250 ml bottles is adequate for the small boards created and a half-hour to one hour are the etch times at ambient room temperatures. The boards must be clean before etching as fingerprints can act as resist if not removed. Soap and water or a mild kitchen abrasive such as Vim can be used to prepare the board before the application of the resist and etching. A shallow pool of etchant in a plastic dish can be used as an etching tank, and warming the etchant solution will decrease the time required to etch the board.

PCBs that require drilling should be center punched, and the fine drills used to make holes compatible with electrical or electronic connections should be mounted in a high-speed rotary tool such as a Dremel for drilling the copper foil or epoxy board. After preparation of a PCB for a project, test the continuity of all traces on the new board.

There are kits available that use a laser printer to create complex circuit boards from photos. A laser-printed pattern must be hot pressed or ironed on to the board blank to transfer the plastic resist pattern and is a more complex process that the investigator can use if required.

General Comments on Advanced Technologies and Improving Experiments

The following itemized list of generalized suggestions, precautions, and naturally occurring restrictions is presented here as an aid to successfully implementing a modification or improvement to experimental systems:

1) Temperature affects many physical parameters, and often experimental apparatus may need to be insulated, isolated, or even thermostated to minimize temperature variation.

2) Use battery power whenever possible as the line or mains power, USB, and line-driven regulated supplies are very noisy for highly sensitive work.

3) All wiring lines carrying signals of interest should be twisted and shielded against electromagnetic interference with grounded metal shielding.

4) Physical contact between triboelectric active materials can cause static electrical accumulations that interfere with high-sensitivity measurements. Static accumulations vary with room humidity that in turn can vary with the seasons in some climactic regions.

5) Prototype boards (Figure 1-3 in Chapter 1, "Arduino and Raspberry Pi") can be used to test circuits, but for high-sensitivity measurements hard-wired or printed circuit boards should be used and encased in grounded metal cases.

6) As most scale expansions simultaneously increase both signal and noise, it is often necessary to use some form of digital signal processing (DSP) to maximize the signal-to-noise ratio.

7) Resistors create electrical noise in proportion to the magnitude of the resistance and the temperature of the resistor. Wire-wound resistors are the least noisy, and metal films are less noisy than carbon-based devices.

8) Visible, UV, and IR light can affect solid-state devices such as diodes and transistors.

9) Air currents can cause variation in temperature, pressure, moisture, and dust movement or deposition.

10) Often in trace quantity chemical analysis, greater sensitivity can be achieved by collecting and processing a bigger sample. When measuring very low values of variables such as resistance and capacitance, if discrete units are available consider measuring several units in series or parallel as required. For conductivity a larger area of contact can create a larger signal across the sample cell plates.

11) Measurements can often be divided into the two classifications of being relative or absolute. Absolute measurements require calibration of the measurement apparatus with known or defined standards. Relative measurements monitor the change in the parameter being monitored. Generally speaking, if an experiment can be devised to create a relative measurement rather that an absolute, a better measurement will result.

12) Current- and voltage-measuring systems using op-amps with very high input impedances, often referred to as electrometers, require a great deal of care in assembly and application in order to produce accurate results. Grounded metal boxes, shielded external measurement probe wires, battery power, and close adherence to the manufacturer's recommended installation and wiring practices will greatly improve system performance.

CHAPTER 1

Arduino and Raspberry Pi

Arduino is the name originally given, in 2005, to an Italian educational project intended to teach physical computing to industrial and commercial design students who did not have an electronics background. Raspberry Pi is the name given, in 2012, to a British educational project aiming to create a single-board computer that could be used to introduce basic computer science in the early phases of childhood education. In both projects, the creators reasoned that by offering very low-cost hardware, more students would have access to computer science and physical computing. As the two educational projects developed far beyond what was imagined possible at the time of their inceptions and introductions, the names have come to represent the hardware boards extensively in use today. Although both Arduino and Raspberry Pi were teaching concepts, they are very different devices with different purposes that display some overlapping capabilities. Each device is uniquely suited to its designed purpose.

Arduino

Originally envisioned as a digitally programmable electronic platform for designers to impart a human interaction option into their work, the Arduino had to be simple to use for those without formal training in

© Richard J. Smythe 2021
R. J. Smythe, *Advanced Arduino Techniques in Science*,
https://doi.org/10.1007/978-1-4842-6784-4_1

electronics. Simplicity was achieved by the creation of the integrated development environment (IDE) software program. An IDE allowed the user to assemble a series of relatively simple basic instructions based upon the C programming language into an executable microcontroller program. The program created in the IDE was able to control the actions of a remote microcontroller, resident on a small circuit board, that provided augmented and extensive input and output capabilities plus electronic control of the design to which it was connected.

Additional simplicity for the Arduino board was achieved by using the USB connection to a host computer to eliminate having a complex operating system on the microcontroller boards, and to provide the computational and graphics capabilities required for the IDE program to assemble, debug, and transfer the code required for programming the board's microcontroller. The program assembled in the IDE resident in the host PC that is downloaded to the Arduino to manage or collect data from sensors or peripherals is called a "sketch".

The augmented input–output capabilities of the Arduino board were achieved by installing an accurate crystal-controlled time clock on the board, and using firmware and application-specific integrated circuitry to implement analog-to-digital conversion, digital input and output, pulse width modulation output, and 5- or 3.3-volt power, all under the control of an AVR ATmega328P 8-bit, 16 MHz microcontroller chip.

Since the Arduino concept was intended to impart interactivity to designed products and artwork, the board has the ability to accept several forms of power. When not driving a load such as an LED, the Arduino Uno board is reported to draw approximately 47 mA. Battery, solar, and generator/alternator power in a DC format within the voltage levels given in Table 1-1 can be supplied to the microcontroller board through the 2.1 mm auxiliary power input jack on the board. The center pin in the male plug is the positive connection for the external supply, and the auxiliary jack is connected to the internal 5-volt regulator of the system power controller.

Table 1-1. *Arduino Uno Specifications*

Microcontroller	ATmega328
Operating Voltage	5V
Input Voltage (recommended)	7–12V
Input Voltage (limits)	6–20V
Digital I/O Pins	14 (of which 6 provide PWM output)
Analog Input Pins	6
DC Current per I/O Pin	40 mA
DC Current for 3.3V Pin	50 mA
Flash Memory	32 KB (ATmega328) of which 0.5 KB used by bootloader
SRAM	2 KB (ATmega328)
EEPROM	1 KB (ATmega328)
Clock Speed	16 MHz (Arduino boards use a crystal clock)

The Arduino board of Figure 1-1 is 3 in. long by 2⅛ in. wide (76 mm x 55 mm) and is an earlier model with a B type USB connection and a through-hole socket-mounted microcontroller chip. Newer boards are populated with surface-mount ICs and a C type USB connection.

Figure 1-1. *Arduino Uno*

To facilitate the creation of compact circuitry, printed circuit boards are available that can be mounted directly on top of the Uno boards to provide a mounting platform for prototyping circuitry, mounting sensors, or items such as mechanical connections. Top-mounted prototyping boards for the Arduino are referred to as "shields," as depicted in Figures 1-2 and 1-3.

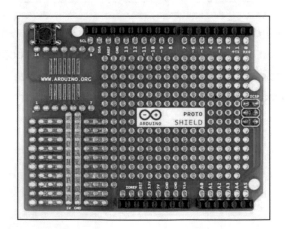

Figure 1-2. *Top view of a blank Arduino shield*

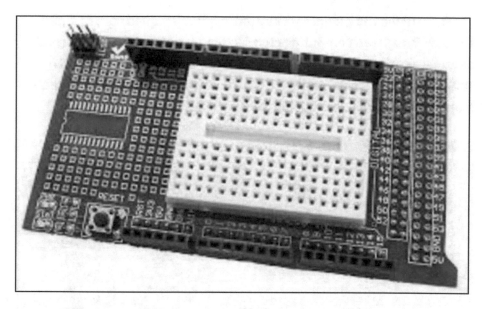

Figure 1-3. *An Arduino shield with a small prototyping breadboard*

The Arduino concept and evolving hardware are solely for physical computing when interfacing sensors or electro-mechanical peripherals to computing devices.

Raspberry Pi

The declining number of students entering the field of computer science led to the concept of creating a very inexpensive computer to increase student interest at the primary levels of education. A non-profit organization called the Raspberry Pi Foundation introduced the first model of the Raspberry Pi (RPi) computer in 2012. The project created and distributed a single-board computer (SBC) for $25 each. The original design has passed through four phases of revision, and as of November 2016 a reported 11 million devices have been sold.

In 2019 the RPi model 4 was introduced with a quad core 64-bit, 1.5 GHz Broadcom computing chip. The model 4 is available in several hardware configurations with prices ranging from $60 to $100 (CDN). Table 1-2 illustrates the growth of the SBC through its first three iterations, many of which are still available from suppliers.

Table 1-2. *Various Models of Raspberry Pi*

	Raspberry Pi 3 Model B	Raspberry Pi Zero	Raspberry Pi 2 Model B	Raspberry Pi Model B+
Introduction Date	2/29/2016	11/25/2015	2/2/2015	7/14/2014
SoC	BCM2837	BCM2835	BCM2836	BCM2835
CPU	Quad Cortex A53 @ 1.2GHz	ARM11 @ 1GHz	Quad Cortex A7 @ 900MHz	ARM11 @ 700MHz
Instruction set	ARMv8-A	ARMv6	ARMv7-A	ARMv6
GPU	400MHz VideoCore IV	250MHz VideoCore IV	250MHz VideoCore IV	250MHz VideoCore IV
RAM	1GB SDRAM	512 MB SDRAM	1GB SDRAM	512MB SDRAM
Storage	micro-SD	micro-SD	micro-SD	micro-SD
Ethernet	10/100	none	10/100	10/100
Wireless	802.11n / Bluetooth 4.0	none	none	none
Video Output	HDMI / Composite	HDMI / Composite	HDMI / Composite	HDMI / Composite
Audio Output	HDMI / Headphone	HDMI	HDMI / Headphone	HDMI / Headphone
GPIO	40	40	40	40
Price	$35	$5	$35	$35

The model 3 iteration of the computer used a Broadcom BCH2837, 64-bit ARMv8 QUAD Core, 64-bit processor with a 1.2 GHz clock. The model 3 SBC is available for $60 (CDN 2017). The credit card–sized computer board is depicted in Figures 1-4 and 1-5.

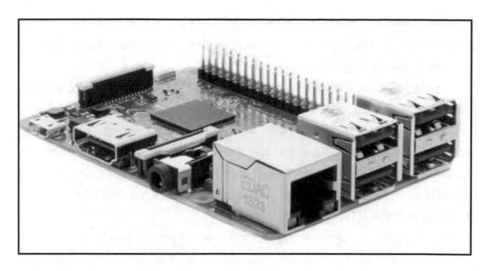

Figure 1-4. *Side view of the RPi model 3*

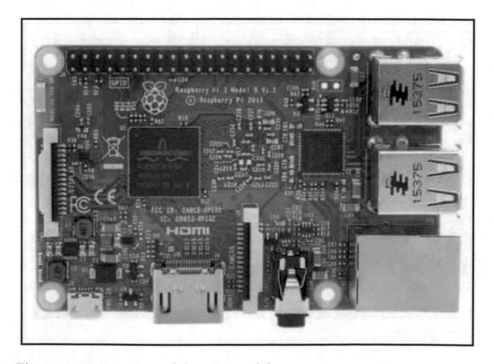

Figure 1-5. *Top view of the RPi model 3*

The model 3 RPi is compatible with 802.11n wireless local area networks (LAN) communications, Bluetooth 4.1 communication, and near-field low-energy protocols.

A very low-cost device was made possible by eliminating virtually all the peripherals normally associated with a computer. All models of the RPi SBC need a power supply and keyboard, must use an SD card to hold the computer operating system, and require cables to connect any peripherals or networks to the processor. A high-definition multimedia interface (HDMI) allows the processor to interface to a wide variety of digital displays, including home televisions.

When properly supported with the required power and I/O peripherals, the RPi is a fully functional computer with a windowed graphical user interface, as depicted in Figures 1-6, 1-7, 1-8, and 1-9.

Figure 1-6. *RPi Pixel "desktop" with the terminal program and file manager open*

Figure 1-7. *Pixel menus*

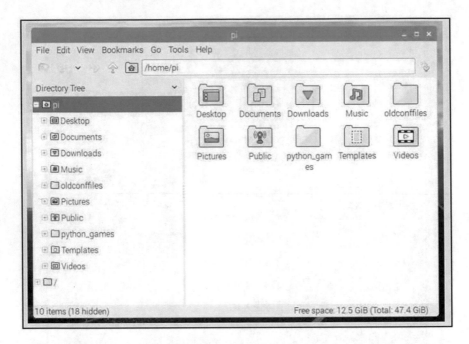

Figure 1-8. *Pixel file manager*

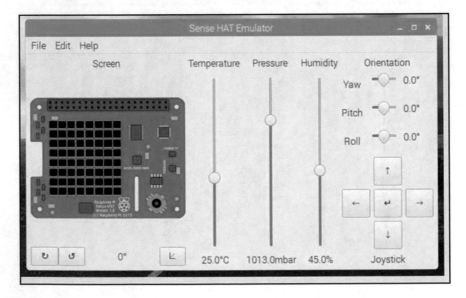

Figure 1-9. *HAT Sense board emulator screen*

Early models of the RPi were equipped with a dual row of thirteen pins that formed a twenty-six-pin array called the general purpose input–output (GPIO) array that enabled the CPU to communicate with peripherals connected to the pins. With the production of the Model B, a modification was made, and the Model B+ was introduced with a forty-pin GPIO array. Drawing from industrial practice, the newer RPi computing systems are able to load and recognize stackable add-on hardware boards that can be fitted over the forty-pin array. The add-on boards are known as hardware added on top (HAT). HATs are available for a large number of sensors, motors, liquid crystal displays, analog-to-digital converters, and a host of other applications, such as the multiple-sensor system depicted in Figure 1-9.

However, the RPi has some inherent limitations in the performance and use of the GPIO facility. The software operating system for the RPi can have a higher-priority process running at the same time as a GPIO operation, which can result in the temporary neglect of the input or output signal. The conflict can sometimes be seen as the "flickering" of LEDs controlled by the GPIO pin array.

In addition to the lower priority of the input–output operations, the RPi does not have any analog-to-digital conversion (ADC) facility. Analog-to-digital conversions can be achieved with software in some cases and by added external hardware connections to the GPIO pin array in others. (The original models of the RPi were produced with a twenty-pin GPIO array that has essentially the same pin assignments as the first twenty pins of the newer models.) The identity of the pins in the GPIO array is depicted in Figure 1-10.

Pin	Top row	Pin	Bottom row
2	5V power	1	3V3 power
4	5V power	3	GPIO2 SDA1 I2C
6	GROUND	5	GPIO3 SCL1 I2C
8	GPIO14 UARTO_TXD	7	GPIO4
10	GPIO15 UARTO_RDX	9	GROUND
12	GPIO18 PCM_CLK	11	GPIO17
14	GROUND	13	GPIO27
16	GPIO23	15	GPIO22
18	GPIO24	17	3V3 power
20	GROUND	19	GPIO10 SPIO_MOSI
22	GPIO25	21	GPIO9 SPIO_MISO
24	GPIO8 SPIO_CEO_N	23	GPIO11 SPIO_SCLK
26	GPIO7 SPIO_CE1_N	25	GROUND
28	ID_SC I2c ID eeprom	27	ID_SD I2c ID eeprom
30	GROUND	29	GPIO5
32	GPIO12	31	GPIO6
34	GROUND	33	GPIO13
36	GPIO16	35	GPIO19
38	GPIO20	37	GPIO26
40	GPIO21	39	GROUND

Raspberry Pi 2 (GPIO)

Figure 1-10. *RPi GPIO pin assignments*

In summary, the GPIO array has twenty-six configurable pins labeled as GPIO 2 to 27 that can be programmed as either digital inputs or outputs. The array has four power pins, two at 5 volts and two at 3.3 volts, with eight ground connections. Two pins are assigned to serial communications. For implementing communications with single integrated circuits such as the MCP3008 analog-to-digital converter, the serial peripheral interface (SPI) protocol is used. (Implementation of the SPI protocol is achieved by selecting the SPI option from the Interfaces tab of the Raspberry Pi Configuration window. The Configuration window is accessed from the main menu by selecting the "Preferences" entry and then "Raspberry Pi Configuration." In order to activate the protocol for use in programming the GPIO pins, the RPi must be rebooted.)

The Raspberry Pi Foundation has produced a series of teaching materials with programming exercises on basic physical computing with the RPi that demonstrate the various forms in which analog-to-digital conversions can be achieved.

Light-dependent resistors (LDR) display a resistance proportional to the intensity of the light incident upon their active surface. Digital logic is characterized by its defined use of high or low levels of voltage. The RPi can distinguish between high- or low-logic-level voltages on any one of the available GPIO pins. If a precision resistor and a capacitor are used in a series RC circuit then the time required for the pin to transit from a low-to a high-logic state is directly proportional to the voltage applied to the circuit. The LDR can be connected in series with a precise capacitor to a GPIO pin, and the time required for the pin to transit from a low to a high logic level can be measured and correlated directly to the quantity of light illuminating the sensor.

A more accurate digital conversion technique using an MCP3008 IC chip is presented in the RPi Foundation teaching materials. An MCP3008 is a \$4 (CDN), 16-pin, dual inline plastic (DIP) package that can be mounted directly onto a prototyping board to connect with GPIO pins and sensors. The chip is an 8-channel 10-bit ADC that uses the SPI protocol to collect data from sensors and transfer it to the RPi. A 10-bit conversion is able to divide an analog signal into 2^{10} or 1024 divisions. With 10-bit resolution the converter can resolve any input voltage into 1024 units. As an example, for a voltage of 3.3 volts the converter can measure down to 3.3/1024 or 3.22 mV. Figure 1-11 illustrates the connections to be made to interface the MCP3008 to the GPIO array of the RPi.

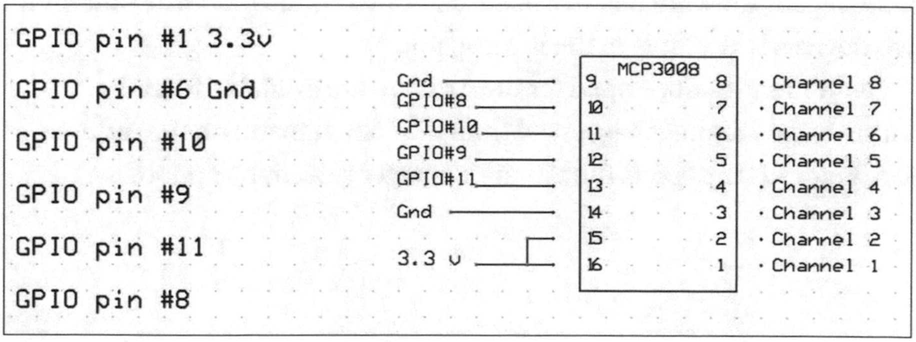

Figure 1-11. RPi GPIO pin–MCP3008 connections

If a higher 12-bit resolution is required, the single-channel MCP3201, 8-pin, plastic DIP IC (\$4 CDN) can be used, or one of the commercially available multichannel ADC boards can be purchased.

The Python code to use the GPIO pins of the Raspberry Pi for physical computing is contained in a library called gpiozero that is part of the operating system. As noted previously, extensive online documentation for using the gpiozero library is available from the RPi Foundation. The formal programming documentation is supplemented with teaching materials illustrating the basics of physical computing by detailing the connection to and control of LEDs, switches, motors, sensors, and other peripherals to the RPi.

Raspberry Pi Arduino Combinations

A relatively low-cost option for the implementation of physical computing on the RPi system is the Arduino microcontroller. An Arduino can function as an "intelligent" USB-connected input–output peripheral for a RPi.

The Arduino IDE software is easily downloaded onto the RPi, which can then be used to program the Arduino for the required sensor monitoring or peripheral control. By combining the two platforms, much of the legacy software that has been generated by the online forums for the two devices is available to the investigator.

New libraries developed for the Arduino are available from the online library manager accessed from the Sketch menu on the Arduino IDE. Figure 1-12 depicts the Library Manager selection window.

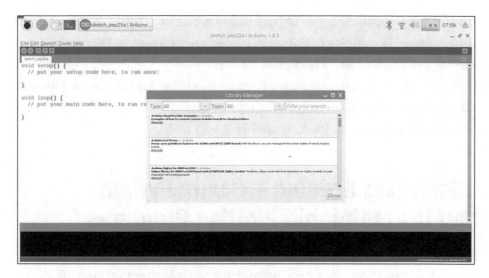

Figure 1-12. *Arduino Library Manager selection window*

Older library files that may not be in the new online compilation can be manually inserted into the Linux-based RPi Arduino IDE. Often an investigator may find that a significant number of programs and utilities have been developed on a particular version of the Arduino IDE and have been deployed into service and validated to the point that a reluctance to disturb the working code arises. In such cases, a second, more up-to-date IDE can be downloaded onto the RPi desktop and will operate independent of the original legacy installation.

Library management has evolved from a somewhat complex process for new programmers into a very easy-to-follow process well supported by online assistance.

From version 1.6.6 of the Arduino IDE onward, a new utility has been added to the serial port of the microcontroller. In addition to the "Serial Port" selection in the Tools menu there is also a "Serial Plotter" selection available. The serial plotter will generate a strip chart recorder–style data display that moves from left to right. The y-axis (vertical) is auto-ranging, and the x-axis is fixed at 500 units and is "tick" activated. An x-axis increment occurs each time a `Serial.println(y-data)` operation is executed by the Arduino sketch. Several examples of the serial plotter are depicted in Figures 10-1 and 10-2 in Chapter 10, "The Kalman Filter."

In revision 1.6.7, the serial plotter was modified to plot two variables if a blank line is "line printed" (`Serial.println(" ")`) between the two data variables being plotted. (See Figures 10-1 and 10-2).

Interfacing Arduino – C with Python and the Matplotlib Plotting Programs

Physical computing with the Arduino and its IDE uses a form of C code. A serial port provides for input and output communications that allow the microcontroller to communicate with many forms of external devices capable of serial transmissions. A number of serial transmission protocols exist that permit one- and two-way communications between devices that must share data or command instructions in either a coordinated synchronous or a random asynchronous manner.

In many experimental investigations, sensor data is generated in a random manner, and hence the simplest form of communication between two devices consists of the source device streaming out the observed data on a serial communication line. The receiving device continuously listens for the data and collects it as it arrives for interpretation.

In very simplified terms, binary systems are represented by ones and zeros consisting of high or low voltage levels in an electrical circuit. Groups of binary digits in the form of 8-bit words can form the basis of a communication by representing numbers, alphabetic characters, and printing control characters such as carriage returns, line feeds, tabs, and even non-English language, or mathematical symbols with 16-bit and larger words. The symbolic relationships are defined by the ASCII codes.

Data sent out from the Arduino on the serial port with the `print();` statement just streams out the bracketed data, while `println();` streams out the bracketed data followed by the newline and carriage return characters, \r and \n.

Care must be taken when programming in Python with the length function len(), to determine the length of a character string, and slice functions since these count the carriage control characters such as new line \n and carriage return \r as single units.

As noted previously, the RPi and Arduino can be connected with a USB communications protocol to form a complementary, low-cost, very flexible physical computing platform. In the following text, a general method for creating the Python programming required to receive and process the serial port data streamed out by an Arduino microcontroller is presented.

In order to begin the development of a Python code to receive and extract the numerical data from a serial port character stream, two small utilities and their usage are described in Listings 1-1 and 1-2. (Note that code listings are provided at the end of the chapter.)

To develop a code for separating or to parse out the numerical data portion of a continuous stream, the experimenter must know the length of the repetitively transmitted units of character and string are adjectives in this context string information streamed out to the RPi serial port. Listing 1-1 is a small utility to print out, on the console, the character string being received in the serial port input buffer.

Figure 1-13 is a console printout of the type K thermocouple temperature data being sent out by an Arduino monitoring an AD595 IC–type K thermocouple combination. As can be seen from the data stream, the input character string consists of the string b'22.48\r\n'. The b' can be considered as the first part of a formatting instruction, while the print controls \r and \n count as single units, and the trailing single quote ' is the final part of the initial formatting statement giving the countable string as 7. Only the four number symbols, the decimal point, and the two print control symbols are counted to create the sum of 7. The slice function is thus [0:5] or in older notation (line)[slice(0,5)].

To use the utility, the investigator must, if possible, know the length of the character string being sent to the port so the correct value can be inserted into the `if (len(line) < 7):` that skips over any fractional portions of the full character string caused by the asynchronous nature of the transmission. If the length of the full character string is not known, an estimate of the suspected size can be entered into the comparison and adjusted as required to get the correct full string length and produce the appropriate console display, as seen in Figure 1-13.

Figure 1-13. *A console output from the ReadSerialPort utility*

Listing 1-2 is a second utility that can be used to isolate the numerical character strings that must then be converted from character strings to valid Python numerical values of integers or floats. In a numerical format the serial port data are suitable for use in matplotlib for realtime plotting.

Figure 1-14 is the console output from Listing 1-2. The utility shows an example of a slice function used to isolate the numerical symbols of the serial port input string and their conversion to numerical float values in the case at hand.

The example depicted in Figure 1-14 has been coded for a numerical value of a two-digit decimal with two decimal places. If the sensor were to register less than 10 degrees or more than 99, the plotter program would "throw an error" or "crash" unless provision is made for the contraction or expansion of the data numerical values by changing the string-length logic and the slice notations for the longer or shorter numbers.

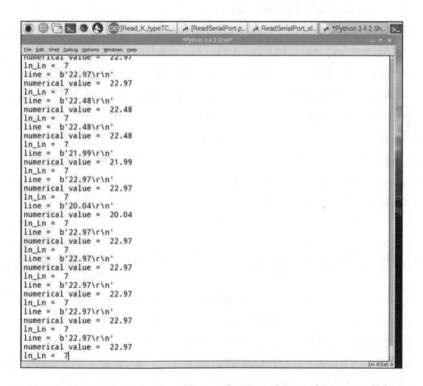

Figure 1-14. *A console output from the ReadSerialPortandSliceData utility*

Listing 1-3 in the code listings is the modified code that has been used to isolate numerical data from an Arduino microcontroller data stream for plotting with the matplotlib strip-chart recorder program. The code is able to accept several orders of magnitude of change in the integer size of the pulse-width differential measured by the 555 timer in high-resolution thermistor temperature measurement readings.

If an application to read a serial port data program terminates unexpectedly with an error such as `ValueError: could not convert string to float : '1.0.1.0'` an additional Python method for catching errors and handling them in order to continue uninterrupted program execution can be added to the code.

The block of logic code that uses the input string length statements, `if (len(inPutln) == 6):`, should be encased in a `try: / except ValueError:` block followed by a `continue` statement. If a `readline()` statement picks up only a partial numerical value or a noisy signal has corrupted the serial port input character string, any of the attempts to convert the character string to a numeric value could fail and generate the `ValueError` exception that would then be caught by the `except ValueError:` statement, which would then force the error to be ignored by continuing the `readline()` loop.

Arduino Interrupts and Timing Applications

RPi errors in time keeping involving spans that are measured to the nearest second do not usually present any significant problems in either measurement or display. Timespans involving fractions of a second require more care in both software creation and event detection. Combining an RPi with an Arduino can resolve many timing issues.

An Arduino microcontroller is equipped with a 16 MHz crystal oscillator to drive the digital logic chips with a well-defined and regulated clocking signal. Software functions can be used to access the clock signal to measure time. Arduino has two time-measuring functions called millis() and micros() that return the millisecond or microsecond clock count value at the time at which the function is called. Any variables that use either the millis or micros counts must be declared as unsigned long types or unusual or inexplicable results will be generated in printouts or calculations.

There are numerous tutorials and demonstrations available that use push-button switches as examples of external events that may represent the initial or final events of a time period to be measured. Erroneous values often result in timing operations using mechanical switching in the form of contact bounce. Time delays and capacitors (100 nF) across the switch contacts can compensate or eliminate some of the bounce problem. Photogates do not bounce, but the passage of a model or air-track car, pendulum bob, rolling ball, or the bars on a "picket fence" acceleration measurement device all produce an initial blocking of the IR beam and unblocking of the beam following device or obstruction passage. Timing software that is monitoring the voltage on a digital pin must be configured with the RISING, FALLING, or CHANGE options on the input pin under test in order to keep track of both the passage time and the light beam–obscuring object as required by the measurement problem at hand.

Each time a sketch is started, the millis() and micros() counting clocks begin. Since millis() is 1/1,000 of a second while micros() is 1/1,000,000 of a second, failure to declare variables attempting to hold these values as unsigned long numerical values will have unpredictable results from numerical overflow.

The registers holding the millis() value will "roll over" after about fifty days of continuous use, while the micros() register will reset to 0 after seventy minutes. Millis() requests are able to resolve time to the nearest single-digit millisecond, while micros() requests resolve time to the nearest four-microsecond multiple. (The resolution can be changed by accessing the pre-scaler register and adjusting the value found there in accordance with the ATmega 328 documentation. The nominal 16 MHz oscillator frequency is divided by an appropriate factor to get the `micro()` and `millis()` clock times.)

Interrupts stop the normal program flow of the central processing unit (CPU) so that important events can be recognized. Interrupts are used to signal to the CPU that a program called an interrupt service routine (ISR) that must be processed immediately to satisfy the conditions for which the interrupt was created. External electro-optical-mechanical switches turning on or off and internal software such as completion of the `millis()`, `micro()`, and pulse-width modulation functions all use interrupts to enable the software to perform as expected.

An Arduino provides two pins, D2 and D3, that can be connected to two external electrical or optical sensors to trigger interrupts and service routines according to rising or falling voltages on the pins. If more than two interrupts are needed, the Pin Change interrupt system built into the ATmega 328 chip must be invoked.

To implement the multiple-interrupt capability, the enableinterrupt library must be downloaded and installed in the Arduino IDE. At the time of writing (2018), the library is at `https://bintraycom/greygnome/generic/EnableInterrupt/view#files` and was in the file enableinterrupt-0.9.8.zip.

In essence, the library allows the experimenter to declare twenty-one pins on the Arduino as interrupts. Details on the usage, pins available, and examples of code are posted on the download page for those using the facility. Listing 1-4 uses five of the six analog input pins available on the Arduino Uno as "Pin Change" interrupts for timing applications that can be used in experiments such as the sloped track or pendulum swing timing used in repetitions of Galileo's classical experiments.

In essence, Listing 1-4 monitors the A0 to A4 ADC inputs on the Arduino's ADC. Interrupts are set up or assigned to each of the five inputs, and as the voltage on each interrupt is activated the interrupt service routine is processed, recording the time on the nominal interrupted pin.

In keeping with the philosophy of starting any experimental development project with the simplest apparatus available, the following multiple-interrupt demonstration can be configured by connecting the first five analog input pins on an Arduino to ground through normally open momentary contact push-button switches. Recalling that switches are prone to bouncing, the code has been set to monitor for five interrupts with a while loop monitoring the analog pins. Originally conceived to measure the four quarters of a sloped track with photogates, the code development was conducted with the five push-button switches for simplicity in construction. However, photogates do not produce false signals, and in a sloped track timing application the order in which the gates are to be read is fixed from start to finish with the three intermediate quarter-distance photogates between the end timers. Although the sloped track code does not require identifying the gate signaling an interrupt, application of the code to a five-lane racetrack circuit would do so. Inclusion of code to identify the pin requesting an interrupt is also a useful feature to have during the code development when bounce-prone switches are substituted for optical photogates. The line of code before the inclusion of the library as seen here allows the experimenter to identify the pin initiating an interrupt and simultaneously identifies the chronological order in which events occurred:

```
#include <EnableInterrupt.h>         // required for pin change
                                     // interrupt use
#define EI_ARDUINO_INTERRUPTED_PIN   // enable interrupt pin
                                     // identification
```

Confusion that may arise in the code-testing phase when the five interrupt times are displayed after only three or four button pushes is eliminated when the same pin number appears twice in the data display with virtually the same clock reading, as depicted in the double gate 15 entry in Figure 1-15.

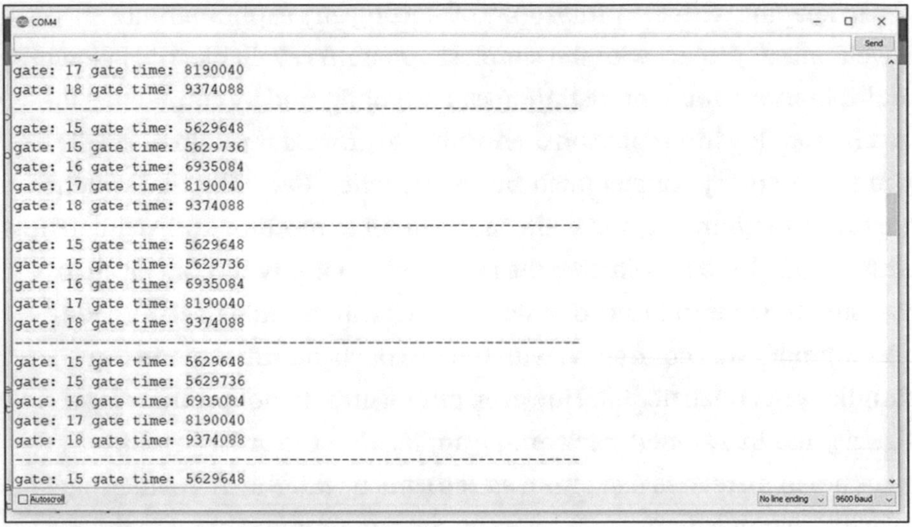

Figure 1-15. *An input switch bounce detected*

Interrupt service routines must be short and fast so as not to disrupt the normal timing of the operating system. As can be seen in the program code for the author's interrupt-driven timing operation, only the time count, the number of the active interrupt pin, and the counter index are assigned to volatile variables. The five array variables storing the time-count data must be declared as unsigned long in order to accommodate the length of the time clock count integers.

Figure 1-16 is the circuit for a series of photogates fabricated onto two circuit boards for mounting on experimental setups requiring accurate timing operations. A pair of these boards was mounted on a prototyping board and the output was connected to the ISR active A0 input on the Arduino.

To demonstrate an optically active high-speed timing exercise, the photogate was connected to the A0 input of Arduino, and the five times at which the gate is blocked by a pen swung back and forth quickly through the gate are recorded in Figure 1-17.

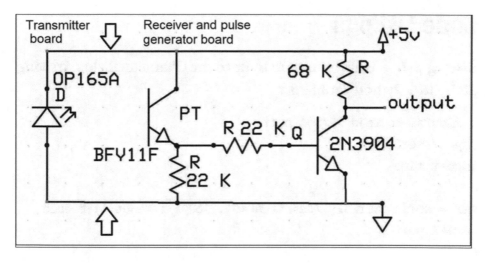

Figure 1-16. *A photogate circuit*

```
● COM4                                                              −   □   ×
                                                                        Send
gate: 14 gate time: 23749972
gate: 14 gate time: 26073796
-----------------------------------------------------------------------
gate: 14 gate time: 18059908
gate: 14 gate time: 18060688
gate: 14 gate time: 22705368
gate: 14 gate time: 23749972
gate: 14 gate time: 26073796
-----------------------------------------------------------------------
gate: 14 gate time: 18059908
gate: 14 gate time: 18060688
gate: 14 gate time: 22705368
gate: 14 gate time: 23749972
gate: 14 gate time: 26073796
-----------------------------------------------------------------------
gate: 14 gate time: 18059908
gate: 14 gate time: 18060688
gate: 14 gate time: 22705368
gate: 14 gate time: 23749972
gate: 14 gate time: 26073796
-----------------------------------------------------------------------
gate: 14 gate time: 18059908
☐ Autoscroll                                         No line ending ∨  9600 baud ∨
```

Figure 1-17. *A five-photogate blockage timing record*

An event requiring an interrupt is determined by the requirements
of the experiment at hand. Figure 1-17 records the times of a photogate
passage and four bounce-free button pushes.

Code Listings

Listing 1-1. A Utility Program to Read the Character String Arriving at the RPi–Python Serial Port

```
# Program to read serial port
import serial
import time
#
ser = serial.Serial('/dev/ttyACM0', 9600, timeout=1) # open
serial port
#
while True:
    ser.flushInput()         # clear the input buffer
    line = ser.readline()    # read to end of line marker
    ln_Ln = len(line)        # determine length of input string
    if (len(line) < 7):      # compare length of input string
        continue             # to known length
    time.sleep(0.1)
    print("ln_Ln = ",ln_Ln)
    print('line = ', line)
```

Listing 1-2. Read the Serial Port Character String and Slice Out the Numerical Symbols for Conversion to Numerical Values

```
# Program to retrieve numerical values from serial port input.
# when the length of the input string appearing on the port varies
# with varying numerical values the max and min possible lengths of
# the string must be determined and a slicing operation set up to
# accommodate each of the possible input string lengths.
#
```

```python
import serial
import time
#
# determine the input string parameters
ser = serial.Serial('/dev/ttyACM0', 9600, timeout=1) # open
serial port
#
while True:
    ser.flushInput()        # clear the input buffer
    line = ser.readline()   # read to end of line marker
    ln_Ln = len(line)       # determine length of input string
    if (len(line) < 7):     # compare length of input string
        continue            # to known length
    time.sleep(0.1)
    print("ln_Ln = ",ln_Ln)
    print('line = ', line)
#
# construct a slicing operation to isolate the numerical
characters for
# conversion to integers or floats
#
    if (ln_Ln == 7): # recall len/slice count 7 characters
        num_dgts = float((line)[slice(0,5)])
        print("numerical value = ", num_dgts)
```

Listing 1-3. Modified Code for matplotlib Strip-Chart Recorder Plotting of Serial Port Data

```
#
ser = serial.Serial("/dev/ttyACM0", 9600)
#
def rd_data():
    while True:
        line = ser.readline()
        #print("line = ", line)
        ln_Ln = len(line)  #determines # digits in temp
        #print("Len line = ", ln_Ln)
        if (ln_Ln < 35):
            continue
        time.sleep(0.1)
        if (ln_Ln == 35): # the IR temp is < 10
            line = float((line)[slice(27, 31)]) # parse out &
            convrt to digits
        if (ln_Ln == 36): # the IR temp is < 100
            line = float((line)[slice(27, 32)]) # parse out &
            convrt to digits
        if (ln_Ln == 37): # the IR temp is = or > 100
            line = float((line)[slice(27, 33)])
        # decimal and single-digit temperature values are
        processed by the code
        # double-digit minus value may require additional
        processing code.
        print(time.asctime())            # console print out of
        print("Temperature =",line," deg. C")   # timestamped
        data with a
        print()                          # formatting blank line
        yield (line)
```

Listing 1-4. Arduino pin interrupt code

```
// Five Photogate Timing
// Pin-change interrupts assigned to A0 to A4 and millis() /
   micros read for
// each photogate blockage recorded by the analog input pins.
//
#include <EnableInterrupt.h>          // required for pin-change
                                         interrupt use
#define EI_ARDUINO_INTERRUPTED_PIN  // enable interrupt pin
                                       identification
//
#define ARDUINOPIN A0
#define ARDUINOPIN1 A1
#define ARDUINOPIN2 A2
#define ARDUINOPIN3 A3
#define ARDUINOPIN4 A4
//
volatile unsigned long intrptTm;
volatile int intrptPin;
volatile int flag = 0;
int gate[5]; //5 element int array for gate / switch number id
unsigned long gateTm[5]; //5 element gate time value
int i; // indexing counter
//
void setup() {
  Serial.begin(9600);                    // initialize serial port
                                            at a reasonable rate
  pinMode(ARDUINOPIN, INPUT_PULLUP); // set the pull up
                                        resistors
  pinMode(ARDUINOPIN1, INPUT_PULLUP);
  pinMode(ARDUINOPIN2, INPUT_PULLUP);
```

```
  pinMode(ARDUINOPIN3, INPUT_PULLUP);
  pinMode(ARDUINOPIN4, INPUT_PULLUP);
//
enableInterrupt(ARDUINOPIN, interruptFunction, RISING);
enableInterrupt(ARDUINOPIN1, interruptFunction, RISING);
enableInterrupt(ARDUINOPIN2, interruptFunction, RISING);
enableInterrupt(ARDUINOPIN3, interruptFunction, RISING);
enableInterrupt(ARDUINOPIN4, interruptFunction, RISING);
}
//
void loop() {  // in loop the gate passage times are displayed
  while (flag < 5) {
    gate[flag] = intrptPin;
    gateTm[flag] = intrptTm;
  }
  //
 Serial.println("----------------------------------");
  delay(1000);
  for (i = 1; i < 6; i++)
  {
    Serial.print("gate: ");
    Serial.print(gate[i], DEC);
    Serial.print(" gate time: ");
    Serial.println(gateTm[i], DEC);
  }
}
  // the ISR or interrupt service routine
void interruptFunction() {
  intrptTm = micros(); // or millis
  intrptPin = arduinoInterruptedPin;
  flag = flag + 1;
  }
```

Summary

- Both the Arduino and Raspberry Pi projects began as educational concepts designed to provide very low-cost introductory hardware support for students to learn computer programming and physical computing.

- Both projects have grown far beyond their original educational purpose and are used commercially and industrially and have generated a large online community of amateur and professional researchers and engineers in need of rapid-prototyping capabilities.

- Although envisioned in two different countries and brought to market seven years apart, each device is complementary to the other and in combination form an extremely flexible and powerful physical computing and SCADA system.

- In Chapter 2, a basic outline is developed for implementing a Python–Arduino SCADA system.

CHAPTER 2

Development of a Simplified Python Supervisory Control and Data Acquisition System

Supervisory control and data acquisition (SCADA) software has been in use for many years, having been implemented on mainframe computers to manage remote installations such as hydroelectric plants, water treatment facilities, and sewage treatment works. Advances in electronics technology that reduced mainframe computer systems to laptop dimensions, object-oriented programming software advances, and the "unit operations" concepts of chemical engineering now allow the individual experimentalist to create very small, dedicated SCADA systems to interface with equipment on desk- or benchtops, between laboratories, or even between laboratories and mobile, remote, "in-field" experimental setups.

This chapter is designed to introduce the general concept of using open source systems for experimental monitoring and control. As noted in the

© Richard J. Smythe 2021
R. J. Smythe, *Advanced Arduino Techniques in Science*,
https://doi.org/10.1007/978-1-4842-6784-4_2

introduction to this book, investigators will need sufficient familiarity with
the concepts of programming and electronics to be able to adapt the code
sequences and circuit diagrams depicted here into workable systems on the
hardware–software combinations being used in their investigative work.

Open source, freely available software such as Python, with its built-in
Tkinter graphical user interface (GUI), when combined with inexpensive
hardware such as the Arduino and Raspberry Pi systems, allows the
experimenter to assemble customized GUI control systems for their
experimental setups at very low cost, measured in dollars and tens of
dollars rather than in thousands. Internet capability allows investigators to
work in both local and remote locations.

A significant concern with open source systems is being current
or "up to date." Many minds are developing new and better methods
for both hardware and software data acquisition with ever increasing
computational capabilities. The experimentalist choosing to use an open
source system must keep up to date with the current stable version of
the system in use. Open source software and hardware systems change
with time and at the time of writing, Python is up to version 3.6, Python's
Tkinter is at version 8.5, and Arduino is at version 1.8.13, while the
Raspberry Pi board advanced from its first implementation to its fourth
revision.

The following six Python program examples have been developed
throughout the implementation of two Raspberry Pi (RPi) releases. These
programs are working examples of Python–Tkinter–Arduino systems that
are able to execute the desired functions of digital data display, component
activation, component selection, component adjustment, and realtime
analog data recording from a GUI resident on a Model B Raspberry Pi.

Prior to embarking on developing an experiment or process-control
system with the Raspberry Pi, the investigator must be aware that the Pi is
a Linux system operating on a very inexpensive computing facility with no
graphics chips, math co-processor, or large amount of memory to vastly
boost system performance.

34

The very simple USB cable serial interfacing of an Arduino to the
RPi greatly increases the control capabilities and range of measurement
available to the experimenter. Pulse-width modulation, analog-to-digital
conversion (ADC), and substantial computing power from the Arduino's
potent C language–based integrated development environment (IDE)
programming aid are readily available from the microcontroller. Although
GUI displays place a large demand on available computing resources
and require simpler, more utilitarian interfaces, substantial digital signal
processing such as time averaging can be performed by the high-speed
microcontroller before sending the processed data to the RPi for display.

Because the concept and initial development of the core of this book
pre-dates the Raspberry Pi, Arduino, and Python, projects in this chapter
will also be behind the current technology when reviewed by experimental
investigators. However, the initial code and hardware specified in the
following pages is reproducible. The code was developed on different
computing platforms, but the final revisions all have been tested and
debugged on the RPi Model B with the NOOBs 2.1.0 operating system
resident on an 8 GB SD card. The supporting microcontroller was the
Arduino Uno or revision 3 boards.

To provide some assistance to those developing their own SCADA
system, a series of six programs spanning the primary unit operations
required to invoke a working experiment control system are presented.
The RPi programs are written in Python, and an Arduino microcontroller
provides a signal for display. The microcontroller programs are presented
in as simple a form as possible and do not include any significant signal-
noise reduction, which can be achieved by more programming of the
microcontroller.

As noted earlier, prior to any use of the Python language, RPi, or
Arduino components, obtain the latest updates and upgrades for the RPi
operating system. The Python language is open source and extensively
documented in numerous online tutorials and reference books. Python
programs should be developed on the computing system being used

to control the experiments at hand. Several Python–Tkinter–Arduino
programs developed on Microsoft or Apple systems have been found to
be incompatible with RPi systems. The RPi operating system has been
designed to facilitate the download of the required supporting software
packages, such as the numerical calculation package Numpy; the plotting
library Matplotlib; the scientific computing package SciPy; and other
specialized libraries, such as the serial port communications library
called serial, and the experimenter is advised to use them. Many of
the Python–Tkinter GUI screens developed for the RPi do not run on
Microsoft- or Apple-based operating systems.

This chapter contains the following exemplar unit operations:

- The basic Tkinter display frame

- An auto-updating, numerical-input screen display

- Screen-controlled On/Off buttons

- A mouse-activated screen slider for power control or
  fine adjustment

- Radio button exclusive selection of one option from a
  group

- Graphical data displays: a realtime strip-chart recorder

Program 1: Display Frame

A very simple display frame is created by the code in Listing 2-1.

Listing 2-1. Creating an Empty Basic GUI Display Frame with Python

```
# Arduino Advanced Techniques SCADA GUI Development with Python
  and Tkinter
#
```

```
import tkinter

mw = tkinter.Tk()
mw.option_add("font",("Arial", 15, "normal"))
mw.title("Arduino Advanced Techniques")
mw.iconname("Advanced Arduino Techniques")
mw.geometry("320x240+325+200")

lab1 = tkinter.Label(mw, text="Data to Display!",background=
"white",foreground="red", font="Arial 20")
lab1.pack()

mw.mainloop()
```

The output from Listing 2-1 is depicted in Figure 2-1. On screen, the size of the display can be varied by dragging the corners of the image frame out or in. The Minimize, Maximize, and Delete buttons all are functional, while the image itself can be "dragged" to a convenient screen location by the usual technique of placing the cursor on the frame's empty space to the right of the Arduino Advanced Techniques heading and depressing the left mouse button (all Tkinter exercises have been developed on the RPi Pixel OS).

In the simple Tkinter-based window seen in Figure 2-1, the basic outer frame and functional resizable display area are all created by the first six lines of code. Three lines of code define a label, its size, background color, text content, and display font, and paint it into the display window.

The parameters of the label display in Figure 2-1 showing the "Data to Display!" text are all fixed by the code and do not change as the outer frame of the small display window is varied. Although unused in this static demonstration, the bottom line implements the mainloop() function on the mw window display and automatically scans the screen area of the window display for mouse-cursor activity or, if programmed, keyboard activity. In-depth details of the mainloop() function can be found in the Tkinter documentation.

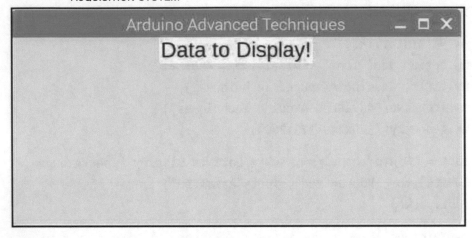

Figure 2-1. *A static sub-window display*

Program 2: Display of Changing Data in Realtime

In the example in Figure 2-1, a simple label displays the static text coded
into the text= option of the Tkinter label method. By substituting special
Tkinter variables (see Tkinter documentation) for the "Data to Display!"
text message, the label can display the actual value of the variable. By
setting the value of the variable to that of an input data stream arriving at
the serial port, the label can provide a "realtime" display of incoming data.
Analog sensor outputs being monitored by an Arduino board can then
be streamed out to the serial port for collection and display on the RPi
monitor. With the aid of a Python program, the data arriving at the serial
port can be processed into a format compatible with a realtime display in a
Tkinter-based GUI.

Monitoring an output signal from a remote sensor with a USB serial
connection to a host computer running a Python, Tkinter, GUI display
window requires forming a coordinated process for data transfer and
display. In terms of relative speeds, the GUI display has a large software

overhead and is thus relatively slow to respond to changing experimental
data. An easily implemented coordination of the one-way data-flow
system is to adjust the rate of delivery from the source of the data stream
to the GUI display so that the visual display operates at its normal rate
and the delivered data displays correctly. The data delivery rate must be
slow enough that the large resource consumption by the GUI neither fails
to display nor distorts the incoming data. In the visual digital display of
Figure 2-2 the display response is fast enough that a manual turning of the
potentiometer shaft is seen virtually immediately in the values observed
in the screen display. Timing on Arduino–RPi host displays is often best
adjusted experimentally.

In the code provided in Listings 2-2 and 2-3, the base display
window of Program 1 has been modified to hold static standard labels
identifying the source of the data stream and a second label that displays
the contents of a changing Tkinter variable that follows the Arduino
ADC values. Tkinter labels have been designed to accept one of the four
defined Tkinter variable types to provide a label readout that tracks the
changes in the original variable value. By reading the data on the port
in fractions-of-a-second intervals, a virtually continuous display of the
values arriving at the port is realized.

Listing 2-2. Python Tkinter GUI Code for Realtime Data Display

```python
import serial
from tkinter import *
from time import sleep
#
ser = serial.Serial('/dev/ttyACM0')
ser.baudrate = 9600
#
```

```python
def update():  # a normal python function definition
    while 1:        # main program loop
        reading.set(ser.readline()) # serial port data read and
        set to "readings" tkinter string variable
        data_strng = ser.readline() # serial port data string
        for examination and conversion
        print(data_strng)             # console display
        print(len(data_strng))        # string length determined
                                      for slicing operation
        if len(data_strng) == 10:   # limit on number of digits
                                      for conversion code
            adcVal = int(data_strng[0:3])  # extraction of integer
                                            ADC value
            print("ADC value = ", adcVal)  # display of three-
                                            digit ADC values only
        root.update()
        sleep(0.125)  # time value for real time display
#
root=Tk()                                   # tkinter window
reading = StringVar()                       # tkinter string
                                            value for display
                                            in label
w = Label(root, text="Serial Port String") # a static text label
w.pack()                                    # place label in window
w = Label(root, textvariable = reading)     # couple label
                                            content to serial
                                            port data string

w.pack()                                    # place label in window
root.after(1,update)                        # tkinter timing function
root.mainloop()                             # window loop
```

Listing 2-3. Arduino Code to Read Data and Write Values to the
Serial Port

```
/*
  AnalogRead and Calculation of 100 KΩ wiper voltage output
  from 5 volts input.
  Reads an analog input on pin 0, prints the result to the
  serial monitor.
  Attach the center pin of a potentiometer to pin A0, and the
  outside pins to +5V and ground.
  Pgm calcs wiperVoltage and sequentially sends int ADC
  (analog-to-digital converter) value and 3 decimal place value
  for the wiper voltage.
 */

// the setup routine runs once
void setup() {
  // initialize serial communication at 9600 bits per second:
 Serial.begin(9600);
}

// the loop routine:
void loop() {
  // read the input on analog pin 0:
  int sensorValue = analogRead(A0);
  float wiperVoltage = float(sensorValue * 5) / 1023; // NB
  double float req'd
  // print out sequentially the ADC and wiper voltage:
  Serial.print(sensorValue);
  Serial.println(wiperVoltage, 3); // NB 3 decimals
  delay(250);        // delay in between sensor reads for stability
}
```

The small windows displaying the data are termed widgets, and for simplicity the default properties of the individual label windows have been used in order to minimize the complexity of the GUI creation code. There are a large number of label options available to alter the appearance of the widget display, and as noted the minimize, maximize, and close widget functions are all active, along with the widget cursor-dragging size-adjustment functions.

In Figure 2-2 the widget display from Figure 2-4 has been enlarged for clarity and to display the static text label and the corresponding Tkinter string variable display. As the shaft of the potentiometer connected to the Arduino ADC is rotated, the character string below the static text identifier changes in virtually realtime.

Figure 2-2. *A realtime data display widget*

Depicted in Figures 2-3 and 2-4 are the graphical widget displays of the Arduino output data stream in the "as received" string format and the Python console display. Tkinter is a GUI creation package, and the ability to display the character string passing through the serial port, although limited, is in most cases probably all that is necessary to use the incoming data stream. A character stream to be used solely as a visual display can be configured to display in the specific format desired by the system operator. If however, the serial port character stream is to be used in a mathematical function or control operation, then the character string must be converted into integers or floating point numbers. Parsing of the character string for conversion to numerical values is best accomplished with Python code.

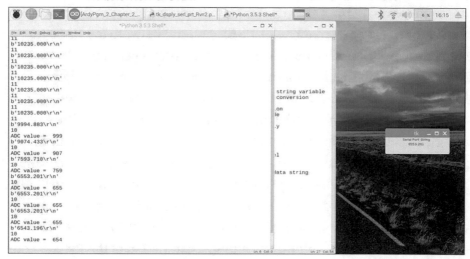

Figure 2-3. *A realtime data display high- to low-digit width
transition*

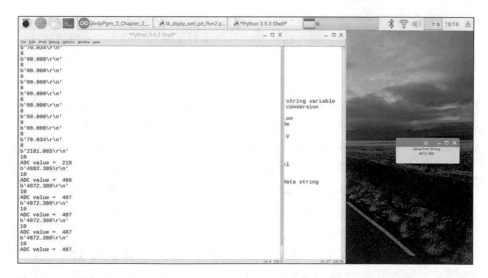

Figure 2-4. *A realtime data display low- to high-digit width
transition*

In these two figures, the smaller Tkinter windows on the right contain a text label naming the data being displayed, and beneath the static text is a character string of values. This character string is generated by the Arduino program that is streaming the integer ADC counts from the microprocessor and the actual calculated floating-point wiper voltage in a continuous stream to the serial port. The Python code receives the stream as a character string that can vary from six to nine units in length as the potentiometer is rotated to either extreme. The console output recordings in Figures 2-3 and 2-4 have captured the voltage transit from the 1023 ADC counts and the 5.000V level to the most common mid-range three-digit values then to the transition to the 0 ADC counts and 0.000V at the low-end extreme of the potentiometer setting. Examination of the Python code shows that in this simple demonstration the string-to-integer conversion is fixed in code at ten digits; that is far larger than the midrange three-digit value most likely to occur during potentiometer-shaft rotation. Shaft positions within the limits of 100 and 999 ADC counts trigger the slicing-logic code that picks out only the three-digit ADC values and converts the string characters into integer numbers that are displayed on the console.

To aid the programmer in setting up the slice function, the actual character stream to parse is displayed along with the len() function value that indicates how the Python code is counting characters. Note that the string reportedly arriving at the port as depicted in Figure 2-2 is 4872.380, which the Python code reports as b'4872.380\r\n', which in turn has a counted character length of ten. When creating the slice function, the programmer can see that the Python len() function counts the b' and \r\n' as single characters.

A point of caution is noted here, and will be repeated later, that involves the nature of the data being streamed out by the Arduino's analog-to-digital converter (ADC). At either extreme of the potentiometer rotation, the data stream can vary from a single digit to four, and hence the Python

code receiving the stream must be able to accommodate the variation in
the size of the serial data stream with multiple slice functions to cover the
expected width range.

In spite of the large overhead created by the Python software, the speed
of the RPi enables the graphic display to keep up with the experimentalist
turning the shaft of the potentiometer without any noticeable delay.

Program 3: Activation of Experimental Devices from Button Displays

To create a functioning unit operation such as activating an LED
connected to an Arduino microcontroller board, a more complex process
must be followed.

The creation of a display-screen button that when pressed by a
mouse click or a keyboard entry initiates a desired remote action requires
implementation of "event-driven programming." Event-driven systems
require two programs: the first creates an RPi screen displaying a button
that is monitored for activation, and the second, resident on the remote
device, monitors the serial communications stream for instructions
from the button-display monitor program. In this simple demonstration,
our screen button will activate an LED already mounted on the remote
Arduino microcontroller board.

Tkinter event-driven "objects," such as buttons and checkboxes, use an
internal loop to scan over the possible actions associated with the object
in the screen display. "Pressing" the button image with a mouse-button
click is caught by the scanning loop software code of the image-object, and
an action is initiated that can consist of sending a serial command to the
Arduino, which in turn switches on the power to an LED. In the current
exercise, event-driven programming is initiated by the user's activating a
screen image that in turn invokes the USB serial communication system
between the host computer and the Arduino microcontroller board. Since

both the display software and the Arduino microcontroller are activated by
looping software code, our event-driven system needs to be coordinated.

To begin the assembly of the button-activated Arduino-LED system,
the screen in Figure 2-5 is created with the Python–Tkinter code (Listing 2-4
and 2-5).

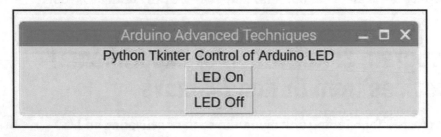

Figure 2-5. *A simple on/off dual button control panel*

Listing 2-4. Python Tkinter GUI for Button Control of Remote
Arduino LED

```
# Event handlers join a widget to a type of event and a desired
# resulting action. Command is the method used to detect mouse
  "<Button-1>"
# events (clicks on the left mouse button) When a button is
  left clicked with
# mouse, the self.buttonClick() method is invoked to initiate a
  serial
# transmission of a signal to activate an Arduino action that
  controls
# an LED.
#
import tkinter      #lowercase t for current python installation
import serial
from time import *
#
```

```python
#open the COM port in use
ser = serial.Serial("/dev/ttyACM0", 9600)
#
# define the myWindow class
class myWindow:
    def __init__(self):

        self.mw = tkinter.Tk()
        self.mw.title("Arduino Advanced Techniques")
        self.mw.option_add("*font",("Arial", 15, "normal"))
        self.mw.geometry("+250+200")
# GUI function title
        self.lab_1 = tkinter.Label(self.mw, text = "Python
        Tkinter Control of Arduino LED")
        self.lab_1.pack()
#
# add two buttons to the ui
        self.btn_on = tkinter.Button(self.mw, text = "LED On",
        command = self.btnOnClick)
        self.btn_on.pack()
        self.btn_off = tkinter.Button(self.mw, text = "LED
        Off", command = self.btnOffClick)
        self.btn_off.pack()
#
#

        self.mw.mainloop()
#
    def btnOnClick(self):
        ser.write('y'.encode())
        sleep(1)
#
```

```python
    def btnOffClick(self):
        ser.write('n'.encode())
        sleep(1)
#
if __name__ == "__main__":
    app = myWindow()
```

Listing 2-5. Arduino Sketch for Response to Python GUI Button
Activation

```c
//Arduino monitors serial port for Python command code
//
char serialreader = ' '; // variable to hold data from serial port
//
void setup(){
  // open serial connection
  Serial.begin(9600); // bps rate
  pinMode(13, OUTPUT); // on board led
  Serial.write("1"); //acknowledge readiness
}

void loop() {
  // assign data sent over serial port to serialreader variable
  while (Serial.available() > 0){
    serialreader = Serial.read();
  }
  // turn Led on/off if y/n transmitted
  if (serialreader == 'y') {
    digitalWrite(13, HIGH); //led on
    Serial.print("Led on\n");//confirm activation
    serialreader = ' '; // clear contents
  }
```

```
else if (serialreader == 'n') {
  digitalWrite(13, LOW); // led off
  Serial.print("led off\n");
  serialreader = ' ';
  }
}
```

This relatively simple on-screen GUI does not have an indicator to
confirm activation of the LED illumination, as the exercise assumes that
the Arduino board is within the field of view of the user. If, however, the
device being controlled is remote and out of sight, the researcher may
want to have the remote unit send back conformation that the LED or
experimental operation is actually powered up by having the code of the
remote device send a message back to the initiating GUI to display some
form of message label or background-color change to indicate power
application to the LED. Alternately, a photoelectric signal derived from
light output from the remote device that confirms both power delivery and
light-source functionality could be returned to the local GUI.

Program 4: A Sliding-Scale Implementation

Listings 2-6 and 2-7 are the pair required to implement Program 4, which
illustrates the use of a sliding-scale selection capability for a screen
component that can be used to simulate an analog-type control
(Figure 2-6). Rough control of the output signal can be achieved by
dragging the scale position-indicator rectangle along the "trough" of the
slider image. Fine control of the movement can be achieved by placing
the mouse cursor over the trough above or below the rectangular index
position indicator and clicking on the mouse button. When the mouse
cursor is over the trough between the end of the scale and the indicator,
each mouse-button click will move the index indicator one unit toward the
scale end at hand.

In this example, the slider output varies the "analog" value written
to a pulse-width modulation pin on an Arduino microcontroller. On
the PWM pin of the Arduino, a current-control resistor and an LED are
mounted so the slider variation can be seen as a dimming of the LED
illumination intensity. In addition to the hardware–software interaction,
this particular system demonstrates an advantage of the PWM technique.
If our hardware–software control system were to instruct the Arduino to
apply a normal analog voltage to the output pin, from the 0 voltage to
approximately 1.5V the LED would be dark because the applied voltage
would be below the device's "turn-on value." A PWM technique, however,
applies a full 5V to the diode (hence the need for the current-control 220
ohm resistor), and the diode is illuminated at full power for a timed period.
By adjusting the duty cycle the illumination can be smoothly varied from
nothing to full illumination intensity, and the diode minimum turn-on
voltage properties of the LED are bypassed.

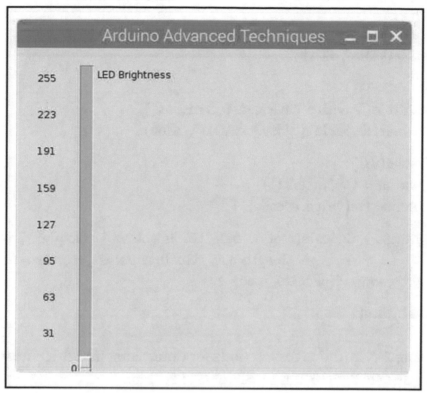

Figure 2-6. *A power-control sliding scale ("slider")*

Listing 2-6. Python Tkinter GUI Code for Implementation of the
Analog Slider Control

```
# A Sliding-Scale Serial Connection for Power Control.
# A tkinter sliding-scale screen widget is used to provide a
  continuously
# adjustable serial signal that controls pulse-width variation
  of a 5 volt
# power signal, applied by an Arduino board to a current-
  limited LED.
# Sliding the scale tab up or down increases or decreases diode
  luminosity.
```

51

```python
#
import serial
import tkinter as tk

root = tk.Tk()
root.title("Arduino Advanced Techniques")
ser = serial.Serial("/dev/ttyACM0", 9600)

def send(val):
    value = chr(int(val))
    ser.write(value.encode())

brightness = tk.Scale(root, label="LED Brightness", from_=255, to=0,
                      length=400, tickinterval=32, command=send)
brightness.grid(padx=20, pady=20)

tk.mainloop()
```

Listing 2-7. Arduino Sketch Code for Controlling LED Brightness in Response to Python Tkinter Slider GUI Position

```
// Tkinter Slider -- Arduino Dimmer Code
// An integer from 1 to 255 is used to control the brightness
   of an LED.
// the integer is created in a Tkinter GUI with a "slider
   scale." Python
// serial code sends an ASCII-coded value between 1 and 255
   that constitutes
// the brightness value

const int ledPin = 9;  // the pin with the LED

int brightness = 0;
```

```
void setup()
{
  // initialize the serial communication:
  Serial.begin(9600);
  // initialize the ledPin as an output:
  pinMode(ledPin, OUTPUT);
}

void loop() {
  //check for serial data
  if (Serial.available() > 0)  // check to see if at least one
                                        character is available
  {
      brightness = (int) Serial.read();
      analogWrite(ledPin, brightness);
    }
}
```

Program 5: Radio Button Controls

GUI radio buttons function in the same manner as the push buttons used in numerous consumer entertainment electronics and electrical appliances. A single button depression exclusively selects a single option from the number of choices available. Program 5 is implemented with Listings 2-8 and 2-9.

In the example created here, the Tkinter panel in Figure 2-7 has been activated with a mouse click to select the third option available, and consequently the third or middle LED in a row of five LEDs connected to an Arduino microcontroller board is illuminated.

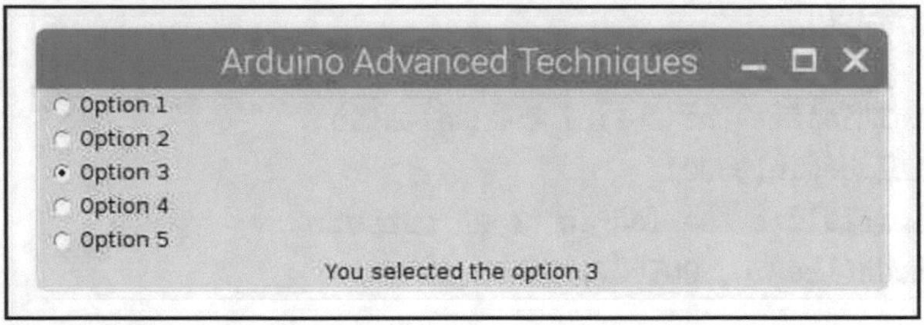

Figure 2-7. *A radio button selection panel*

Listing 2-8. Python Tkinter GUI for a Radio Button Selection Panel
Display

```
# Radio button Exclusive Selection of One Option from a Group
# A GUI is created with the Python Tkinter module that contains
  five labeled
# radio buttons and a display label. Clicking on an empty
  button ring causes
# the solid center of the button to appear, the display label
  to indicate the
# identity or number of the button depressed, and serially
  transmits the number
# of the keyed button to, in this example, an Arduino board
  with 5 LEDs.
# The logic creating the selection exclusivity is easily
  implemented with the
# Arduino code.
#

from tkinter import *
import serial

ser = serial.Serial("/dev/ttyACM0", 9600)
```

```python
def sel():
    selection = "You selected the option " + str(var.get())
    label.config(text = selection)
    #print(str(var.get())) # code for pgm dvlpmnt
    ser.write((str(var.get())).encode('ascii')) # object to
    string conversion

root = Tk()
root.title("Advanced Arduino Techniques")

var = IntVar() # a Tkinter integer variable object

R1 = Radiobutton(root, text="Option 1", variable=var,
value=1,command=sel)
R1.pack(anchor = W)

R2 = Radiobutton(root, text="Option 2", variable=var,
value=2,command=sel)
R2.pack(anchor = W)

R3 = Radiobutton(root, text="Option 3", variable=var,
value=3,command=sel)
R3.pack(anchor = W)

R4 = Radiobutton(root, text="Option 4", variable=var,
value=4,command=sel)
R4.pack(anchor = W)

R5 = Radiobutton(root, text="Option 5", variable=var,
value=5,command=sel)
R5.pack(anchor = W)

label = Label(root)
label.pack()
root.mainloop()
```

Our radio-button example uses Tkinter variable objects that cannot be passed as normal integer values on the serial bus. (See Tkinter documentation.) Conversion of the object to a string that is compatible with both the serial bus transmission and Arduino C code is required to implement the interfacing of the two system components. The author has left in place one of the "commented out" print statements used in the initial development of the code. Printing variables is a technique that can be used to see what the code, in an experimental passage, is actually producing. Leaving or "commenting out" the invisible statement in place can be an aid in future maintenance or code-modification operations.

For ease of code development and to minimize USB traffic, the exclusivity logic of the radio button selection should be implemented in the Arduino code. When a button is selected in the Tkinter GUI, the button identity can be transmitted to the Arduino for diode illumination, and the Arduino code can then turn off the last LED illuminated.

Listing 2-9. Arduino Sketch for Implementing the Radio Button Selection from the Python Tkinter GUI Panel

```
/*
Switch statement with serial input

Pgm uses a switch statement to choose which LED to illuminate
and which LEDs to turn off.
Serial monitor on Arduino should be used to confirm
microcontroller
operation before configuring the entire system from Serial
Monitor to send any number between 1 and 5 to turn on the
appropriate LEDs. Any other character will turn off the LEDs.

 The circuit:
 * 5 LEDs attached to digital pins 2 through 6 each requires a
 220-ohm resistor
```

```
*/

void setup() {
  // initialize serial communication:
  Serial.begin(9600);
   // initialize the LED pins:
      for (int thisPin = 2; thisPin < 7; thisPin++) {
        pinMode(thisPin, OUTPUT);
      }
}

void loop() {
  // read the sensor:
  if (Serial.available() > 0) {
    int inByte = Serial.read();
      {

    switch (inByte) {
    case '1':
      digitalWrite(2, HIGH);
      digitalWrite(3, LOW);
      digitalWrite(4, LOW);
      digitalWrite(5, LOW);
      digitalWrite(6, LOW);
      break;

    case '2':
      digitalWrite(3, HIGH);
      digitalWrite(2, LOW);
      digitalWrite(4, LOW);
      digitalWrite(5, LOW);
      digitalWrite(6, LOW);
      break;
```

```
    case '3':
      digitalWrite(4, HIGH);
      digitalWrite(3, LOW);
      digitalWrite(2, LOW);
      digitalWrite(5, LOW);
      digitalWrite(6, LOW);
      break;

    case '4':
      digitalWrite(5, HIGH);
      digitalWrite(3, LOW);
      digitalWrite(4, LOW);
      digitalWrite(2, LOW);
      digitalWrite(6, LOW);
      break;

    case '5':
      digitalWrite(6, HIGH);
      digitalWrite(3, LOW);
      digitalWrite(4, LOW);
      digitalWrite(5, LOW);
      digitalWrite(2, LOW);
      break;
    default:

    // turn all the LEDs off:
      for (int thisPin = 2; thisPin < 7; thisPin++) {
        digitalWrite(thisPin, LOW);
      }
    }
   }
  }
}
```

Program 6: Graphical Data Display—A Realtime Strip-Chart Recording

Many experimental investigations use graphical data displays that may be divided into two basic types: those that use previously recorded or theoretically generated data to create the display and those that monitor and display the present and recent past values of a data stream. Static files of data, collected over years or microseconds and maintained in stored format, can be used to create static or animated images for visual analysis with two- or three-dimensional plotting software, as provided by the Matplotlib facilities of Python. Matplotlib also has the ability to generate continuous graphical displays of streamed, varying data with minimal time delays between the change in data-stream values and the alteration of the visual display. A visual display that tracks a varying-value data stream is commonly referred to as a "realtime" display. Realtime displays are often required in setting up experimental apparatus or following slowly changing signal measurements such as weather conditions, animal movement, or titrations in chemical analysis determinations.

Oscilloscopes electronically record and display relatively high-speed electrical signals over very short time scales, while strip-chart recorders monitor longer time bases for displaying varying signals. Strip-chart recorders are electro-mechanical devices in which a pen draws a trace on a paper strip chart, moving at a constant velocity beneath the potentiometrically balanced pen drive mechanism.

An audio frequency range oscilloscope display can be created from a monitor and a PC sound card with software programs obtained commercially or from internet download. Xy recording and audio-frequency measurements are accessible for more advanced investigations through these various freeware and moderate-cost options.

Python's plotting library, known as Matplotlib, contains a generic strip-chart recorder program in its list of animation program examples.

There are other plotting facilities available in commercial, free, and open source formats obtainable from the internet. (See DAQFactory Express, PL Plot, etc.)

Python's strip-chart recorder is based upon the animations capability found in the Matplotlib module, and the example program provides its own internal series of "random spiking" events to record for demonstration purposes.

Program 6 is implemented with the Arduino and Python–Matplotlib pair of Listings 2-10 and 2-11.

An easily fabricated experimental setup, capable of providing a continuously varying analog signal that can be digitized, transmitted over a serial connection, and displayed back, in analog form, can be created by coupling a TMP36 integrated-circuit temperature sensor to the analog input on an Arduino microcontroller board, which in turn outputs a temperature reading to the RPi GUI for display. The circuit for the wiring is depicted in Figure 2-8.

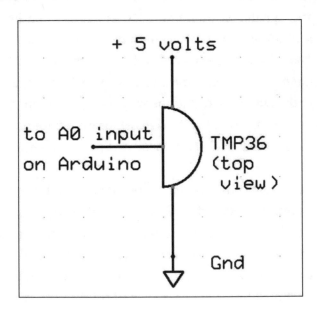

Figure 2-8. *A circuit configuration for realtime temperature recording from a TMP36 IC*

Listing 2-10. Arduino Sketch for Digitization and Serial
Transmission Streaming of TMP36 Temperature Data

```
// TMP-36 Temperature sensor monitor
//
// The TMP36 is biased with +5 volts and the IC signal is
// output on the serial port. IC resolution is 10mv/deg C
// and a 500 mv offset is used to allow for sub-zero
// temperature readings.
//
// TMP36 pin assignments
int temperaturePin = 0;
//
void setup()
{
  Serial.begin(9600);
}
//void loop()
{
  float temperature = getVoltage(temperaturePin);
 temperature = (temperature - .5) * 100; // conversion code
 // 10 mv/degC with 500mv offset x 100 to get degC
 Serial.println(temperature); // output value
 delay(1000);   // once per second
}
//
//
float getVoltage(int pin)
{
  return (analogRead(pin)*0.004882814); // convert from
  // 0 -1023 ADC out to 0 - 5 volts.
}
```

Listing 2-11. Python Matplotlib Strip-Chart Recording Code for
Streamed TMP36 Data

```python
# Arduino Temperature Monitor
import serial
import numpy as np
from matplotlib import pyplot as plt
ser = serial.Serial('/dev/ttyACM0', 9600)
#
plt.ion() # set plot to animated
#
ydata = [0] * 50
ax1 = plt.axes()
#
# create the plot
line, = plt.plot(ydata)
plt.ylim([10,40])
#
#
# start data collection
s = [0]
while True:
    read_serial = ser.readline() # read arduino output string
    from serial
    s[0] = str(ser.readline())
    # use slicing to isolate the TMP data
    if len(s[0]) == 12:
        data = float((s[0][2:7]))
        ymin = float(min(ydata))-10
        ymax = float(max(ydata))+10
        plt.ylim([ymin,ymax])
        ydata.append(data)
```

```
    del ydata[0]
    line.set_xdata(np.arange(len(ydata)))
    line.set_ydata(ydata)  # update the data
    plt.draw() # update the plot
else:
    print("error in data")
```

The plotting code originally posted by B. Welt in 2013 and modified by
the author only accepts two-digit temperature values but works well as a
demonstration of realtime recording.

In Figure 2-9, the RPi screen contains the Python console on the left
and the Matplotlib strip-chart recorder output on the right.

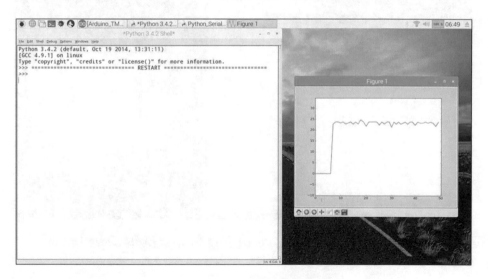

Figure 2-9. *The RPi console and a SCR display of a TMP output*

In the examples section of the Matplotlib documentation an actual
strip-chart recorder (SCR) program is presented in which a random-
number generator is used to provide data for the program display.
A modification of the SCR program to record the streamed output of
an Arduino microcontroller monitoring the ambient room light near a

window on a cloudy day is presented here. The Arduino and RPi–Python
code pair of Figure 2-12 and Listing 2-12 are presented together with a
screen display from the RPi in Figure 2-10 and a detail of the actual plotter
output in Figure 2-11.

The functions of the buttons in the lower left-hand corner of the
graphical display are detailed in the Matplotlib Interactive Navigation
documentation. The coordinates of any point on the recorded graphic line
can be displayed in the lower right-hand corner of the display by placing
the mouse pointer over the desired location.

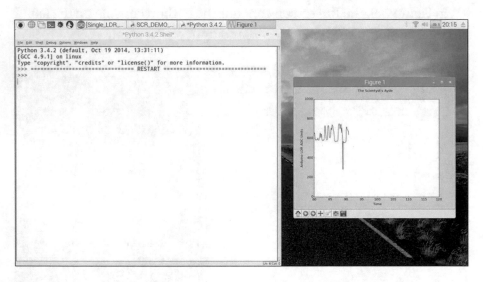

Figure 2-10. *An illumination recording from a light-dependent
resistor on a cloudy day*

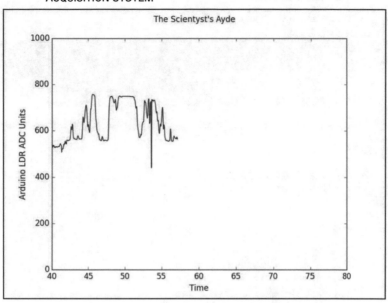

Figure 2-11. *The illumination recording from Figure 2-10*

Arduino Sketch to Monitor, Digitize, and Serially Stream LDR Data for
Python–Matplotlib SCR Presentation shown in Figure 2-12.

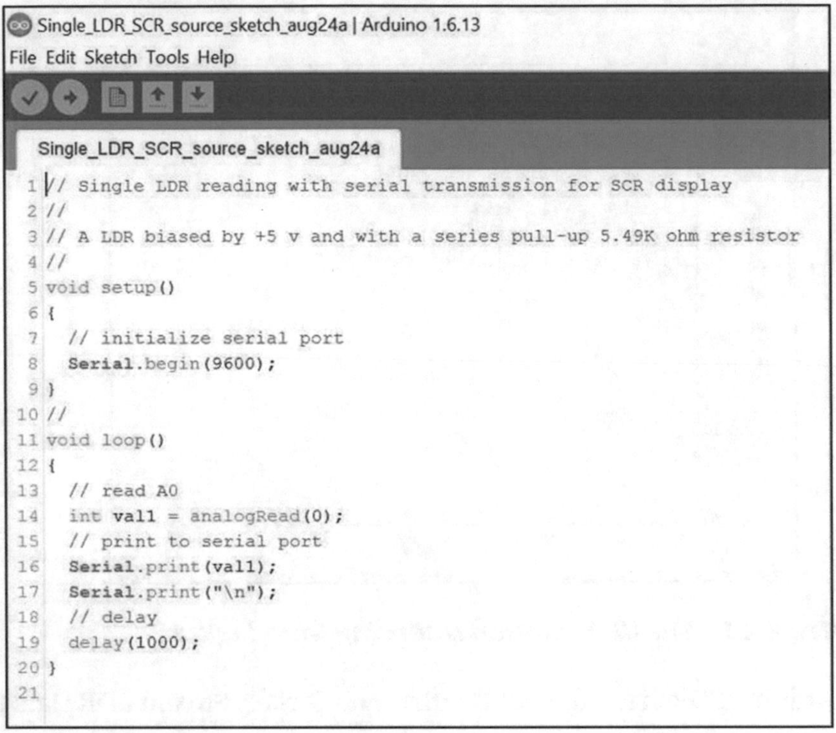

```
Single_LDR_SCR_source_sketch_aug24a | Arduino 1.6.13
File Edit Sketch Tools Help

Single_LDR_SCR_source_sketch_aug24a
 1 // Single LDR reading with serial transmission for SCR display
 2 //
 3 // A LDR biased by +5 v and with a series pull-up 5.49K ohm resistor
 4 //
 5 void setup()
 6 {
 7   // initialize serial port
 8   Serial.begin(9600);
 9 }
10 //
11 void loop()
12 {
13   // read A0
14   int val1 = analogRead(0);
15   // print to serial port
16   Serial.print(val1);
17   Serial.print("\n");
18   // delay
19   delay(1000);
20 }
21
```

Figure 2-12. *An Arduino IDE code listing for LDR response*

Listing 2-12. Python Matplotlib SCR Display Code

```
"""

A Strip Chart Recorder Graphical Display for Raspberry Pi
"""

# The RPi display is driven by an Arduino serial port output
#
import matplotlib
import numpy as np
from matplotlib.lines import Line2D
import matplotlib.pyplot as plt
import matplotlib.animation as animation
import serial
```

```python
class Scope:
    def __init__(self, ax, maxt=40, dt=0.02):
        """maxt time width of display in minutes"""
        self.ax = ax
        self.dt = dt
        self.maxt = maxt
        self.tdata = [0]
        self.ydata = [0]
        self.line = Line2D(self.tdata, self.ydata)
        self.ax.add_line(self.line)
        self.ax.set_ylim(0.0,1000.0)  # y axis scale
        self.ax.set_xlim(0, self.maxt)

    def update(self, y):
        lastt = self.tdata[-1]
        if lastt > self.tdata[0] + self.maxt: # reset the arrays
            self.tdata = [self.tdata[-1]]
            self.ydata = [self.ydata[-1]]
            self.ax.set_xlim(self.tdata[0], self.tdata[0] +
            self.maxt)
            self.ax.figure.canvas.draw()

        t = self.tdata[-1] + self.dt
        self.tdata.append(t)
        self.ydata.append(y)
        self.line.set_data(self.tdata, self.ydata)
        return self.line,

ser = serial.Serial("/dev/ttyACM0", 9600)
#
```

```python
def rd_data():
    while True:
        inPutln = ser.readline()
        #print("inPutln = ", inPutln)
        line = int(str(inPutln)[slice(2,-3)]) # convert arduino
        serial output stream to a Python string, parse out the
        numerical symbols, and convert to a value.
        #print(line)
        yield (line)

fig = plt.figure()
fig.suptitle("The Scientyst's Ayde", fontsize = 12)
ax = fig.add_subplot(111)
ax.set_xlabel("Time")
ax.set_ylabel("Arduino LDR ADC Units")
scope = Scope(ax)

# use rd_data() as a generator to produce data for the update
  func, the delay(n)
# in the Arduino code determines rate of data feed to the
  animated
# screen display. Software overhead limits response speed of
  display.
ani = animation.FuncAnimation(fig, scope.update, rd_data,
interval=50,
blit=True)

plt.show()
```

When Listing 2-12 is run on the RPi, it generates the dual screens of
Figure 2-10, with Python on the left and the graphic display trace depicted
on the right and in close up in Figure 2-11. The SCR display is divided
into forty-minute increments, and data display is initiated and timed

from the loading and running of the Python code. After the accumulation and display of forty minutes of data, the program advances to the next forty-minute window, as is visible on the time axis in Figures 2-10 and 2-11. The SCR program code does not have any provision for storing the data from a previous window time increment other than the ability to save the current graphical display provided by the Save button on the right-hand end of the lower left panel of buttons. The area of the plot window can be dragged to any convenient size by the usual mouse window-edge manipulation techniques.

All of the programs and code presented in this chapter are very simple, have no signal-to-noise reduction code, and are uncalibrated. Most of the code has been commented, and some contains print statements for diagnosing malfunctioning code that have been "commented out" for actual use. Where applicable, cautions have been added with respect to processing the incoming data-stream variations that may occur. The analog-to-digital converter on an Arduino can output values from 0 to 1023. In other words, the incoming stream can vary from a single-digit value to a four-digit value together with the control characters required to uniquely define the transmission of the data stream. There are numerous serial data-transmission protocols used in various sensors, and the experimenter must accommodate these protocols when modifying the Python codes presented here for data display.

The programs work and can be used as a known starting point for the development of more-complex, very low-cost, small-scale, Linux–Python–based SCADA systems.

Summary

- A series of six basic "unit operations" that can be used to assemble a SCADA system are developed.

- Data displays and analog-and-digital control functions
  are developed in Python–Tkinter–based GUI screen
  displays resident on the RPi, and serial data or
  operational commands are streamed back and forth
  with an Arduino microcontroller functioning as an
  intelligent peripheral or interface.

- A Python–Matplotlib continuous strip-chart recorder
  data display is demonstrated by providing a continuous
  recording of Arduino data streams following ambient
  temperature and lighting conditions.

In Chapter 3, the care required when generating and working with high
heats and high temperatures in experimental investigations is explored.

CHAPTER 3

Experimental Work at High Temperatures and High Heats

In this introductory book, only high heat and temperature created by electrical current–based Joule heating is considered in accordance with its simplicity of application and low cost. Non-contacting induction heating is a much more complex and expensive technique suitable for more advanced projects and investigations.

Small volumes are the key to safely creating high-heat, high-temperature environments with the regular line voltages available in North America. Most domestic and commercial electrical-distribution systems are wired for 15 amp currents at a nominal 115 volts AC, which limits usable power to approximately 1.5 kilowatts. (The wiring of 220 volt systems is beyond the simplified nature of this book and should only be designed and assembled with the aid of qualified electrical technicians familiar with local electrical safety codes.)

© Richard J. Smythe 2021
R. J. Smythe, *Advanced Arduino Techniques in Science*,
https://doi.org/10.1007/978-1-4842-6784-4_3

71

Safety Considerations

- All materials melt.

- Create high heat slowly.

- Molten materials can dissolve anything.

- Water is a violent explosive when contacting any material at red heat.

- Heat accelerates corrosion, so in hot areas use stainless steel fasteners.

- Fuel gases are odorless, dangerously flammable, and explosive.

Safety concerns mandate that live mains electrical connections be completely enclosed and that the outer surface of the case or shell enclosing the hot volume and electrical connections is allowed to be warm or hot to the touch but not so hot as to burn skin. Steel sheet metal coated with zinc known as galvanized steel is a good, readily available material for an outer casing. The zinc coating will retard corrosion, and since the outer surface of any high-temperature device should never get hot enough to burn skin, the zinc-metal protective coating should provide an excellent service life. If an accidental overheating condition occurs, the glossy crystalline outer surface of the zinc "galvanizing" in the hot zone will turn matte gray as the zinc coating oxidizes in the presence of oxygen to provide a visual alert of the dangerous failure condition (Figure 3-21).

Good insulation is required to both keep the external case at a reasonable temperature and to contain the heat in the interior hot chamber. Ceramic oxides in brick, sheet, and crushed small-particle format or as woven fiber cloths or wool batts are common materials able to significantly restrict the flow of heat.

Many homes have wood-burning fireplaces for heat or decoration and thus many building suppliers can be a convenient source of refractory and insulation materials. High-temperature equipment such as kilns and accessories are available from industrial and pottery or ceramic hobby suppliers.[1]

Experimental work involving high heat and temperatures often uses "pot," "tube," and "muffle" furnaces. (A muffle or a retort furnace is one in which the material being heated is completely isolated from the source of heat.) An open to the air pot furnace in which a material such as a glass or clay mineral must be dissolved or fused with a salt-based flux to provide a water-soluble salt solution for further analysis can be assembled from readily available materials. Production of a high-purity material such as metallic iron may require conducting a reduction reaction at high temperatures in a hydrogen atmosphere, and a tube furnace would be an appropriate reactor selection.

Construction of either of the two types of high-temperature furnace will require a similar design approach. A cube 2 or 3 in. on a side (5–7.5 cm) forming a pot furnace for a 50 ml crucible or a 1 to 2 in. (2.4–5 cm) diameter cylinder 12 to 18 in. (30.5–45.5 cm) in length to accommodate a 2 to 3 ft. (1 m) long Pyrex, fused silica/quartz glass or ceramic tube can be heated with flexible, coiled resistance-wire heaters. Shaped conductors used for resistance heating applications or spiral-wound resistance wire filaments encased in refractory ceramic supports are often referred to as heating elements.

Electrically powered nichrome wire-heating elements powered by the 110 volt line and fused at 15 A are a convenient source of high-temperature heat. Table 3-1 indicates that nichrome heating wires melt at 1400°C. At temperatures between 500°C and 600°C, most metals are a dull red, and hence near the melting point of nichrome heating elements the wires will emit bright white light. To measure temperatures above the bright white light seen in the 1200°C range, special optics or N and

---

[1] www.thermcraftinc.com
[2] www.sheffield-pottery.com

K type thermocouples are required. Experimental work at temperatures above that attainable with nichrome heating-wire elements requires more specialized techniques than those being considered in this chapter. For experimental work at such elevated temperatures the investigator may begin with information available in works such as *Building Scientific Apparatus*.[2]

Power control systems for heating can be divided into two categories consisting of low-voltage, high-current DC systems that often use PWM to control heating, and higher-voltage AC systems. Power control systems drawing AC from the mains must be implemented in accordance with local electrical codes. High-current, low-voltage power control systems should be implemented with the same care and precautions as are given to higher-voltage AC wiring.

AC electronic power-switching systems can often produce electromagnetic interference that may interfere with nearby thermocouple sensors. In keeping with safety considerations, enclosing power control systems in grounded metal housings can minimize the radiated electromagnetic interference.

Creating a stable temperature one or two hundred degrees above ambient is a relatively simple procedure, as has been described and reviewed in the section on dry wells. A controlled, variable voltage can be used to heat a suitable high-wattage resistor embedded in a large thermal mass to a desired calibrated set point, as depicted in Figure 3-3.

For working at elevated high-heat, high-temperature levels using only the electrical energy available from the mains requires special heaters, insulated enclosures, and various methods of power control. The design of high-temperature heaters is not a trivial exercise, and commercially available heaters should be used whenever possible.

---

[2]*Building Scientific Apparatus*, 4th Edn., Moore, Davis, and Coplan, Cambridge University Press, ISBN 978-0-521-87858-6.

If an investigation requires higher temperatures and a commercially manufactured heating element is not available, then an experimental development process can be followed to create the required heater.

Electrical potential energy is converted into heat energy when a voltage forces a current through a resistance. A filament-type resistance has a surface temperature proportional to the current flowing through it. A balance must be established in which the resistance of the wire and the voltage available permit a current flow that will generate the desired temperature at the surface of the filament resistance wire.

To pass the currents required to attain temperatures near the limits available from nichrome wires with 115 volts, fine, narrow-gauge wires are required. To avoid melting the fine filaments of heater elements, precise power control is mandated. Whenever possible, simple manual controls are easily implemented, adjustable, and reliable.

Because of the filament's fine, narrow structure, careful power control to obtain the current required to develop the desired wire surface temperature and maintain it at several hundred degrees above ambient can be achieved by several methods that in turn depend upon the size and end use of the heated chamber or surface. Many applications, such as dry wells or pot furnaces, only require the continuous application of sufficient energy to achieve the desired temperature and offset the heat transfer from the thermal mass to its environment to maintain a constant elevated temperature, as depicted in Figure 3-3 and the calibration curve of Figure 3-4. Virtually any type of power control can be used for systems regulated by constant heat loss from a large thermal mass. Variable-voltage AC transformers (Variac), triac controls (110 volt "light dimmer"), or for DC systems using high-current pulse-width modulation (PWM) programs from a microcontroller, can be used to provide the input energy required to maintain the desired constant temperature in a substantial thermal mass.

An adjustable, higher-power set-point control system can be assembled with an Arduino microcontroller and a PID algorithm. A 40 A AC, zero-crossing, optically isolated, solid-state relay (SSR, see item D in Figure 3-1) can be automatically controlled by a PID controller program that switches the SSR on and off in accordance with the set-point temperature requirements of the controller program and the temperature measurements made within the heated cavity. (See Chapter 4 and the following.)

When attempting to implement a PID controller system to regulate a resistance-wire heating source, the experimenter must ensure that the proportional function in the controller algorithm does not create large enough power demands to damage the heater wire element.

Wires carrying either electrical power or sensor signals must be insulated to prevent short circuiting or possibly heat damage to nearby components. Wires can either be routed through holes in high-temperature ceramic refractory materials or encased in appropriate lengths of refractory ceramic sleeves or tubing. (See Figure 3-9.)

Table 3-1 tabulates some physical and electrical properties of the metals and alloys often used for electrical resistance heating and making electrical connections, and details assorted thermal and physical limitations.

As can be seen in Table 3-1, many of the metals used in the construction of high-temperature sources have melting points that are too high for fusion welding. Fusion welding of dissimilar metals requires special skills, equipment, and knowledge that are not compatible with the introductory nature of this work. Many of the problems involved in fabricating the connections required to make mechanical structures and electrical contact can be achieved by brazing, which is discussed in much greater detail in the brazing section.

Table 3-1. *Thermo-electric Properties of Materials Used in Resistance Heating*

Element or alloy	TCR at 20.0 degrees C	Melting point °C	comments / alloy composition
aluminum	0.004308	660.3	
constantan	-0.000074	1210	55/45 cu/ni
copper	0.004041	1085	
gold	0.003715	1064	
iron	0.005671	1538	
kanthal		1425	fe/cr/al
manganin	+/- 0.000015	1020	84/12/4 cu/mn/ni, tcr about 0
molybdenum	0.004579	2623	
nickel	0.005866	1455	
nichrome	0.00017	1400	80/20 ni/cr, high resistance heater
nichrome C	0.00013	1000	60/16/24 ni/cr/fe
platinum	0.003729	1768	very inert material
silver	0.003819	961.8	solder/brazing -/+ 450°C
steel	0.003	1370	
tin/lead		188	60/40 sn/pb
tungsten	0.004403	3422	
zinc	0.003847	419.5	coating on galvanized sheet steel

Figure 3-1 depicts some of the commercially available components that can be used to assemble high-heat experimental apparatus. Hot electrically heated resistance wires often need to be encased in an insulating refractory ceramic support or completely protected from possible short circuiting. Items A and B in Figure 3-1 are a pair of commercially available ($225 CDN), 2½ in. (64 mm) long by 3¼ in. (83 mm) outer diameter (o.d.) and 2¼ in. (58 mm) inner diameter (i.d.) 200 watt, 115 volt AC nichrome wire heater elements. Each semicircular element is cast from an alumino-silicate mullite type of refractory able to withstand temperatures above the melting point of nichrome wires, reported to be 1000°C to 1400°C. (Recall that at elevated temperatures some alkali metals and alkali earth oxides can melt and in a liquid format dissolve many materials that melt at much higher temperatures. Numerous salts melting at lower temperatures are often used as "fluxes" to dissolve refractory materials.)

Each of the "D"-shaped elements has a resistance of 15 Ω. An individual "D"-shaped element can thus pass approximately 7.7 A of current at line voltages. The nichrome wire filament is a 20 ga. (0.8118 mm) size that will attain a surface temperature of approximately 425°C with a 6.2 A current.

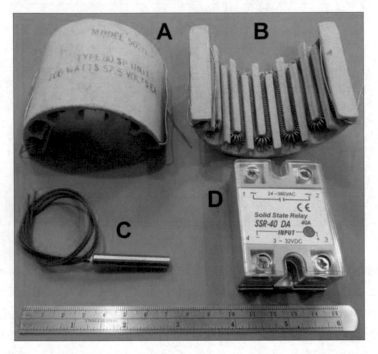

Figure 3-1. *High-heat, high-temperature heating elements and a power control SSR*

Item C is an Omegalux CSS series, stainless steel, 30 watt, 120 V heater cartridge ($75 CDN) for use up to 675°C. For safety, since the electrical lead insulation is Teflon, the power wiring should not be exposed to temperatures over 260°C. Item D is a 40 A solid-state relay (SSR, $15 CDN). (See below for application details.)

To create environments with temperatures hundreds of degrees above ambient, more heat energy must be added to a system than is lost. Heat loss cannot be stopped but can be reduced through the use of insulation and system design to reduce mechanical and radiative energy transfer.

An energy transfer rate is proportional to ΔT, and thus for a material

$$Q = \lambda A \, dT/dx$$

where Q is the heat transfer in watts, λ is the thermal conductivity value in watts / °K – m, A is the cross-sectional area in square meters, and dT/dx is the thermal gradient in °K/m, i.e., the first derivative of temperature with respect to distance.

Recalling that in very simplified terms heat is a measure of molecular motion in the mass of material at hand and that temperature is a measure of the vibrational amplitude of that heat energy, it has been shown that different materials require different inputs of heat to change their temperature. The heat input required to raise a material's temperature through one degree Celsius is known as the specific heat and can be defined as the product of

$$Q = C_p \, m \, \Delta T$$

where Q is the heat added in Joules to the mass m in grams, ΔT is the change in temperature, and C_p is the specific heat. Specific heat is measured in units of energy per unit mass per degree of temperature, typically in joule/kg °C in the SI, or calorie/g °C in a widely used older system.

Thermal conductivity is a measure of a material's ability to transfer heat, and specific heat is a measure of the energy required to raise the temperature of a unit mass of the material by a unit degree. To achieve high temperatures from low-power electrical sources, chamber construction materials of low thermal conductivity and low mass are required.

With limited power inputs, the chamber to contain the heat should be small, fabricated from lightweight refractory materials, surrounded by a good, thick insulation layer, and as physically isolated from the ambient atmosphere as possible. A chamber can be supported in the midst of a bed of small particles of insulation with small cross-sectional area contacts to minimize thermal connections to the supporting outer metal case. Tungsten total inert gas (TIG) welding electrodes of $\frac{1}{16}$ in. (1.5 mm) diameter by 6 in. (152 mm) long are brittle enough to be broken with hand-held pliers into lengths suitable for use in supporting or "pinning" blocks of firebrick insulation drilled to receive the pins.

A portion of any heat generated in a chamber will be transferred out of the system by the emission of electromagnetic radiation. The amount of radiation emitted is proportional to the fourth power of the temperature of the heated body. Infrared radiation is the main transport mechanism by which hot objects transfer heat. Higher-frequency visible light and UV do not carry away much heat in comparison to the longer-wavelength infrared radiation.

Recall that in general terms black surfaces are better at absorbing and emitting radiation than white or reflective surfaces, which can be poor absorbers and emitters of radiation. Hot surfaces radiate heat to colder surfaces in their line of sight, and the rate of heat transfer increases with the fourth power of the absolute temperature.

Experiments involving high heat and high temperature must be designed and built in accordance with the heat-loss limitations reviewed. In essence, the more power that is available the larger the volume of a high-temperature chamber that can be created.

In the following experimental section, temperature measurement and power control with an Arduino will be developed. Some methods for power control for both low-voltage DC and higher-voltage AC systems, together with temperature maintenance through high-mass thermal inertia and with feedback control, will also be presented for investigator use in experimental research.

Experimental

A collection of six subtopics follow that describe an experimental approach to the measurement and creation of moderately and substantially elevated controlled temperatures.

Simple Measurement of Elevated Temperatures

Temperature measurement above 250°C is usually accomplished with thermocouples. An Arduino microcontroller program reading data from an AD594 or AD595 is a very convenient method for displaying temperatures accessible with the J- and K-type thermocouples ($35 CDN). AD594 and AD595 ICs are available in ceramic 14-pin DIP configurations for use in prototyping breadboards. Newer, more sensitive thermocouple amplifiers AD8494 and AD8495 for J- and K-type sensors are available in a small, low-power, SMT, 8-lead MSOP format. Output signals from the SMT chips are reported as 5mV/°C. As noted, the SMT formats can be mounted on "breakout" boards for use with prototyping breadboards ($25 CDN). See "Roadmap to the Exercises" in *Arduino Advanced Techniques in Science, Integrated Circuitry, and Surface Mount Technology SMT*. See also MAX31855 breakout boards from Adafruit Industries.

A K-type thermocouple can be connected to an AD595 integrated circuit to measure elevated temperatures up to 1250°C. An Arduino's ADC can be used to measure the AD595 10mV/°C output and convert the value into a Celsius degree temperature value for display on the serial monitor, as depicted in Figure 3-2. Listing 3-1 contains the Arduino sketch that produces the stream of temperature data in Figure 3-2 (all code listings are provided at the end of the chapter). The code is simple, contains no time averaging, and can be combined with more complex code that requires a feedback temperature value for a process controller, such as in a PID loop configuration.

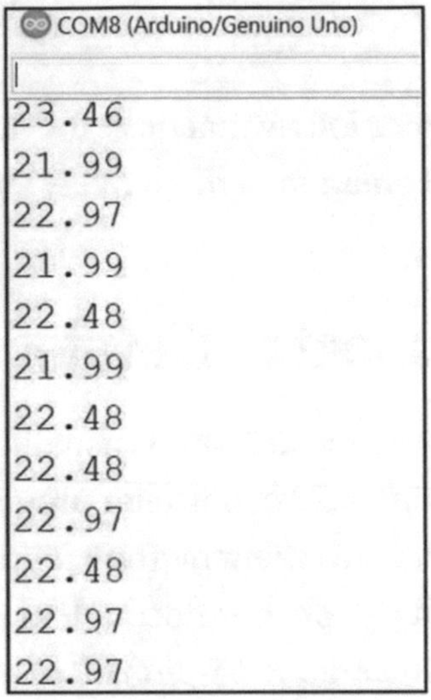

Figure 3-2. *Streamed K-type thermocouple temperature data on the Arduino serial monitor*

A set of NIST thermocouple tables at the end of the code listings for this chapter list the unit-degree milli-volt readings for the K-type device over its usable range. Similar tables are available from the NIST for other types of thermocouples (`https://srdata.nist.gov`).

Dry Wells

A dry well is a cavity in a large thermal mass, usually a substantial block of metal such as aluminum or steel, that is situated inside an insulated box to minimize thermal fluctuations. Figure 3-3 is a typical dual-well dry-well block built in the author's lab from an aluminum flat bar. Three or four 3 in. long (76 mm) pieces of 2 in. wide (50 mm) by ⅛ in. thick (3 mm) bar stock were cut and all drilled to accept ⅜ in. (9 mm) stainless steel bolts that formed the body of the dry well when the plates were bolted together. The bolts were fitted ½ in. (12 mm) to ¾ in. (18 mm) from each end to provide room for the wells and heating element. To drill the wells the bolts were tightened, and to cut or shape the openings for the heater element the bolts were removed in order to free up the thinner plates for drilling, filing, or machining.

Figure 3-3. *A typical dry well*

Dry wells are simple constructs without any feedback control of their set-point temperatures. Normally, the power temperature curve as depicted in Figure 3-4 is used to adjust the power input to the block to get the desired temperature, which is maintained by the equilibrium between heat input and loss from the insulated thermal mass.

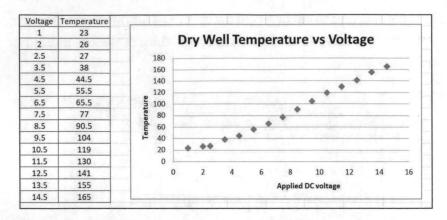

Voltage	Temperature
1	23
2	26
2.5	27
3.5	38
4.5	44.5
5.5	55.5
6.5	65.5
7.5	77
8.5	90.5
9.5	104
10.5	119
11.5	130
12.5	141
13.5	155
14.5	165

Figure 3-4. *A dry well calibration*

Heat was created in the dry well with a 5 watt, 22 Ω, 5% tolerance resistor that was supplied with electrical power from a 30V, 2 A adjustable lab supply to provide a reproducible semi-predictable temperature-reference compartment for calibrating thermistors.

Dry wells and other equipment that must be heated often use cartridge heaters. A typical cartridge heater is depicted as item C in Figure 3-1. The heater has a stainless-steel outer case and is capable of reaching 675°C, but the Teflon insulation on the power leads of the unit must be kept to 250°C or less.

Low-voltage, high-current DC can also be used to power small heating elements with the same type of PWM power-control circuitry, as depicted in Figure 3-6.

Dry wells for use at higher temperatures can be fabricated from iron and steel blocks and heated with resistance wires encased in ceramic refractory materials. Insulation for the higher-temperature devices can be fabricated from firebrick or refractory cement, and the insulated block can be mounted on "stand-offs" inside a protective metal case filled with rock-wool insulation or perlite. (See "Refractories and High-Temperature Insulations" section.)

Resistance-Wire Heating

To build or assemble a small, high-temperature apparatus, the project can be divided into manageable portions by following a series of suggested selections, as listed in Figure 3-5. The design of resistance-wire heating elements is not a trivial matter. For the experimenter an empirical approach to heater design is more realistic.

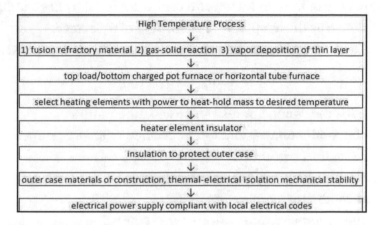

Figure 3-5. *A high-temperature apparatus design process*

An experimental development program based upon initial calculations made from several well-known, reasonably accurate approximations is suggested for creating the heater to be fabricated for use in new experimental designs. An initial start for the construction of a custom-built heating element is to determine the temperature range at which the new system is to operate. Nichrome resistance wire has been selected for this exercise as it is readily available in many different gauges of wire thicknesses.

Heat is generated by the passage of current through an electrical resistance. Quantitatively, power can be expressed as the product of voltage and current or as the product of resistance and the square of the current.

$$P = VI = I^2R$$

Application of a voltage to a conductor at ambient temperatures creates an electron flow through the circuit, developing heat as the resistance of the conductor impedes the current. In simplified terms, it is suggested that increased thermal motion at the atomic scale increases the temperature of the conducting mass and increases its resistance. As the wire temperature increases, its resistance increases and the current is marginally reduced. Metal wire resistance is known to be a function of the temperature of the conductor, and each metal or alloy has a unique quantity known as the temperature coefficient of resistance.

Recall that the resistance temperature relationship is expressed as:

$$R = R_{ref}\left[1 + \alpha(T - T_{ref})\right]$$

Where R is the conductor resistance at temperature T.

R_{ref} is the conductor resistance at a specified reference temperature, usually 20°C or 0°C.

α is the temperature coefficient of resistance for the conductor at hand.

T is the conductor temperature in °C.

T_{ref} is the reference temperature at which the value of α has been specified.

Values of α for many metals and alloys are tabulated and available online and in handbooks.[3] The desired experimental temperature and the voltage of the power supply available are fixed quantities, and with Ohm's law and the TCR, heater-element parameters can be calculated.

Nickel-chrome alloys are one of the main sources of electrically controlled heat creation and temperature generation. The alloy elements are readily available, relatively inexpensive, have a relatively high electrical resistance, and oxidize in air to form a protective refractory oxide coating. The documentation for nichrome use as an electrically controlled heat source has been accumulated for over a hundred years (see Figures 3-15 and 3-16).

---

[3] *Handbook of Chemistry and Physics,* 100th Edn., Rumble, CRC Press, Boca Raton, FL. ISBN 13-978-1-13836-7296.

To build an electrically controlled heat source for an experimental design, the investigator can begin with the development of the wire-filament characteristics that will be needed to realize the temperature at which the new apparatus must operate. Tables are available based upon the temperature coefficient of resistance calculations relating approximate current flow, wire resistance, and conductor temperature from several sources.[4]

An established temperature requirement can thus be used to find the wire-filament resistance and current combination that will result in the desired heater-element surface temperature. An established resistance and current requirement for a given temperature can be used with Ohm's law to calculate the required length of filament resistance wire. The data compiled into the current-temperature tabulations is for straight lengths of resistance wire.

If the wire is coiled to fit into a particular shape, the resistance of the filament element increases. Care must also be taken when coiling the wire around a mandrel that the wire is not twisted, as strained sections will also increase the resistance. (See item 2 in Figure 3-10.) Localized increased resistance can cause hot sections that can contribute to a shortened heater service life.

Heating elements such as A, B, and C in Figure 3-1 have been manufactured with completely enclosed resistance-wire heating elements in C and partially enclosed wires in A and B. If a heated chamber is to be accessed to change furnace loads or samples, the energized resistance-wire filaments, for safety, should be recessed in the refractory filament support or enclosed in continuous refractory ceramic tubing or closely spaced short segments to avoid accidental electrical contact. (See Figure 3-10, items 3 and 4.)

---

[4] 1) https://assets.omega.com/pdf/cable-and-wire/heating-wire/Ni80.pdf
2) https://en.wikipedia.org/wiki/Nichrome
3) https://wiretron.com/nichrome-resistance-wires

Isolation can often be built into an experimental heater design through the use of a shaped refractory insulator core or mold. Embedding the heater filament into a molded shape or wrapping the heater filament around the outside of a shaped refractory core can create an effective electrical isolation safety margin.

Cores and molds can be created by coating appropriately shaped forms made from materials such as plastic, wood, or cardboard coated with a release agent such as a paraffin oil, wax, or thin plastic film. The release agent is used to facilitate separation of the shaped core or mold form and the dried, castable, refractory material chosen for the application at hand.

A convenient refractory insulation material is available in a dry-powder format that when mixed with water forms a castable paste. The Imperial Group manufactures several formulations of refractory furnace cements in both premixed and dry-powder formulations for both repair and the forming of castable shapes. The various products are serviceable from 1000°C to 1400°C when dried and cured. (Available from home improvement and hardware stores, 1.36 Kg or 3 lb., $20 CDN.) The refractory furnace cement can be used to embed a heater core filament in a molded casting or form a hollow core shape to be wrapped with the desired length of resistance wire. (See items C and D in Figure 3-12.)

Single or multiple layers of wire insulated from short circuiting can be embedded in layers of cement to achieve the final configuration of the heating element. To increase the total length and resistance of the heating filament, the wire can be close coiled through winding around a mandrel such as an appropriately sized threaded rod. (See item 2 in Figure 3-10.) The close-coiled filament can then be expanded to not more than three times the original close-coiled length to avoid short circuiting as the spiraled filament is wound on the heater refractory core. (See items A and B in Figure 3-1.) Larger shaped insulated constructs used as heater cores or as shaped heat insulation can be fabricated with the refractory cement and fillings such as rock-wool insulation, perlite, vermiculite, or crushed firebrick, as detailed in the "Refractory Insulations."

Powering Heating Elements

For higher temperatures, such as those that would be used with thermocouple or silicon-carbide thermistor temperature-measurement systems, a power controller able to handle over 2 A in either a DC or AC format is desired. A high-current DC format power-control circuit has been used by the author with the circuit depicted in Figure 3-6 to control thermoelectric heat pumps. In the previous work, the heat-pumping elements were in the circuit position labelled as "heater coil" in the control circuit. In the heat pump project, an Arduino microcontroller is used with a PWM pin output to regulate the gate voltage on a high-power MOSFET switch. Listing 3-4 contains the microprocessor code for power control. An FQP33N10, 100V, 33 A, N channel enhancement-mode MOSFET mounted on a 2 in. x 2 in. (50 mm x 50 mm) finned heat sink was used to control a 12V 8.5 A DC current to a thermoelectric heat/cool module load. Power is controlled by sending an "i" for increase or a "d" for decrease from the serial port monitor screen to the Arduino, which in turn appropriately adjusts the width of the PWM signal and the high-current DC power delivered to the thermoelectric elements.

DC power control systems are reasonably simple in design and can manage the application of a wide range of current. Enhancement-mode metal oxide field-effect transistors are available in numerous formats, from the 2N7000 in the TO-92 case able to handle 200 mA to the FQP50N06 TO-220 case able to handle 50 A with an appropriate heat sink.

Small heater elements created from fine iron, steel, or resistance-wire materials can be tested and ultimately powered with PWM output from a microcontroller using the simple circuit depicted in Figure 3-6.

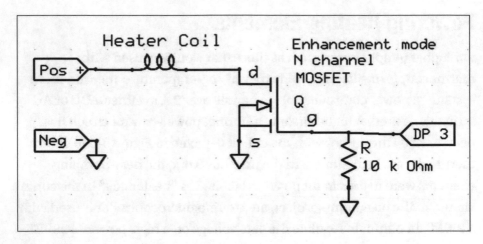

Figure 3-6. *An Arduino high-current DC power-controller circuit*

DP 3 in the schematic is the lowest digital pin on the Arduino capable of a PWM output. The signal from the microcontroller is applied to the gate of an enhancement-mode N channel MOSFET that switches the FET on and off in accordance with the power settings sent from the serial monitor. Power settings are varied by sending "i" for increase by 5% or "d" to decrease by 5% the on/off time setting of the control program from the serial monitor. The serial monitor displays the output stream of the most recent power setting as % power and as a power level on a 0–255 scale, in addition to the chamber temperature. Figure 3-7 displays the data streamed from the serial monitor during a test in which a 12V DC, 5 A supply applies 50 percent power to a lightbulb filament. A J-type thermocouple connected to an AD594 is pressed against the glass envelope to monitor the outside surface temperature in the incandescent bulb "test chamber."

```
COM5 (Arduino/Genuino Uno)

|

Power = 50 PLevel = 128
Thermocouple temperature = 64.97
Power = 50 PLevel = 128
Thermocouple temperature = 64.97
```

Figure 3-7. Serial monitor output for Arduino PWM power control

A complete power control with heated chamber or surface temperature monitoring capability can be implemented by adding the K-type thermocouple temperature-sensing system, using Listing 3-1, to a heated chamber, as depicted in Figure 3-9. A similar thermocouple monitor could be added to the circuitry in Figure 3-8.

Figures 3-13 and 3-14 depict the open-air testing of a heating element of 30 ga. (0.010 in. or 0.254 mm) 80/20% nichrome wire. The heater filament has been spiral wound on a ¹⁄₁₆ in. (1.6 mm) mandrel and has a 1.5 inch long (40 mm) close-wound length and a total resistance of 7.9 Ω. A 100 watt power supply (18V @ 5 A) used in the circuit configuration of Figure 3-6 with an Arduino PWM control program can bring the filament to a dull red heat at 50 percent PWM power and to the red heat depicted at 84 percent power.

Higher heats can be realized with higher-wattage DC power supplies. (See "Discussion.")

Figure 3-8 depicts a circuit for an AC power controller that has been developed from components and code drawn and modified from several sources.[5]

---

[5] 1) www.bristolwatch.com
2) https://cdn.hackaday.io/files/1597066832861504/SimpleIsolatedZero
CrossDetector.pdf

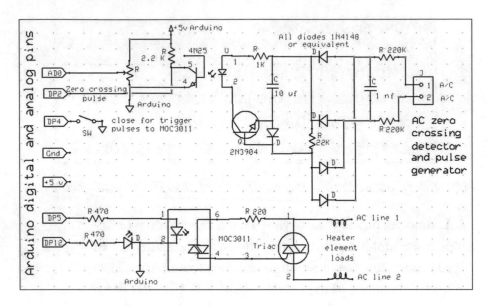

Figure 3-8. *A zero-crossing AC power-control circuit for triacs*

Figure 3-8 has three distinct optically isolated components, the first of which consists of a circuit to detect the point at which the 115V power line, high-voltage AC waveform passes through the zero-voltage point as it changes phase. The zero-passage-phase voltage change causes the 2N3904 to drive a power pulse through the interior LED in the 4N25 optical-coupler chip, which activates the phototransistor to pass a current through the 2.2 K Ω resistor on the low-voltage side of the coupler. The transistor pulse-generator circuit eliminates the need for a transformer to step down the higher power-line voltage.

The microcontroller operates at 5 volts DC and provides both the sequencing timing and logic used to proportion out the amount of the high-voltage power cycle applied to the load. The sequenced triggering signals created by the microprocessor are passed back through another optical-isolator chip (MOC 3011) to preserve the separation of the voltage levels and fire the triac at the desired portion in the power cycle.

The third portion of the circuit consists of the high-power triac, the line power, and the heater-element load. The triac device is not specified, as the power-handling capability of the device is determined by the energy required by the heating load. Development work for the prototype circuit in Figure 3-8 was conducted with a 400V AC, 6A, BTA06 triac in a TO-220 case from STMicroelectronics with a simple ballast lamp load and suitable heat-sink and device-mounting assembly for the triac.

Lab testing of the high-heat, high-temperature equipment used the BTB16-600BWRG 600V, 16 A, TO-220 case, triac power semiconductors.

Triac power control is achieved by applying an adjustable portion of the AC waveform to the load. When the circuit of Figure 3-8 is used, there is no voltage applied to the filament load when the pulse control switch is open. However, when the pulse control switch is closed, 10V AC is applied to the load, even with the control potentiometer in the minimum voltage position. (See Figure 3-17 in "Observations" and "Discussion.")

A K-type thermocouple temperature monitor using the AD595 with the circuitry seen in Figure 3-9 has been added to the Arduino zero-crossing code in Listing 3-2 for this exercise. However, the thermocouple amplifier output is connected to A1 on the Arduino ADC inputs, as the A0 channel is used by the interrupt service routine in the triac control code.

Solid-State Relays (SSR)

A solid-state relay is a device used to control higher-voltage alternating-current power. An inexpensive SSR is the Fotek SSR-40 DA device ($12 CDN). The device is able to use a 5 volt DC signal from a microcontroller or computer to switch on or off up to 40 A of AC current at voltages between 24 and 380 volts. The SSR is designed to switch current only at the zero-crossing point of the AC cycle to minimize the radio frequency interference (RFI) emitted during the switching. The input circuitry uses photo diodes to trigger a photo triac on the high-voltage side of the relay and thus provides over 50 MΩ of isolation for safety.

In Figure 3-9, an SSR under microprocessor control is used to manage the AC power delivered to a heater load. However, a relay can only be on or off, and hence some form of control similar to PWM must be used to regulate the temperature within the heated chamber. An Arduino library is available for managing the power delivered by solid-state relays. The Arduino library implements a form of slow pulse-width modulation called time proportioning. In combination with the thermocouple temperature monitor measuring the temperature within the heated chamber, a PID control algorithm switches the relay on or off for a certain period of time in proportion to the difference between the present chamber temperature and the desired set-point temperature. PID control is detailed in Chapter 4, "The PID Process-Control Algorithm," and in Listing 3-3.

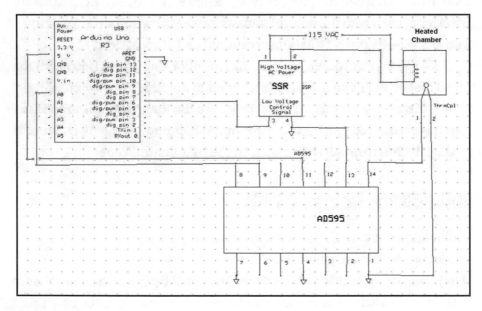

Figure 3-9. *An Arduino-hosted PID temperature controller for a heated chamber*

Heated chambers can take a number of forms, such as the low-volume, top-loading "pot furnace," front-load ovens, or cylindrical-tube furnaces. A pot furnace has a small cylindrical heat chamber with a removable top that allows small crucibles to be inserted and removed from the round heated chamber. Two of the commercially available semi-cylindrical heating elements depicted in Figure 3-1 as items A and B can be placed inside a metal tin with a carved firebrick base support to form the heated core of a high-temperature chamber. The curved ceramic heater elements, lined with coiled nichrome resistance heating wire, form the halves of a cylindrical chamber 2.5 in. (64 mm) long by 3 in. (7.5 cm) in diameter when placed edge to edge. The heater elements will form the core of the pot/tube furnace, and various methods can be used to regulate the chamber temperature by controlling the power supplied to the heater coils. Variable-voltage transformers (Variacs), triacs, and SSR devices can be used to regulate the power delivered to the heavier-gauge, commercially manufactured wire heating elements. (For incandescent heating temperatures, the heavy-gauge wire elements must be powered from 220V sources.)

Tube furnaces consist of long supported tubes passing through the heated zone of a horizontally positioned heating element. Inorganic synthesis and organic elemental analysis are probably the two major uses for these devices. The material used to form the tube must be compatible with the intended operating temperature and chemical operation to be conducted. Usually the length of the tube must be long enough that the heat from the hot zone does not affect the fittings on either end of the tube that passes gases and allow for sample introduction or recovery.

To control or regulate the temperature in a heated zone, a PID controller can be used. PID controllers should not be used with fine wire heating elements. Heavy-gauge wires are able to absorb the high-power applications created by the proportional phase of the PID cycle without overheating. Fine-gauge heating wires (> 20) will often fuse at 50°C to 100°C set points during startup operations using the default Arduino PID library settings for SSR operations. For adequately heavy heater element wires, a fixed but adjustable level or programmable temperature profile can be created by varying the set-point value in the code of the electronic controller. (See Chapter 4, "The PID Process-Control Algorithm.")

In order for a PID controller to operate in a temperature-control mode, there must be a feedback loop to compare the heated chamber temperature with that of the desired set point. For high-heat experimental setups, thermocouple temperature sensors such as the K-type perform well up to their upper limit of 1200°C (2192°F). Recalling that heat energy is transferred by radiation, conduction, and convection, the positioning of the temperature sensor in the heated chamber will depend upon both the configuration of the experimental setup and its intended use. A temperature sensor should be in a position to respond quickly to any temperature changes in the environment under control.

An electric heating element can only produce heat, and the effectiveness of the insulation will determine the rate at which the chamber cools and the temperature drops. Intuitively, one expects that the better the chamber is insulated, the lower the heat loss and the better the degree of temperature regulation the PID controller system should exhibit.

Finer wire heating elements fabricated from 24 ga. nichrome as depicted in Figure 3-10 are best controlled manually.

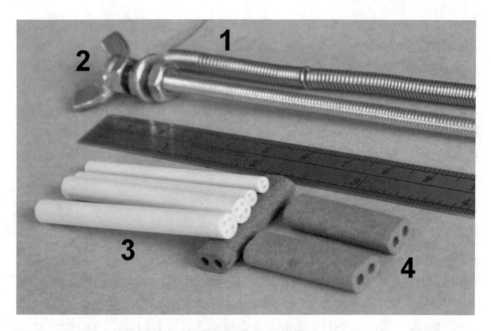

Figure. 3-10. *A spiral-coiled 8-32 heater element, winding form, and ceramic insulators*

Item 1 is a tight wire spiral of the nominal nichrome wire that was wound on the 8-32 threaded rod depicted as item 2 in Figure 3-10. (8-32 stands for a ⅛ in. diameter rod with 32 threads per inch, or 3 mm diameter with 32 threads per 24.5 mm.) The threaded rod has been fitted with a wing nut locked in position with a spring-lock washer and a standard nut in order to provide a means of turning the rod during the formation of the coiled-wire spiral. At caption 3 are refractory insulators bored with holes to receive and support fine wires for thermocouples or heating elements. The shorter, dual-wire channel, ceramic sleeves at caption 4 are used for providing a more flexible, segmented heat-resistance insulation for wiring exposed to higher temperatures.

For work at elevated temperatures, the number of refractory materials available for providing effective insulation for thermal and electrical isolation becomes limited. Electrical isolation can be provided by ceramic sleeving such as items 3 and 4 in Figure 3-10. Two- and four-bore sleeves are available in alumina (white) and other refractory materials (tan) for separating signal- and power-carrying electrical conductors at elevated temperatures. Odd sizes and shapes of insulating refractories can be made from the castable refractory furnace cements, such as that available from the Imperial Group. (See Figure 3-12, items C and D, and entry vi in supplier list.)

Refractory Insulation

In addition to having low volumes as an aid to creating high-heat, high-temperature enclosures, efficient insulations must be used to contain the heat. Recalling that heat energy is transferred through conduction, convection, and radiation, each method of loss must be minimized by some form of insulation or chamber design. Table 3-2 tabulates data on high-temperature insulations.

Table 3-2. *Refractory Insulations, Service Temperatures, and Thermal Conductivities*

Insulation Material	Servicable Temperature °C	Thermal conductivity Watts/meter.°C or K
alumino silicate wool (ASW or RCF)	600 -1400	0.1 - 0.65 (°K)
aluminum oxide (alumina)	2050	18 (°K)
boron nitride	2973	27 (°K)
calcium silicate	2130	0.07 - 0.17 (°K)
ceramic fiber wool	1650	0.12 (°K)
fire brick high density	up to 1648	1.3 - 1.2 (°C)
fire brick low density	up to 1500	0.13 - 1.1 (°C)
fuzed quartz	1723	1.38 (°K)
fused silica	1650	1.38 (°K)
glass wool	230 - 260	0.04 (°K)
kao wool	1650	0.06 - 0.3 (°K)
magnesium oxide	2798	30 - 8 (°K) (inverse wrt temp.)
mullite	1840	6 (°K)
perlite	soften 871-1093	0.06 - 0.14 (°K)
perlite	melt 1260-1343	
pyrex glass (type 7740)	softens 820	1.1 (°K)
rock wool	up to 1177	0.03 - 0.2 (°K)
silicon cardide	2500	120 (°K)
silicon nitride	1900	30 (°K)
soda lime glass	softens 700 - 900	0.94 (°K)
still air		0.05 (°K)
stone wool	700 - 800	0.022 (°K)
vermiculite	1093	0.058 - 0.071 (°K) (> Density)
zirconia	2715	2.7 (°K)

Although many exotic materials are available to retard heat flow, only readily available, inexpensive, and easy-to-work materials are being examined in this chapter.

ASTM C71 from the American Society for Testing and Materials defines refractories as "non-metallic materials having those chemical and physical properties that make them applicable for structures, or as components of systems, that are exposed to environments above 1,000°F (811°K; 538°C)."

There are no insulation materials that can completely block the flow of heat. Heat energy always flows from higher temperatures to lower. As detailed earlier, the rate of heat transfer is proportional to the temperature difference or gradient over which the insulation must retard heat flow.

Examination of the values in Table 3-2 indicates that solid materials have relatively high thermal conductivities when compared to fiber-based insulation materials such as mineral wools and calcium-silicate fiber boards. Refractory materials formed into fibers are generally limited to temperatures below 1000°C, while solid alumina, mullite, and other ceramic oxide–based materials can be used above this limitation.

Firebrick and ceramic sheets, tubes, and sleeving can be cut and shaped with diamond wheels on a tile saw, drill press, or hand-held rotary tool. Small heater filaments compatible with lower-amperage power sources will not be able to heat small chambers in massive insulators such as whole firebricks to incandescent temperatures. To create the higher temperatures, smaller, thinner sections of commonly available high-temperature insulators such as firebrick can be cut and fitted together to form small, low-mass, and hence low–thermal load, high-temperature chambers in small, experimental development programs.

Since materials heated to incandescence must be contained and isolated from contact with the ambient atmosphere for both safety and maintenance of temperature, a rigid, protective, outer metal case is often a convenient and readily available means to support and enclose the insulation surrounding heated components.

An outer metal case can be a container for free-flowing insulations such as perlite, vermiculite, or crushed firebrick. Flexible fiber-based insulations can be used to line the inside of an outer case or wrap the inner heated chamber as it is supported in a bed of free-flowing insulation. Various custom shapes of rigid insulation can also be cast into molds or created by mixing quantities of a free-flowing thermal insulation with refractory cement.

It has been reported that an optimal mix ratio of 1:4 by volume of furnace cement to perlite can be used to make a castable insulation. A mix of 1:5 produces a friable structure while a 1:3 mix seals voids in the perlite and will not dry properly. It is suggested that a small amount of water, no more than 2 cups/gallon (an 8:1 vol./vol. thinning of cement to water), can make the refractory cement easier to work with and that exposed surfaces of the composite casting should be sealed with a thin layer of refractory cement.[6] Prior to applying heat to the casting, the piece must be completely dry to ensure there is no entrapped water that will cause a steam explosion when the piece is put into service. (See second and fourth "Safety Considerations," earlier.)

Circular, readily formed metal casings are available from most home improvement outlets or building suppliers in the form of 4 to 8 in. (10.2 to 20.4 cm) diameter lengths of galvanized home-heating air ducting. (6 in. [150 mm] diameter duct tubing was found to be a convenient size for the initial experimental development of small heated chambers.)

Semicircular heater elements such as items A and B in Figure 3-1 can be wired in series and either clamped together with perforated steel straps or enclosed in a heavier steel container such as can be cut by hand with a hacksaw from a spent propane cylinder. Before cutting open an empty propane cylinder, fill it completely with water then empty it to remove the last vapors of the fuel gas. If the commercial elements are fitted inside a convenient-sized crimped sheet-metal foodstuff tin can, the experimenter must be careful not to let the heater element temperatures get close to the melting/boiling points of the tin (Mp. 231.93°C, Bp. 2602°C) or zinc (Mp. 419.53°C, Bp. 907°C) coating on the container. The heater elements can be placed on a pad of firebrick that can serve as the bottom of the heated chamber. The firebrick can then be placed inside a sheet-metal tube cut from a length of the 6 in. (150 mm) galvanized air ducting to provide an outer wall for the chamber. Typically the 4 in. (102 mm) curved semicircular elements when clamped together will have a 1 in. (24.5 mm) annular spacing between the ceramic support and the outer wall of the case. The space can be filled with an appropriate insulation. Depending upon the upper temperatures to be created in the inner chamber, flexible or free-flowing insulation

---

[6]https://makezine.com/2012/04/05/how-tohomemade-castable-refractories/

such as rock wool, perlite, or vermiculite—available at hardware stores, home improvement centers, or garden suppliers—can be used. For higher temperatures, the castable refractory cement, granular firebrick, or other suitable refractories can be used.

A convenient bottom for the structure can be made from a "blanking plate" made to fit or from an end covering often called a "clean-out" plate for the 6 in. (15.2 cm) ducting.

Figure 3-11 illustrates a small high-temperature test chamber carved from four medium-density fire ricks available locally in the smaller imperial sized 4 x 1¼ x 8 in. and the larger metric-sized 3 x 11 x 23 cm units. The chamber is closed and aligned with the four threaded rods in the corners of the bricks.

Figure 3-12 illustrates the main components of a pot furnace outer case, with item A, a corrugated-edged blanking plate, forming the bottom of the device and a short length of duct pipe, item B, forming the cylindrical wall.

Items C and D are economically sized 3 lb. plastic tubs (1.3 kg) of the premixed grey and dry-mix castable refractory cements from the Imperial Group (supplier vi in listing).

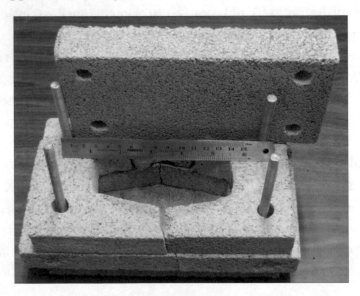

Figure 3-11. *A small high-temperature testing chamber from carved firebrick*

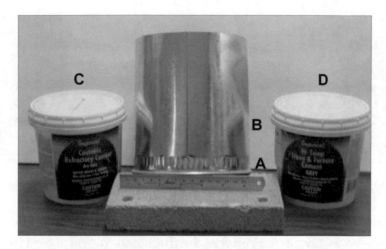

Figure 3-12. *Refractory cements and a two-piece pot furnace outer case*

Observations

Figure 3-13. *An open-air, firebrick heater filament test jig with thermocouple monitor*

Figure 3-14. *A DC MOSFET power-control heater filament test*

For small-size, custom-built heating elements assembled from fine resistance wires, it is important that the thermocouple be placed in close proximity to the heater filament to ensure that the temperature of the system can be monitored and the current controlled to keep the filament below the melting point of the resistance wire.

In Figures 3-15 and 3-16, the surface of the 30 ga. 80/20% nichrome wire is depicted before and after being heated to red heat in the open air.

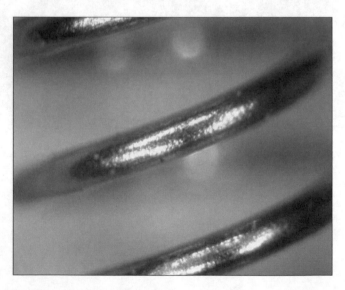

Figure 3-15. *New 30 ga. 1/16 in. (1.6 mm) spiral-wound heater filament*

Figure 3-16. *Nichrome wire surface after heating to red heat*

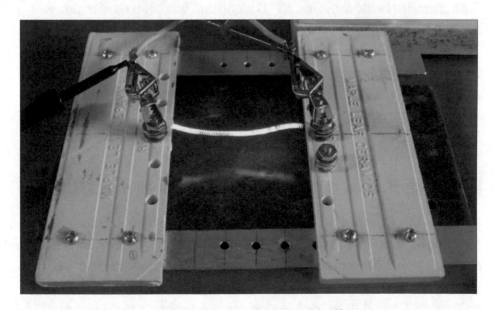

Figure 3-17. *A 10V AC minimum triac signal effect on a low-impedance heater filament*

The adjustable test jig depicted in Figure 3-17 has been assembled from two ceramic tiles 2 in. (50 mm) by 6 in. (15.2 cm) by ³⁄₁₆ in. (5 mm). The glazed side of the tiles is facing down so the porous, unglazed side could be used to lay out the positions for the holes required to position the tiles on the ¾ in. (20 mm) drilled aluminum angle bases. The 6-32 bolts to which the filament is attached are all stainless steel to minimize corrosive actions. The mounting bolts through the legs are zinc-plated carbon steel, as their exposure to heat is minimal. The jig is placed on the glazed surface of a 4 in. (10.2 cm) by 8 in. (20.4 cm) tile to protect the benchtop from the radiant heat.

As discussed in Chapter 4, "Control of Process Operations," the proportional, integral, and derivative (PID) algorithm is able to regulate the temperature in a heated apparatus to within the temperature resolution limitations imposed by the digital hardware used to implement the controlled heated system. A PID algorithm has been used to power heaters for several of the experimental systems described in this chapter.

However, when the PID control system is used with fine, small heater filaments as depicted in Figures 3-13, 3-14, and 3-17, the investigator must ensure that on start-up of the heater system the proportional demand of the PID algorithm does not draw excessive current beyond what the filament at hand can sustain.

Failures Involving High Heat and Temperatures

In the series of Figures 3-18 to 3-21, the results of a failed experiment attempting to utilize materials at hand to develop a high-temperature chamber are displayed. In order to place a thermocouple in close proximity to the filaments of a commercial cylindrical heater as depicted in Figure 3-1 A and B, an easy-to-drill clay-based ceramic tile was used as a chamber top. During a PID controller data-collection transition from

400°C to 500°C the tile fused and shorted out the thermocouple in the feedback loop. The controller–SSR loop applied full power to the heater for several minutes before the author was able to shut off the power.

Thermocouples to be used in high-heat, high-temperature measurements near the upper limits attainable with nichrome resistance wires in the 1000°C to 1400°C temperature range must be insulated with materials able to withstand these extremes. Refractory tubes made with single, two, or four bore holes—alumina refractories available from suppliers such as McMaster-Carr Supply Company—are available in ⅛ in. (3 mm) o.d. (p/n 87175K77, $22 USD) by 18 in. (44 cm) lengths and 24 in. (60.8 cm) lengths with 0.040 in. (1 mm) diameter holes through which the individual thermocouple wires can be routed. (See item 3 in Figure 3-10.)

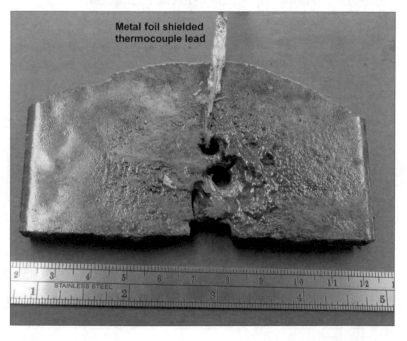

Figure 3-18. *Top surface of overheated chamber top plate*

Examination of the top and bottom surfaces of the top plate as seen in Figures 3-18 and 3-19 illustrates the heat to which the tile material was subjected. The severity of the overheating is evident in the smooth protuberance of the molten fired clay that appears to be in the initial stages of a drop formation in Figure 3-19.

The overheat did not appear to have fused the wires of the K-type thermocouple. There appear to be several possible reasons for the overheat failure. A short circuit may have been caused by the author's using a grounded aluminum-foil wrapping as an EMI noise shield and its being too close to the heated chamber during the 400°C to 500°C temperature transition. It is also possible that the tile used for the chamber top was a lower-melting-point, high-clay-content ceramic that fused and dissolved the aluminum EMI shielding and the interior ceramic fiber insulation of the thermocouple wires. (Recall Al m.p. 660.3°C.)

Figure 3-19. *Bottom surface of overheated chamber top plate*

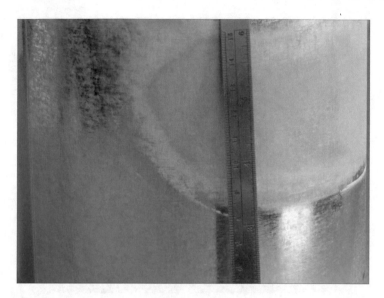

Figure 3-20. *Oxidized zinc of galvanizing on outer case of overheated chamber*

Figure 3-20 illustrates the damage done to a galvanized surface when it is overheated in the presence of oxygen; the surface has formed grey zinc oxide.

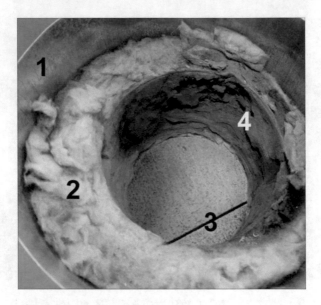

Figure 3-21. *Overheated insulation*

Figure 3-21 depicts the damage done to the internal insulation separating the inner high-temperature heated chamber from the outside casing of the testing device. Caption 1 is the oxidized zinc inside of the outer case, 2 is the intact domestic-grade rock-wool insulation, 3 is the firebrick floor of the chamber, and 4 is the blackened, fused, friable remnants of the overheated insulation.

Discussion

In experimental work with high-temperature, high-heat systems it is important to ensure that all of the materials of construction used in or near the hot zone can withstand the temperatures to which they will be exposed.

By acquiring either a commercially prepared set of heating elements as depicted in Figure 3-1 or hand winding a similar nichrome wire spiral, any furnace temperature from slightly over ambient to approximately 1200°C to 1300°C can be created in a small 3–4 cubic inch enclosure

(75–100 cc) (cubic centimeter). Experiments that require the high-temperature heating of large volumes in excess of several-cubic-inch or half-liter volumes will require substantial amounts of power and specialized equipment and incur greater expense.

While creating high-heat, high-temperature environments, a careful monitoring of the heater resistance-wire temperature must be maintained in order to keep the alloy from which the filament has been manufactured within its safe operating range. Heater-element wires in the 14 to 18 ga. sizes are robust, easy to work with, and stiff enough to hold their shape when bent. Current flow through the heater elements determines the surface temperature of the wire, and heavier wires can tolerate transient current surges better than the thinner heater filaments can. Heavier wires are also of lower resistance and may not be able to be heated to the desired temperature with the power supply available. Careful design and control are required to develop robust high-temperature systems.

AC or DC electrical energy can be used to energize suitable commercially available heater elements, with the DC power option being suitable for low-volume dry wells and AC power being used for high-temperature tube or pot furnace construction. Higher AC voltages as available from the lines are easily controlled with a microprocessor and a solid-state relay, depicted as item D in Figure 3-1. Figure 3-9 depicts the circuit with which a PID controller program running on an Arduino, a K-type thermocouple, a solid-state relay (SSR), and an AD595 IC can be used to control the interior temperature of a heated chamber. SSR devices should be triac-based systems that utilize zero-line-voltage crossing as the power-switching point to minimize the generation of EMI radiation.

Although zero-crossing SSRs produce low EMI emissions, it may still be necessary to wrap temperature-sensor wiring with grounded shielding and ensure that the low-melting metal wrap does not compromise the system integrity at higher operating temperatures.

PID controllers are suggested for the temperature programming of any heated systems. If a steady temperature is required in a smaller mass or for

a calibration operation, either a manual control, such as a variable-voltage
AC transformer, or a PWM–MOSFET control system may be used.

As can be seen in Figure 3-17, the 10V AC minimal signal of the circuit
depicted in Figure 3-8 can supply enough current to heat a low-impedance
filament to red heat, so care must be taken in applying this circuitry to fine
wire heating elements.

Sources of refractory insulations, materials, structures, and lab ware
are as follow:

I.   McMaster–Carr Supply Company www.mcmaster.
     com/alumina-ceramic alumina sleeves, rods, and
     sheets

II. LSP Industrial Ceramics, Inc. https://
     lspceramics.com/products/ crucibles, boats,
     sleeves, rods, tubes, sheets from several refractory
     materials

III. Promat Industries www.promat-hpi.com/en/
     service/what-is-hti, defines high-temperature
     insulations, company has large variety of refractory
     products

IV. Morgan Advanced Materials www.
     morganthermalceramics.com ceramic wool
     blankets, Kaowool, Cerablanket, Cerachem, and
     Cerachrom refractory ceramic fiber

V.   Kumar Ceramics Private Limited www.indiamart.
     com/kumarceramics/ crucibles, boats, sleeves, rods,
     ceramic combustion tubes, thermocouple beads

VI. Imperial Manufacturing Group, refractory cement
     and mortars www.imperialgroup.ca/fireplace_
     maintenanceproducts

High Temperature and High Heat with Fuel Gases

Experimental work at higher temperatures limits the techniques that can be used to join materials together. For ambient and mildly elevated temperatures, soldering and mechanical fasteners have been able to hold structures together and assure electrical conductivity. At elevated temperatures, fusion welding or brazing are two methods that can be used by the investigator to construct experimental setups at moderate cost with readily available materials.

Small-scale gas welding/brazing and metal-cutting kits are available from local hardware and building-supply stores, sold as the BernzOmatic line of gases, torches, and associated supplies for the home-repair and hobby market. The Model WK5500OX kit ($120 CDN) is an excellent home workshop-laboratory gas heating torch.

In previous work, the author had to prepare stainless-steel conductivity probes. Any inert metal probe must provide a low-resistance electrical connection between an electrode, such as one of stainless steel, and a copper-wire conductor while maintaining sufficient mechanical strength to withstand the changing of the calibration and tested solutions or rough handling in field work.

Strong electrically conductive joints can be made between the different metals with the technique of silver soldering. Silver solders vary greatly in the silver content, which can be between 56% and 80%. The balance of the solder can be metals such as copper (Cu), zinc (Zn), nickel (Ni), manganese (Mn), cadmium (Cd), tin (Sn), and silicon (Si), to name only the more common additives. Prior to attempting to produce a silver-soldered joint, the researcher should consult literature from the manufacturers of brazing alloys to select the appropriate alloy for the intended joint to be made, surface preparation techniques, and the nature of any fluxes that may be required. See Table 3-4 for further details.

Silver solders melt from 618°C (1,145°F) for the low silver content alloys up to 740°C (1,370°F) for the higher silver content materials. Silver soldering is similar to the brazing technique discussed later. In both silver soldering and brazing the heat is applied to the base metals being joined, and the silver solder is melted into the area to be joined by the heat of the base metals, not the torch flame. Right-angled joints should display a filleted alloy residue when cooled and lap-jointed fastenings a thin continuous line of alloy between the joined surfaces.

Table 3-3 tabulates the various temperatures obtained when common fuel gases are burnt with air or oxygen.

Table 3-3. *Flame Temperatures of Common Fuel Gases*

Fuel Gas	Oxidant	Deg. C	Deg. F
propane	air	1980	3596
acetylene	air	2550	4622
methane	air	1950	3542
propane	oxygen	2800	5072
acetylene	oxygen	3100	5612
Map	oxygen	2870	5198

Table 3-4. *Brazing Materials' Typical Compositions and Fusion Temperatures*

Filler Metal	Typical Composition	Brazing Temperature	Base Metals
aluminum and silicon	90% Al, 10% Si	600° C (1112° F)	Aluminum
copper	99.9% Cu	1120° C (2048° F)	Nickel Copper
copper and phosphorus	95% Cu, 5% P	850° C (1562° F)	Copper
copper and zinc	60% Cu, 40% Zn	925° C (1697° F)	Steels, Cast irons, nickel
gold and silver	80% Au, 20% Ag	950° C (1742° F)	Stainless steel, nickel alloys
nickel alloys	Ni, Cr, others	1120° C (2048° F)	Stainless steel, nickel alloys
silver alloys	Ag, Cu, Zn, Cd	730° C (1346° F)	Titanium, Monel, Inconel, tool steel, nickel

Brazing

In many cases, brazing is a much more efficient technique for joining metals or materials than fusion welding. In essence, a filler metal is drawn into the close-fitting, heated space between the joint surfaces to form a metallurgical bond between the two substrate surfaces on cooling to the crystalline temperature range of the filler metal.

The melting or softening point of the filler metal thus defines the upper temperature limit to which the brazed joint can be subjected.

Joints to be brazed must be shaped to fit tightly together. A brazing rod should be melted by the heat of the base metals being joined and not by the flame of the torch in use.

Surfaces to be bonded should be prepared by abrasive cleaning followed by a degreasing to remove oil, finger grease, or any other residual coating. If required, apply any fluxes that are recommended for creating the required joint. Clamp the pieces together over a heat-resistant, non-combustible surface and heat the base metals with the torch flame. At the proper temperature, the filler rod tip, when applied to the crevice between the pieces to be joined, will melt, and the liquid metal will be drawn into the joint by capillary action. The filler metal should flow between the total surface area of the joint to act as a bonding agent to join the two pieces of metal together. In many cases the bond covering the entire surface area of contact between the two substrates often results in the base metals failing under stress before the brazed joint.

Discussion

High-temperature torch work requires practice. To gain the experience required to work with high-temperature flame-generated heat, the experimenter can collect or acquire a large number of coupons of the metal or material to be joined, research the literature for the correct technique, and join coupons together until a good, sound joint is produced each time the process is attempted. The skills required for brazing are much easier to acquire than are those for fusion welding.

Joining materials is discussed in detail in chapter one of the fourth edition of *Building Scientific Apparatus*,[7] and it is strongly recommended that researchers without formal training or substantial experience in welding/brazing techniques read the joining section of this definitive text before undertaking any high-temperature joint creation.

A gas heating torch burning propane or MAP (Methylacetylene–propadiene, propane mixtures have been replaced with MAP gases that are >95% propylene) with air or oxygen can be used for glass blowing. The basics of glass blowing are presented in chapter two of *Building Scientific Apparatus*.

As can be seen from Table 3-3, all the listed fuel gases whether burning with air or oxygen are hot enough to fusion melt J- and K-types of thermocouple wires. Gas torches can be used to make or repair J- and K-type thermocouples with J-type sensors of iron (melting point or m.p. 1538°C/2800°F) with constantan (m.p. 1210°C/2210°F) and K-type sensors of chromel (m.p. 1420°C/2588°F) with alumel (m.p. 11399°C/2550°F).

As noted, brazing does not melt the base metals being joined but rather forms a metallurgical bond between the filler metal and the pieces being joined. The filler metal is drawn into the brazed joint by capillary action and often forms a bond stronger than the metals being joined. Brazing is the preferred method for joining dissimilar metals or materials such as carbides, alumina, and graphite. A large portion of the skill required for brazing can be found in the design and engineering of the joint along with the attention given to joint-surface preparation.

---

[7]*Building Scientific Apparatus* 4th Edn. Moore, Davis, and Coplan, Cambridge University Press, ISBN 978-0-521-87858-6.

Code Listings

Listing 3-1. Arduino Sketch to Measure a K-Type Thermocouple and Stream Temperature Data to the Serial Monitor

```
// Read a K-type Thermocouple on A0
//
float temp ;
//
void setup()
//
{
//
Serial.begin(9600);
//
}
//
void loop()
//
{
//
int raw = analogRead(A0);
//
float Vout = raw * (5.0 / 1023.0);
//
temp = (Vout)/0.010;    // for the AD595 10 mV/deg C
//
Serial.println(temp);
//
delay(500);    // adjust if reqired
//
}
```

Listing 3-2. Arduino Control of Triac Power

```
/*
An external circuit is used to detect zero crossing of the
mains power cycle and
create a pulse at digital pin 2, which after a potentiometer
adjustable delay
switches on the triac. An external switch connected between pin
4 and ground controls
the application of gate-triggering pulses to the MOC3011 and
triac.
A K-type thermocouple readout of the heater source temperature
is available on the
serial monitor.
 */

#define triacPulse 5        // digital outut pin for zero
                            crossing synchronizing pulses

#define SW 4                // digital pin connected to switch
                            to enable pulses to MOC3011

#define aconLed 12          // digital pin connected to power
                            on indicator LED

//
float temp;                 // floating point variable for
                            temperature measurement

//
void setup()
{                           // configure the pins
  pinMode(2, INPUT);        // pin 2 receives the zero-crossing
                            pulse from the transistor

  digitalWrite(2, HIGH);    // pull up resistor
```

```
  pinMode(triacPulse, OUTPUT);     // pin 5 set for output
  pinMode(SW, INPUT);              // pin 4 set to input
  digitalWrite(SW, HIGH);          // pull up resistor
  pinMode(aconLed, OUTPUT);        // pin 12 set for output
  digitalWrite(aconLed, LOW);      // ac on indicator turned off
  //
  Serial.begin(9600);              // initialize the serial port
                                   // to display temperature data
}

void loop() {
  // read and calculate heated source temperature
  int raw = analogRead(A1);
  float Vout = raw * (5.0/1023.0);
  temp = (Vout/0.010);    // for the AD595 10 mv/deg C.
  Serial.print("Source temperature = ");
  Serial.println(temp);
   //
  // check that switch on pin 4 is closed enabling synched
  pulses to activate MOC3011
  if (!digitalRead(SW))   {
    // enable power
    attachInterrupt(0, acon, FALLING);
    // HV indicator on
    digitalWrite(aconLed, HIGH);
  }  // end if
  else if (digitalRead(SW)) {
    detachInterrupt(0); // disable power
    // HV indicator off
    digitalWrite(aconLed, LOW);
  }  // else
} // end loop
```

```
    //
    //
    // begin AC interrupt routine
    // delayMicroseconds()must be used to create the empirical-
       experimentally determined value
    // required to control the generation time of the triac turn
       on pulse
    //
void acon()
{
    delayMicroseconds((analogRead(0) * 6) + 1000); // read AO value
                                                    and adjust
    digitalWrite(triacPulse, HIGH);
    delayMicroseconds(200);   // delay 200 uSec on output pulse to
                                turn on triac
    digitalWrite(triacPulse, LOW);
}
```

Listing 3-3. Arduino PID Control of SSR Power

```
/********************************************************

    PID RelayOutput Example
    Heated chamber temperature read by K-type TC and AD595.
    Arduino code converts 0 to 5 volt ADC into degrees C for
    Comparison with set point of PID algorithm. TC on AO.
    Output to a digital pin which is controlling an SSR.
    The PID is designed to output an analog value,
    but the relay can only be On/Off.

    To operate the process a "time proportioning
    control" is used. TPC is in reality a slow version of PWM.
    First, we decide on a window size (default in PID demo code
    is 5000mS )
```

set the PID to adjust its output between 0 and that window size actually chosen or determined by experiment. Finally, logic that
translates the PID output into "Relay On Time" with the remainder of the
window being "Relay Off Time" is added.
```
*******************************************************/

#include <PID_v1.h>
#define RelayPin 6

//Define Variables we'll be connecting to
double Setpoint, Input, Output;
float temp;    // temperature in deg. C from K type TC and AD595

//Specify the links and initial tuning parameters
PID myPID(&Input, &Output, &Setpoint, 2, 5, 1, DIRECT);

int WindowSize = 1000;
unsigned long windowStartTime;
void setup()
{
  Serial.begin(9600);         // start serial port to see
                                 operating parameters and data
  pinMode(RelayPin, OUTPUT);

  windowStartTime = millis();

  //initialize the variables we're linked to
  Setpoint = 100;    // desired heated chamber temperature in
                        degrees Celcius

  //tell the PID to range between 0 and the full window size
  myPID.SetOutputLimits(0, WindowSize);
```

```
  //turn the PID on
  myPID.SetMode(AUTOMATIC);
}

void loop()
{
  int raw = analogRead(0);        // read the mV output from the
                                     TC-AD595
  float vout = raw * (5.0/1023); // convert ADC to mV
  temp = (vout)/0.010;            // convert TC mV from AD595 to
                                     degrees C
  Input = temp;                   // convert chamber temperature
                                     into PID controller variable

  myPID.Compute();

  /************************************************
     turn the output pin on/off based on PID output
   ************************************************/
  unsigned long now = millis();
  if (now - windowStartTime > WindowSize)
  { //time to shift the Relay Window
    windowStartTime += WindowSize;
  }
  if (Output > now - windowStartTime) digitalWrite(RelayPin, HIGH);
  else digitalWrite(RelayPin, LOW);
  Serial.print("Chamber temperature = ");  // begin output of
                                              data in a streamed
                                              line display
  Serial.print(temp);
  Serial.print("  Set point = ");
  Serial.print(Setpoint);
  Serial.print("  Input = ");
  Serial.print(Input);
```

```
  Serial.print("  raw = ");
  Serial.println(raw);
}
```

Listing 3-4. Arduino MOSFET Power Controller

```
// A MOSFET Power Controller with Temperature Monitor
//
// This program uses the #3 PWM pin on an Arduino to regulate
   the power delivered to a load.
// The Arduino controls a high-power MOSFET gate to regulate
   the current flow to the load by
// sending i or d from the serial port to increase or decrease
   the power to the load.
// A K- or J-type thermocouple temperature sensors on A0
   monitors the temperature near the load.
//
int load = 3; // the gate of the N channel MOSFET connects to
                 Arduino pin 3
int power = 0;   // the power level varies from 0 to 99%
int load_level = map(power, 0, 99, 0, 255);   // power level
                                                mapping of %
                                                and 255
//
void setup(void) {
  Serial.begin(9600);
  pinMode(load, OUTPUT); // set the load or MOSFET gate control
                         pin to output
}

void loop(void) {
  uint8_t i;
```

```
  char option;            // action to be initiated; "i" increase,
                             "d" to decrease power input
//
  if(Serial.available() > 0)
  {
    option = Serial.read();
    if (option == 'i') // i sent from the serial port increases
                       the power to the load
    power += 5;
    else if(option == 'd') // d sent from the serial port
                             decreases the power to the load
    power -= 5;
//
  if(power > 99) power = 99;
  if(power < 0) power = 0;
//
  load_level = map(power, 0, 99, 0, 255);
  }
//
Serial.print("Power = ");
Serial.print(power);
Serial.print(" PLevel = ");
Serial.println(load_level);
//
analogWrite(load, load_level); // write the new levels % AND
                               0-255 to the port
//
int raw = analogRead(A0);
float Vout = raw*(5.0/1023.5);
float temp = (Vout)/0.010; // for the AD595 10mV/deg C
Serial.print("Thermocouple temperature = ");
```

```
Serial.println(temp);
delay(500);
}
```

The following table of tabulated data is an exemplar of the downloadable information available for thermocouples from the NIST at https://srdata.nist.gov.

Table 3-5. *ITS-90 Table for type K thermocouples*

```
ITS-90 Table for type K thermocouple
°C     0     -1     -2     -3     -4     -5     -6     -7     -8     -9    -10
                            Thermoelectric Voltage in mV

-270 -6.458
-260 -6.441 -6.444 -6.446 -6.448 -6.450 -6.452 -6.453 -6.455 -6.456 -6.457 -6.458
-250 -6.404 -6.408 -6.413 -6.417 -6.421 -6.425 -6.429 -6.432 -6.435 -6.438 -6.441

-240 -6.344 -6.351 -6.358 -6.364 -6.370 -6.377 -6.382 -6.388 -6.393 -6.399 -6.404
-230 -6.262 -6.271 -6.280 -6.289 -6.297 -6.306 -6.314 -6.322 -6.329 -6.337 -6.344
-220 -6.158 -6.170 -6.181 -6.192 -6.202 -6.213 -6.223 -6.233 -6.243 -6.252 -6.262
-210 -6.035 -6.048 -6.061 -6.074 -6.087 -6.099 -6.111 -6.123 -6.135 -6.147 -6.158
-200 -5.891 -5.907 -5.922 -5.936 -5.951 -5.965 -5.980 -5.994 -6.007 -6.021 -6.035

-190 -5.730 -5.747 -5.763 -5.780 -5.797 -5.813 -5.829 -5.845 -5.861 -5.876 -5.891
-180 -5.550 -5.569 -5.588 -5.606 -5.624 -5.642 -5.660 -5.678 -5.695 -5.713 -5.730
-170 -5.354 -5.374 -5.395 -5.415 -5.435 -5.454 -5.474 -5.493 -5.512 -5.531 -5.550
-160 -5.141 -5.163 -5.185 -5.207 -5.228 -5.250 -5.271 -5.292 -5.313 -5.333 -5.354
-150 -4.913 -4.936 -4.960 -4.983 -5.006 -5.029 -5.052 -5.074 -5.097 -5.119 -5.141

-140 -4.669 -4.694 -4.719 -4.744 -4.768 -4.793 -4.817 -4.841 -4.865 -4.889 -4.913
-130 -4.411 -4.437 -4.463 -4.490 -4.516 -4.542 -4.567 -4.593 -4.618 -4.644 -4.669
-120 -4.138 -4.166 -4.194 -4.221 -4.249 -4.276 -4.303 -4.330 -4.357 -4.384 -4.411
-110 -3.852 -3.882 -3.911 -3.939 -3.968 -3.997 -4.025 -4.054 -4.082 -4.110 -4.138
-100 -3.554 -3.584 -3.614 -3.645 -3.675 -3.705 -3.734 -3.764 -3.794 -3.823 -3.852

 -90 -3.243 -3.274 -3.306 -3.337 -3.368 -3.400 -3.431 -3.462 -3.492 -3.523 -3.554
 -80 -2.920 -2.953 -2.986 -3.018 -3.050 -3.083 -3.115 -3.147 -3.179 -3.211 -3.243
 -70 -2.587 -2.620 -2.654 -2.688 -2.721 -2.755 -2.788 -2.821 -2.854 -2.887 -2.920
 -60 -2.243 -2.278 -2.312 -2.347 -2.382 -2.416 -2.450 -2.485 -2.519 -2.553 -2.587
 -50 -1.889 -1.925 -1.961 -1.996 -2.032 -2.067 -2.103 -2.138 -2.173 -2.208 -2.243

 -40 -1.527 -1.564 -1.600 -1.637 -1.673 -1.709 -1.745 -1.782 -1.818 -1.854 -1.889
 -30 -1.156 -1.194 -1.231 -1.268 -1.305 -1.343 -1.380 -1.417 -1.453 -1.490 -1.527
 -20 -0.778 -0.816 -0.854 -0.892 -0.930 -0.968 -1.006 -1.043 -1.081 -1.119 -1.156
 -10 -0.392 -0.431 -0.470 -0.508 -0.547 -0.586 -0.624 -0.663 -0.701 -0.739 -0.778
   0  0.000 -0.039 -0.079 -0.118 -0.157 -0.197 -0.236 -0.275 -0.314 -0.353 -0.392
```

```
ITS-90 Table for type K thermocouple
°C      0      1      2      3      4      5      6      7      8      9     10
                        Thermoelectric Voltage in mV

  0  0.000  0.039  0.079  0.119  0.158  0.198  0.238  0.277  0.317  0.357  0.397
 10  0.397  0.437  0.477  0.517  0.557  0.597  0.637  0.677  0.718  0.758  0.798
 20  0.798  0.838  0.879  0.919  0.960  1.000  1.041  1.081  1.122  1.163  1.203
 30  1.203  1.244  1.285  1.326  1.366  1.407  1.448  1.489  1.530  1.571  1.612
 40  1.612  1.653  1.694  1.735  1.776  1.817  1.858  1.899  1.941  1.982  2.023

 50  2.023  2.064  2.106  2.147  2.188  2.230  2.271  2.312  2.354  2.395  2.436
 60  2.436  2.478  2.519  2.561  2.602  2.644  2.685  2.727  2.768  2.810  2.851
 70  2.851  2.893  2.934  2.976  3.017  3.059  3.100  3.142  3.184  3.225  3.267
 80  3.267  3.308  3.350  3.391  3.433  3.474  3.516  3.557  3.599  3.640  3.682
 90  3.682  3.723  3.765  3.806  3.848  3.889  3.931  3.972  4.013  4.055  4.096

100  4.096  4.138  4.179  4.220  4.262  4.303  4.344  4.385  4.427  4.468  4.509
110  4.509  4.550  4.591  4.633  4.674  4.715  4.756  4.797  4.838  4.879  4.920
120  4.920  4.961  5.002  5.043  5.084  5.124  5.165  5.206  5.247  5.288  5.328
130  5.328  5.369  5.410  5.450  5.491  5.532  5.572  5.613  5.653  5.694  5.735
140  5.735  5.775  5.815  5.856  5.896  5.937  5.977  6.017  6.058  6.098  6.138

150  6.138  6.179  6.219  6.259  6.299  6.339  6.380  6.420  6.460  6.500  6.540
160  6.540  6.580  6.620  6.660  6.701  6.741  6.781  6.821  6.861  6.901  6.941
170  6.941  6.981  7.021  7.060  7.100  7.140  7.180  7.220  7.260  7.300  7.340
180  7.340  7.380  7.420  7.460  7.500  7.540  7.579  7.619  7.659  7.699  7.739
190  7.739  7.779  7.819  7.859  7.899  7.939  7.979  8.019  8.059  8.099  8.138

200  8.138  8.178  8.218  8.258  8.298  8.338  8.378  8.418  8.458  8.499  8.539
210  8.539  8.579  8.619  8.659  8.699  8.739  8.779  8.819  8.860  8.900  8.940
220  8.940  8.980  9.020  9.061  9.101  9.141  9.181  9.222  9.262  9.302  9.343
230  9.343  9.383  9.423  9.464  9.504  9.545  9.585  9.626  9.666  9.707  9.747
240  9.747  9.788  9.828  9.869  9.909  9.950  9.991 10.031 10.072 10.113 10.153

250 10.153 10.194 10.235 10.276 10.316 10.357 10.398 10.439 10.480 10.520 10.561
260 10.561 10.602 10.643 10.684 10.725 10.766 10.807 10.848 10.889 10.930 10.971
270 10.971 11.012 11.053 11.094 11.135 11.176 11.217 11.259 11.300 11.341 11.382
```

°C	0	1	2	3	4	5	6	7	8	9	10
270	10.971	11.012	11.053	11.094	11.135	11.176	11.217	11.259	11.300	11.341	11.382
280	11.382	11.423	11.465	11.506	11.547	11.588	11.630	11.671	11.712	11.753	11.795
290	11.795	11.836	11.877	11.919	11.960	12.001	12.043	12.084	12.126	12.167	12.209
300	12.209	12.250	12.291	12.333	12.374	12.416	12.457	12.499	12.540	12.582	12.624
310	12.624	12.665	12.707	12.748	12.790	12.831	12.873	12.915	12.956	12.998	13.040
320	13.040	13.081	13.123	13.165	13.206	13.248	13.290	13.331	13.373	13.415	13.457
330	13.457	13.498	13.540	13.582	13.624	13.665	13.707	13.749	13.791	13.833	13.874
340	13.874	13.916	13.958	14.000	14.042	14.084	14.126	14.167	14.209	14.251	14.293
350	14.293	14.335	14.377	14.419	14.461	14.503	14.545	14.587	14.629	14.671	14.713
360	14.713	14.755	14.797	14.839	14.881	14.923	14.965	15.007	15.049	15.091	15.133
370	15.133	15.175	15.217	15.259	15.301	15.343	15.385	15.427	15.469	15.511	15.554
380	15.554	15.596	15.638	15.680	15.722	15.764	15.806	15.849	15.891	15.933	15.975
390	15.975	16.017	16.059	16.102	16.144	16.186	16.228	16.270	16.313	16.355	16.397
400	16.397	16.439	16.482	16.524	16.566	16.608	16.651	16.693	16.735	16.778	16.820
410	16.820	16.862	16.904	16.947	16.989	17.031	17.074	17.116	17.158	17.201	17.243
420	17.243	17.285	17.328	17.370	17.413	17.455	17.497	17.540	17.582	17.624	17.667
430	17.667	17.709	17.752	17.794	17.837	17.879	17.921	17.964	18.006	18.049	18.091
440	18.091	18.134	18.176	18.218	18.261	18.303	18.346	18.388	18.431	18.473	18.516
450	18.516	18.558	18.601	18.643	18.686	18.728	18.771	18.813	18.856	18.898	18.941
460	18.941	18.983	19.026	19.068	19.111	19.154	19.196	19.239	19.281	19.324	19.366
470	19.366	19.409	19.451	19.494	19.537	19.579	19.622	19.664	19.707	19.750	19.792
480	19.792	19.835	19.877	19.920	19.962	20.005	20.048	20.090	20.133	20.175	20.218
490	20.218	20.261	20.303	20.346	20.389	20.431	20.474	20.516	20.559	20.602	20.644
°C	0	1	2	3	4	5	6	7	8	9	10

ITS-90 Table for type K thermocouple

°C	0	1	2	3	4	5	6	7	8	9	10
				Thermoelectric Voltage in mV							
500	20.644	20.687	20.730	20.772	20.815	20.857	20.900	20.943	20.985	21.028	21.071
510	21.071	21.113	21.156	21.199	21.241	21.284	21.326	21.369	21.412	21.454	21.497
520	21.497	21.540	21.582	21.625	21.668	21.710	21.753	21.796	21.838	21.881	21.924

```
 ITS-90 Table for type K  thermocouple
 °C      0       1       2       3       4       5       6       7       8       9      10
                              Thermoelectric Voltage in mV

500 20.644 20.687 20.730 20.772 20.815 20.857 20.900 20.943 20.985 21.028 21.071
510 21.071 21.113 21.156 21.199 21.241 21.284 21.326 21.369 21.412 21.454 21.497
520 21.497 21.540 21.582 21.625 21.668 21.710 21.753 21.796 21.838 21.881 21.924
530 21.924 21.966 22.009 22.052 22.094 22.137 22.179 22.222 22.265 22.307 22.350
540 22.350 22.393 22.435 22.478 22.521 22.563 22.606 22.649 22.691 22.734 22.776

550 22.776 22.819 22.862 22.904 22.947 22.990 23.032 23.075 23.117 23.160 23.203
560 23.203 23.245 23.288 23.331 23.373 23.416 23.458 23.501 23.544 23.586 23.629
570 23.629 23.671 23.714 23.757 23.799 23.842 23.884 23.927 23.970 24.012 24.055
580 24.055 24.097 24.140 24.182 24.225 24.267 24.310 24.353 24.395 24.438 24.480
590 24.480 24.523 24.565 24.608 24.650 24.693 24.735 24.778 24.820 24.863 24.905

600 24.905 24.948 24.990 25.033 25.075 25.118 25.160 25.203 25.245 25.288 25.330
610 25.330 25.373 25.415 25.458 25.500 25.543 25.585 25.627 25.670 25.712 25.755
620 25.755 25.797 25.840 25.882 25.924 25.967 26.009 26.052 26.094 26.136 26.179
630 26.179 26.221 26.263 26.306 26.348 26.390 26.433 26.475 26.517 26.560 26.602
640 26.602 26.644 26.687 26.729 26.771 26.814 26.856 26.898 26.940 26.983 27.025

650 27.025 27.067 27.109 27.152 27.194 27.236 27.278 27.320 27.363 27.405 27.447
660 27.447 27.489 27.531 27.574 27.616 27.658 27.700 27.742 27.784 27.826 27.869
670 27.869 27.911 27.953 27.995 28.037 28.079 28.121 28.163 28.205 28.247 28.289
680 28.289 28.332 28.374 28.416 28.458 28.500 28.542 28.584 28.626 28.668 28.710
690 28.710 28.752 28.794 28.835 28.877 28.919 28.961 29.003 29.045 29.087 29.129

700 29.129 29.171 29.213 29.255 29.297 29.338 29.380 29.422 29.464 29.506 29.548
710 29.548 29.589 29.631 29.673 29.715 29.757 29.798 29.840 29.882 29.924 29.965
720 29.965 30.007 30.049 30.090 30.132 30.174 30.216 30.257 30.299 30.341 30.382
730 30.382 30.424 30.466 30.507 30.549 30.590 30.632 30.674 30.715 30.757 30.798
740 30.798 30.840 30.881 30.923 30.964 31.006 31.047 31.089 31.130 31.172 31.213

750 31.213 31.255 31.296 31.338 31.379 31.421 31.462 31.504 31.545 31.586 31.628
760 31.628 31.669 31.710 31.752 31.793 31.834 31.876 31.917 31.958 32.000 32.041
```

°C	0	1	2	3	4	5	6	7	8	9	10
760	31.628	31.669	31.710	31.752	31.793	31.834	31.876	31.917	31.958	32.000	32.041
770	32.041	32.082	32.124	32.165	32.206	32.247	32.289	32.330	32.371	32.412	32.453
780	32.453	32.495	32.536	32.577	32.618	32.659	32.700	32.742	32.783	32.824	32.865
790	32.865	32.906	32.947	32.988	33.029	33.070	33.111	33.152	33.193	33.234	33.275
800	33.275	33.316	33.357	33.398	33.439	33.480	33.521	33.562	33.603	33.644	33.685
810	33.685	33.726	33.767	33.808	33.848	33.889	33.930	33.971	34.012	34.053	34.093
820	34.093	34.134	34.175	34.216	34.257	34.297	34.338	34.379	34.420	34.460	34.501
830	34.501	34.542	34.582	34.623	34.664	34.704	34.745	34.786	34.826	34.867	34.908
840	34.908	34.948	34.989	35.029	35.070	35.110	35.151	35.192	35.232	35.273	35.313
850	35.313	35.354	35.394	35.435	35.475	35.516	35.556	35.596	35.637	35.677	35.718
860	35.718	35.758	35.798	35.839	35.879	35.920	35.960	36.000	36.041	36.081	36.121
870	36.121	36.162	36.202	36.242	36.282	36.323	36.363	36.403	36.443	36.484	36.524
880	36.524	36.564	36.604	36.644	36.685	36.725	36.765	36.805	36.845	36.885	36.925
890	36.925	36.965	37.006	37.046	37.086	37.126	37.166	37.206	37.246	37.286	37.326
900	37.326	37.366	37.406	37.446	37.486	37.526	37.566	37.606	37.646	37.686	37.725
910	37.725	37.765	37.805	37.845	37.885	37.925	37.965	38.005	38.044	38.084	38.124
920	38.124	38.164	38.204	38.243	38.283	38.323	38.363	38.402	38.442	38.482	38.522
930	38.522	38.561	38.601	38.641	38.680	38.720	38.760	38.799	38.839	38.878	38.918
940	38.918	38.958	38.997	39.037	39.076	39.116	39.155	39.195	39.235	39.274	39.314
950	39.314	39.353	39.393	39.432	39.471	39.511	39.550	39.590	39.629	39.669	39.708
960	39.708	39.747	39.787	39.826	39.866	39.905	39.944	39.984	40.023	40.062	40.101
970	40.101	40.141	40.180	40.219	40.259	40.298	40.337	40.376	40.415	40.455	40.494
980	40.494	40.533	40.572	40.611	40.651	40.690	40.729	40.768	40.807	40.846	40.885
990	40.885	40.924	40.963	41.002	41.042	41.081	41.120	41.159	41.198	41.237	41.276
°C	0	1	2	3	4	5	6	7	8	9	10

ITS-90 Table for type K thermocouple

°C	0	1	2	3	4	5	6	7	8	9	10

Thermoelectric Voltage in mV

°C	0	1	2	3	4	5	6	7	8	9	10
1000	41.276	41.315	41.354	41.393	41.431	41.470	41.509	41.548	41.587	41.626	41.665
1010	41.665	41.704	41.743	41.781	41.820	41.859	41.898	41.937	41.976	42.014	42.053

ITS-90 Table for type K thermocouple										
°C	0	1	2	3	4	5	6	7	8	9	10
				Thermoelectric Voltage in mV						
1000	41.276	41.315	41.354	41.393	41.431	41.470	41.509	41.548	41.587	41.626	41.665
1010	41.665	41.704	41.743	41.781	41.820	41.859	41.898	41.937	41.976	42.014	42.053
1020	42.053	42.092	42.131	42.169	42.208	42.247	42.286	42.324	42.363	42.402	42.440
1030	42.440	42.479	42.518	42.556	42.595	42.633	42.672	42.711	42.749	42.788	42.826
1040	42.826	42.865	42.903	42.942	42.980	43.019	43.057	43.096	43.134	43.173	43.211
1050	43.211	43.250	43.288	43.327	43.365	43.403	43.442	43.480	43.518	43.557	43.595
1060	43.595	43.633	43.672	43.710	43.748	43.787	43.825	43.863	43.901	43.940	43.978
1070	43.978	44.016	44.054	44.092	44.130	44.169	44.207	44.245	44.283	44.321	44.359
1080	44.359	44.397	44.435	44.473	44.512	44.550	44.588	44.626	44.664	44.702	44.740
1090	44.740	44.778	44.816	44.853	44.891	44.929	44.967	45.005	45.043	45.081	45.119
1100	45.119	45.157	45.194	45.232	45.270	45.308	45.346	45.383	45.421	45.459	45.497
1110	45.497	45.534	45.572	45.610	45.647	45.685	45.723	45.760	45.798	45.836	45.873
1120	45.873	45.911	45.948	45.986	46.024	46.061	46.099	46.136	46.174	46.211	46.249
1130	46.249	46.286	46.324	46.361	46.398	46.436	46.473	46.511	46.548	46.585	46.623
1140	46.623	46.660	46.697	46.735	46.772	46.809	46.847	46.884	46.921	46.958	46.995
1150	46.995	47.033	47.070	47.107	47.144	47.181	47.218	47.256	47.293	47.330	47.367
1160	47.367	47.404	47.441	47.478	47.515	47.552	47.589	47.626	47.663	47.700	47.737
1170	47.737	47.774	47.811	47.848	47.884	47.921	47.958	47.995	48.032	48.069	48.105
1180	48.105	48.142	48.179	48.216	48.252	48.289	48.326	48.363	48.399	48.436	48.473
1190	48.473	48.509	48.546	48.582	48.619	48.656	48.692	48.729	48.765	48.802	48.838
1200	48.838	48.875	48.911	48.948	48.984	49.021	49.057	49.093	49.130	49.166	49.202
1210	49.202	49.239	49.275	49.311	49.348	49.384	49.420	49.456	49.493	49.529	49.565
1220	49.565	49.601	49.637	49.674	49.710	49.746	49.782	49.818	49.854	49.890	49.926
1230	49.926	49.962	49.998	50.034	50.070	50.106	50.142	50.178	50.214	50.250	50.286
1240	50.286	50.322	50.358	50.393	50.429	50.465	50.501	50.537	50.572	50.608	50.644
1250	50.644	50.680	50.715	50.751	50.787	50.822	50.858	50.894	50.929	50.965	51.000
1260	51.000	51.036	51.071	51.107	51.142	51.178	51.213	51.249	51.284	51.320	51.355
1270	51.355	51.391	51.426	51.461	51.497	51.532	51.567	51.603	51.638	51.673	51.708

```
1100 45.119 45.157 45.194 45.232 45.270 45.308 45.346 45.383 45.421 45.459 45.497
1110 45.497 45.534 45.572 45.610 45.647 45.685 45.723 45.760 45.798 45.836 45.873
1120 45.873 45.911 45.948 45.986 46.024 46.061 46.099 46.136 46.174 46.211 46.249
1130 46.249 46.286 46.324 46.361 46.398 46.436 46.473 46.511 46.548 46.585 46.623
1140 46.623 46.660 46.697 46.735 46.772 46.809 46.847 46.884 46.921 46.958 46.995

1150 46.995 47.033 47.070 47.107 47.144 47.181 47.218 47.256 47.293 47.330 47.367
1160 47.367 47.404 47.441 47.478 47.515 47.552 47.589 47.626 47.663 47.700 47.737
1170 47.737 47.774 47.811 47.848 47.884 47.921 47.958 47.995 48.032 48.069 48.105
1180 48.105 48.142 48.179 48.216 48.252 48.289 48.326 48.363 48.399 48.436 48.473
1190 48.473 48.509 48.546 48.582 48.619 48.656 48.692 48.729 48.765 48.802 48.838

1200 48.838 48.875 48.911 48.948 48.984 49.021 49.057 49.093 49.130 49.166 49.202
1210 49.202 49.239 49.275 49.311 49.348 49.384 49.420 49.456 49.493 49.529 49.565
1220 49.565 49.601 49.637 49.674 49.710 49.746 49.782 49.818 49.854 49.890 49.926
1230 49.926 49.962 49.998 50.034 50.070 50.106 50.142 50.178 50.214 50.250 50.286
1240 50.286 50.322 50.358 50.393 50.429 50.465 50.501 50.537 50.572 50.608 50.644

1250 50.644 50.680 50.715 50.751 50.787 50.822 50.858 50.894 50.929 50.965 51.000
1260 51.000 51.036 51.071 51.107 51.142 51.178 51.213 51.249 51.284 51.320 51.355
1270 51.355 51.391 51.426 51.461 51.497 51.532 51.567 51.603 51.638 51.673 51.708
1280 51.708 51.744 51.779 51.814 51.849 51.885 51.920 51.955 51.990 52.025 52.060
1290 52.060 52.095 52.130 52.165 52.200 52.235 52.270 52.305 52.340 52.375 52.410

1300 52.410 52.445 52.480 52.515 52.550 52.585 52.620 52.654 52.689 52.724 52.759
1310 52.759 52.794 52.828 52.863 52.898 52.932 52.967 53.002 53.037 53.071 53.106
1320 53.106 53.140 53.175 53.210 53.244 53.279 53.313 53.348 53.382 53.417 53.451
1330 53.451 53.486 53.520 53.555 53.589 53.623 53.658 53.692 53.727 53.761 53.795
1340 53.795 53.830 53.864 53.898 53.932 53.967 54.001 54.035 54.069 54.104 54.138

1350 54.138 54.172 54.206 54.240 54.274 54.308 54.343 54.377 54.411 54.445 54.479
1360 54.479 54.513 54.547 54.581 54.615 54.649 54.683 54.717 54.751 54.785 54.819
1370 54.819 54.852 54.886

°C     0     1     2     3     4     5     6     7     8     9     10
```

Summary

- High-heat and high-temperature work requires care and caution.

- Where possible, commercially available components should be used in experimental investigations requiring the use of high-temperature conditions.

- Heating elements, furnaces, and AC or DC power supplies with feedback or static temperature controls can be assembled with readily available low-cost materials and components if unique, custom-configuration or low-cost heating systems are required.

- An origin and cause analysis on an unexpected furnace failure is reviewed.

- High-temperature work with different fuel gases is reviewed.

Chapter 4 discusses the theory, applications, and limitations of the PID process-control algorithm often used as the basis of a precise furnace temperature controller.

CHAPTER 4

The PID Process Control Algorithm

Proportional, integral, and derivative (PID) controllers are an important technological development that in the past hundred years has become an industrial commodity and an integral part of a host of manufactured laboratory equipment. However, the bulk of the literature available concerning PID control systems is heavily biased toward industrial or engineering applications and theoretical mathematical treatments. The object of this chapter is to review the simple theory of the PID algorithm and apply the robust controller to microcomputer and microprocessor small-scale experimental works.

Theory

When control of experimental or scientific investigation process variables over an extended period of time is required, the PID algorithm can be used. In processes such as maintaining the temperature within an enclosure, the intensity of illumination, the position of a robotic arm, or the speed of a rotating device such as a pump, agitator, or wavelength scanner, the PID algorithm can be used. Virtually any electro-mechanical process can be controlled with the (PID) algorithm. The PID methodology uses a feedback-loop technology that has evolved over the past century

© Richard J. Smythe 2021
R. J. Smythe, *Advanced Arduino Techniques in Science*,
https://doi.org/10.1007/978-1-4842-6784-4_4

into a digital-format algorithm able to be processed in a computing machine to provide automatic or "realtime" process control on a local benchtop, manufacturing facility, or remote field location.

As noted, a full PID algorithm contains proportional, integral, and derivative mathematical operations, but proportional-only and proportional-plus-integral forms of the controller are also used to form a controller loop. Investigators implementing a control process must assess the degree of control required for the process at hand and select the appropriate form of the algorithm to use.

Each individual process that is to be controlled will have a desired "set" or operating point, an actual operating point, which can be measured, and an error value that is the difference between the set point and the actual process operating point. On startup or after a system perturbation, the set point and the actual operating point are different, and when this happens, the PID controller attempts to generate a composite output signal that will bring the process back to the desired set point. A perturbation can upset the process by causing an increase or decrease in the magnitude of the error term, thus requiring a positive or negative corrective action.

Figure 4-1 is a block flow chart for a PID-based control system.

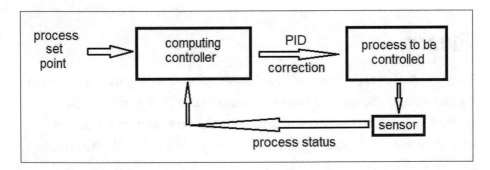

Figure 4-1. *A PID-type control system*

Figure 4-1 is a very simple depiction of the flow of information that can be used to control virtually any electro-mechanical system. In the cycle displayed, a computing device is operating in a continuously interactive mode with a process in a closed-loop configuration. Within the loop the process controls are continuously being manipulated by the controller to keep the monitored process status in accord with the controller's desired set point.

A process set point may be a fixed value such as a furnace temperature or it may be a time-dependent value in a temperature program, such as those used in gas chromatography or in a heat treatment metallurgical process. The set point is a value recognized in the computing controller that is compared to the process status value as monitored by the sensor in Figure 4-1. If an error or difference is found between the set point and the sensor output, the computing controller invokes the PID mathematical algorithm to generate a signal that changes the process controls to reduce the magnitude of the calculated error.

Adaptability is a very important feature of the PID control system that is made possible by the use of five variables. To effectively control the process at hand, the process value and the desired set point are needed to determine the error signal, which is then processed by the PID algorithm in use to evaluate the proportional, proportional-plus-integral, or full PID error correction.

Figure 4-2 depicts the classical theoretical mathematical form of the full PID equation.

$$u(t) = k_p \left(e(t) + \frac{1}{T_t} \int_0^t e(\tau) d\tau + T_d \frac{de(t)}{dt} \right)$$

Figure 4-2. *The PID equation*

In the time-based format of Figure 4-2, the process status is $PV(t)$ and the desired set point is SP, so the error at time t is $e(t)$, the difference between the set point and the process value. $u(t)$ can be considered as the electrical signal to be sent to the process controls to bring the process value and set point closer together. ᴛ is a variable of integration.

The PID formula weights the proportional term by a factor of K_p, the integral term by a factor of K_p/T_I, and the derivative term by a factor of $K_p T_D$, where K_p is the controller gain, T_I is the integral time, and T_D is the derivative time.

Using the notation of K_p, K_i, and K_d values in the following figures, the three empirical numerical "tuning constants" that modify the values determined by the proportional, integral, and derivative mathematical operations working on the calculated process set-point error can be defined.

The proportional term depicted in Figure 4-3 can be considered as a value that is directly proportional to the difference between the set point and the operating point. If the process is operating at its set point the proportional correction term contribution to the output is virtually zero. If the process has drifted or been pushed far from its desired set point, the proportional contribution to the output will be correspondingly larger. In experimental works such as with small, fine wire-heating elements, a power restriction must be applied to the heater circuitry to avoid heater filament destruction on system startup when initial error values are large.

$$P = K_p e(t)$$

Figure 4-3. *The proportional term*

A second contribution to the algorithm's output value that aids in bringing the operating point and set point closer together is provided by the integral term as defined in Figure 4-4.

$$I = K_i \int_0^t e(\tau)d\tau$$

Figure 4-4. *The integral term*

The integral term is derived from the sums of the previous error values over a fixed time interval. If the operating and set points are far apart, a larger contribution will be generated by the error summing. If the set point and operating point are closer together, the error will get smaller and the incremental sum will increase at a slower rate. Thus, depending upon the previous trend the integral contribution will vary in accordance with the size of the calculated error. It is suggested in the general PID literature that the integral term corrects for systematic errors in which the process value and the desired set point differ by a constant value over a given period of time.

A changing error value is detected by taking the mathematical derivative of the series of numerical values constituting the error stream. The derivative term of the controller algorithm is displayed in Figure 4-5. A derivative is a measure of the rate of change of a variable. The derivative component monitors how fast the error value is changing and applies an appropriate corrective action. In a PID loop there may be random noise that may be interpreted by the controller as an error signal requiring a controller output to correct. Excessive unnecessary corrective controller output can cause premature wear and failure in the final control element (FCE) in process loops using mechanical valves as control elements. It is reported in the literature that for many fast-response industrial processes using mechanical control elements the inclusion of the derivative term in the controller algorithm does not contribute enough improvement in control performance to offset the increased equipment maintenance costs. However, for slower response processes such as temperature control loops, pH control, and other slow-response processes the derivative term should be included. The literature also notes that a two-term control algorithm is much easier to tune than the three-term entity.

$$D = K_d \frac{d}{dt} e(t)$$

Figure 4-5. *The derivative term*

As noted, the three mathematical operations monitor the process as it runs and from the stream of error values generated produce three numerical-value contributions to an error-correction signal. The controller output based upon the three values should bring the process operating value and the set point closer together. The three *K* values that precede each of the mathematical operations determine how much "weight" or "influence" the individual mathematical function–created controlling values will have in the overall feedback loop. A great deal of research in the engineering community has gone into finding methods for selecting the optimum values for the tuning constants for the PID algorithm. Researchers using the PID algorithm on a unique experimental setup will probably find that best practice is to follow the Zeigler Nichols methods for estimating the required constants to optimize system performance.

Tuning and Practical Applications of the PID Controller

As noted previously, processes to be controlled can vary substantially in the rate at which they respond to disturbances, perturbations, or control inputs. To control a high-speed process, fast error generation and PID reaction times may be necessary to provide timely process adjustments. A process moving a solar panel to face the sun or keep a furnace at a constant temperature may be considered as having a very slow rate of operation, while maintaining the speed of a motor spinning a mirror in an interferometer may be considered a fast operation. It is highly unlikely that the same set of tuning constants will be applicable to all process control implementations of the algorithm.

A controlled process can operate in one of three possible states: stable, unstable, or marginally stable. A controlled stable process is one that has eventually converged to a steady state of operation and remains that way with increasing time. An unstable process is not in a state of control and oscillates around the desired steady-state point of operation, with irregular oscillation amplitude never reaching a steady-state condition. A marginally stable system will oscillate about the desired steady-state condition with a relatively constant amplitude and is considered to be the intermediate state between controlled and uncontrolled processes.

Processes that require control are usually subjected to both driving and opposing forces. The opposing entities are typically mechanical friction; electrical, gas, liquid, and magnetic resistances; thermodynamic heat flow; or gravity, and are often termed the damping force.

A very simplified division classifies process control into underdamped, overdamped, and critically damped systems. Disturbances or perturbations may cause the system to oscillate about its normal steady-state condition. An overdamped system can be said to reach or return to its steady-state condition after a disturbance or from startup without

oscillation about the steady-state value. An underdamped system will
return to its steady state after a series of gradually decreasing oscillations
about the steady-state value. A critically damped system returns to its final
steady state in the shortest time possible and without oscillation from a
perturbation or system startup. In some systems there can be a fourth
state in which the system oscillates at a relatively constant frequency and
amplitude about the steady-state value after a disturbance; this fourth
state can be considered as the situation in which the damping force is
small enough to describe the system as undamped. A theoretical graphical
depiction of the four states is displayed in Figure 4-6.

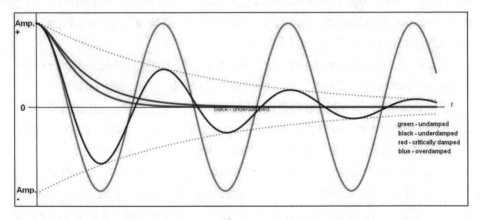

Figure 4-6. *Theoretical system response to perturbations*

Figure 4-6 and the discussion on system response to disturbances
have been presented as an aid in understanding adaptations of the PID
controller algorithm to experimental processes. Prior to implementation of
the controller algorithm, it is assumed that an investigator has assembled
a system that can run safely for at least a period of time of sufficient length
that the controller output and the process variable can be recorded.
A documented record of process variables is required to support an
experimental development program that is used to determine the values of

the three controller constants that are depicted in Figures 4-3, 4-4, and 4-5 so as to get satisfactory process control.

In 1942 a pair of methods was presented to the American Society of Mechanical Engineering by J.G. Ziegler and N.B. Nichols for determining a set of PID constant values that could control a process or serve as a base from which the process operator could modify the values to obtain the desired degree of control.

Prior to examining Ziegler and Nichols's two methods, the four terms for describing a controlled system's response to a perturbation or disturbance will be discussed. *Rise time* is the initial time it takes for the process output to rise beyond 90 percent of the desired set-point level. *Overshoot* describes the amount above the desired set point that the controller drives the output on startup or during recovery from a disturbance. *Settling time* is the time required for the process to settle back to its steady-state condition after a disturbance. A *steady-state error condition* exists in a process if there is a difference between the steady-state value and the desired set point. As previously noted, this systematic error is usually eliminated by the integral term of the algorithm.

To implement the first of the two methods used to generate an initial set of algorithm constants, the process at hand must be running in a closed-loop configuration and be in a steady-state condition. A known sized-step perturbation or disturbance must be made to the system, and the system response should form an "S" shape as it returns to the steady-state value, as depicted in Figure 4-7.

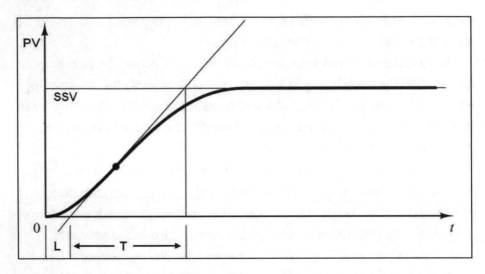

Figure 4-7. *Steady-state system response to a step disturbance*

Once a satisfactory curve has been recorded, the inflection point of the transition curve from disturbed state to steady-state value is located, as represented by the black dot in Figure 4-7. A line tangential to the straight portion of the transition curve at the inflection point is then drawn to intersect the zero-point disturbance value and the steady-state value. A vertical line is drawn from the point of intersection of the tangent line to the time axis to generate a pair of measured values known as the lag time L and the process time constant T.

A generally accepted application of the "S" step data response for a proportion-only controller is to set K_p equal to T/L, usually in seconds. The K_p and K_i constants for a proportional and integral controller are $0.9(T/4)$ and $L/3$, respectively. A complete set of possible constants for a full PID controller using K_p, K_i, and K_d can be calculated from $1.2(T/4)$, $2L$, and $L/2$, respectively.

The second procedure described by Ziegler and Nichols sets the values of K_i and K_d to zero and increases K_p until the system under test exhibits the theoretical undamped response as seen in the green trace of Figure 4-6. In Figure 4-8, the author's small, heated chamber's PID temperature controller exhibits a typical in-service undamped response.

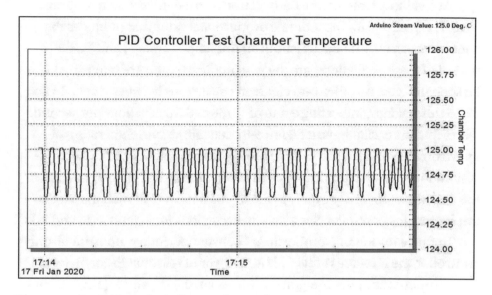

Figure 4-8. *Induced undamped steady-state system response*

The system response depicted in Figure 4-8 was eventually obtained by setting K_p to 128. To find the 128 value, the code in the microcontroller program defining the three PID parameters was initially altered to set K_p to 1 and K_i and K_d to 0. The microcontroller code was then launched and the system response recorded for five to ten minutes. A trace consisting of recorded random noise near the system set point was deemed a failure for the K_p value in use for the present iteration of the testing cycle. After such a failure, the next iterations used binary doubling of the coefficient until a pattern in the observed random noise began to appear. The doubling process was continued until the system response was found to produce the image recorded in Figure 4-8. Increasing the value of K_p above that producing the relatively symmetrical oscillation about the nominal set point increased the distortions seen just before the halfway point between the 17:15–17:16 time stamps and just before the 17:17 time stamp. As noted, the least distorted, most symmetrical oscillating display as seen in Figure 4-8 was realized at $K_p = 128$.

Two values of interest are derived from the recorded system response seen in Figure 4-8. K_u, the ultimate proportional value that produces the controller response characteristic of an undamped system, and P_u, the period of these oscillations, are the two predictive values of interest. As can be seen in Figure 4-8, there are eighteen oscillations between the 17:14 and 17:15 time stamps, indicating a rate of 18/60 or 0.3 oscillations per second. (Note that the oscillations in Figure 4-8 occur about the temperature of approximately 124.8°C rather than the system set point of 125°C. The systematic error can be partially attributed to the lack of an integral term in the PID algorithm and partially to the digital hardware limitations used to implement the controller. See also the discussions for Figures 4-10 and 4-11.)

To find a reasonable proportional constant K_p for a proportional-only controller, the K_u value is divided by 2. A pair of reasonable coefficients for a proportional-plus-integral controller are $0.45K_u$ and $1/(1.2\,P_u)$. For a full PID control algorithm, K_p is found by multiplying K_u by 0.6. The K_i coefficient is found by dividing the ultimate P_u by 2, and the K_d coefficient is determined by dividing P_u by 8.

There is a very large amount of literature on control engineering available to the investigator that provides many variations on the methods by which the PID coefficients can be estimated and how they can be adjusted to create a desired system performance. Only the traditional, more rudimentary process has been outlined in this chapter for use in experimental investigations.

Once the initial set of coefficients has been determined for the system at hand, the performance or dynamics of the controller can be adjusted if required in accordance with the data tabulated in Table 4-1.

Table 4-1. *Effects on System Dynamics of Increased PID Constants*

Effects of Increasing PID Parameter Values				
System Response	Rise Time	Overshoot	Settling Time	Error
K_c	decrease	increase	no effect	decrease
K_i	decrease	increase	increase	eliminates
K_d	no effect	decrease	decrease	no effect

PID for Thermal Control

If employing the circuit displayed in Figure 4-9, you would need to ensure that changing the PID coefficients would not cause damage to the process equipment being tested (i.e., heater filament destruction). Listing 4-1 was used to provide the system performance depicted in Figure 4-10, which was recorded with the DAQFactory plotting sequence shown in Listing 4-2. (All code listings provided at the end of the chapter.)

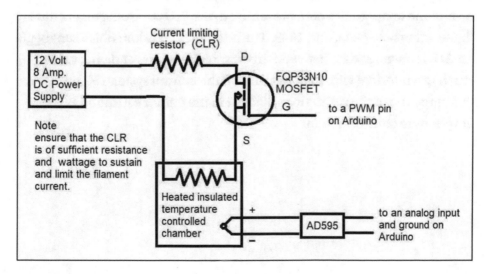

Figure 4-9. *A heated chamber power control circuit*

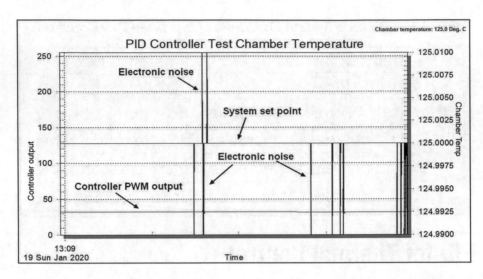

Figure 4-10. *The PID-controlled temperature of a heated chamber*

In Chapter 9, "The Analog Front End," the limitations of the typical microcontroller's built-in ADCs are addressed. In essence, most microcontrollers use a 10-bit ADC to convert a 0 to 5V input signal into a 0 to 1023 digital value. Although the thermocouple signal is amplified and conditioned by the AD595 and averaged to lessen the noise, the final form of the temperature data presented to the PID controller algorithm is a digital value between 0 and 1023. The addition of random noise can toggle the ADC converter data between the next higher or lower digital value, which can interfere with the operation of the control system. Figure 4-11 illustrates one of the restrictions evident in the author's Arduino PID temperature control system.

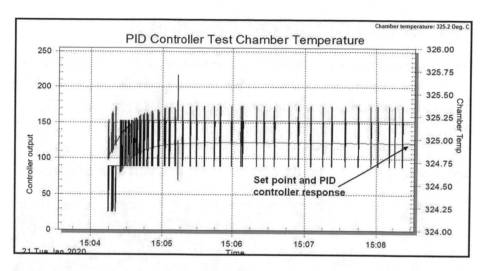

Figure 4-11. *The set point and system response for an Arduino PID-controlled temperature in a heated chamber*

Careful examination of the temperature scale and system response indicates that although the microcontroller code requests a set point of 325.0°C the system responds with a median value of 324.95°C. Further examination of the black trace reveals that the system response is oscillating from 324.70°C to 325.20°C—a difference of 0.50°C. The discrepancies evident in Figure 4-11 are consistent with the results of the digital limitations imposed upon the system by the 10-bit microprocessor hardware when it is used over a large dynamic range. If these restrictions are not acceptable to the experiments being conducted, then the PID controller algorithm must be applied to a narrower range of temperature control to achieve a higher degree of resolution.

With proper heat sinking, PID control of a PWM output can manage DC heater element currents up to 33A and 100V with the FQP33N10. Higher AC voltages of up to 400V and currents of 40A can be managed with solid-state relays and the technique known as time proportioning. (See Chapter 3, "Experimental Work at High Temperatures and High Heats.")

PID Control of Optical Brightness

Several educational institutions have made use of a microcontroller with an LED and a photoresistor optically coupled loop as a simple, inexpensive desktop demonstration of a PID controller. Figure 4-12 is a circuit diagram of an Arduino-based cadmium selenide LED optical loop to be controlled by a PID algorithm, via Listing 4-3, resident in the microcontroller. (An auxiliary supply may be used if a larger or brighter light source is desired.)

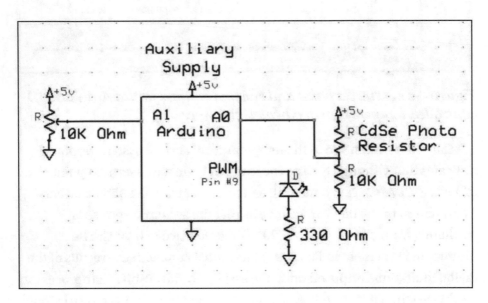

Figure 4-12. *A circuit diagram for an Arduino optical PID demonstration*

In Figure 4-13, the circuit of Figure 4-12 has been assembled on a 2 ⅛ in. (5.5 cm) by 3 ¼ in. (8.2 cm) prototyping breadboard. The microcontroller depicted in Figure 4-13 is a Sparkfun RedBoard Arduino Uno emulator available in volume purchases for $20 (USD).

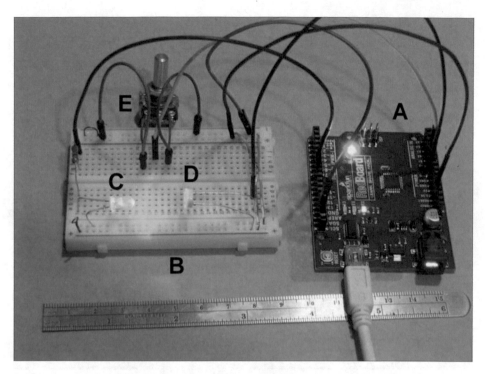

Figure 4-13. *A desktop LED–LDR PID control demonstration*

Item A is an Arduino-type microcontroller, and B is a small prototyping breadboard. Items C, D, and E are the LED light source, the cadmium selenide light-dependent resistor, and set-point potentiometer, respectively.

The academic institutions that used the setup described followed the previously noted industrial practice of creating a proportional, integral-only controller for both inexpensive simplicity and to accommodate a fast response process.

Figure 4-14 depicts the recorded results of interfering with the intensity of the LED emissions. Arduino's 8-bit PWM signal is limited to values between 0 and 255, which defines the full-scale output of the controller output and consequently the set-point limits. The microcontroller ADC is a 10-bit device, and the microcontroller program must scale the LDR output accordingly.

In Figure 4-14, the black trace recording the set point at approximately 200 can be seen to follow a straight line through the noise band of the input controller signal from the LDR recorded in red. The blue trace records the controller algorithm output.

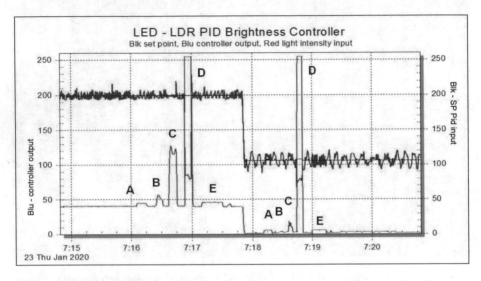

Figure 4-14. *PID LED illumination control during beam-blocking perturbations*

A series of qualitative beam-interference perturbations were made to the system at two different set-point values and were created by altering the settings on the potentiometer, seen as item E in Figure 4-13. Prior to 7:16, the blue trace recording the controller output as generated by the PWM output on pins 5, 9, or any PWM-capable digital pin of the microcontroller remains relatively constant in the absence of a disturbance to the visible light falling upon the LDR. Shortly after 7:16 and 7:18, the first captions A mark the blockage of the overhead light by a simple hand shading. The captions at B mark an approximate quarter blockage of the LDR surface; the C captions approximate a half-surface blockage, and the D disturbances mark a full blockage of the beam. The disturbances marked by the E captions indicate the system response to turning off the overhead lights.

In Figure 4-14, the noise in the input signal is substantial, but interference with the light beam does not appear to cause any hesitation or delay in the system response. Examination of the red input trace during the output trace's heightened power demand at caption D reveals the same apparent signal noise in the lower value of the recorded trace. During normal undisturbed operation on the bench top, the light beam can be seen to pulse and flicker at all set-point values, and hence the recorded noise level is not unexpected.

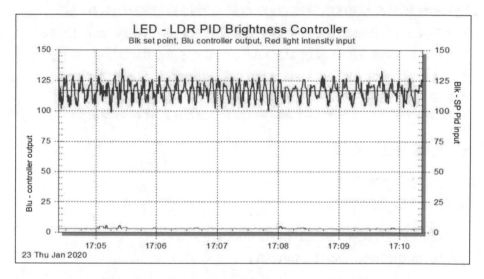

Figure 4-15. *PID LED illumination control scale expansion for noise examination*

Using the scale-expansion capabilities of the DAQFactory software, it can be seen in Figure 4-15 that the controller output in blue is responding with sufficient speed to follow some of the apparent noise variations in the red input trace.

The system used in this demonstration or exercise does have some limitations imposed by the ambient light levels and the limited set-point values over which the system will function. Although the three suggested tuning constants published with the original descriptions of the classroom exercises of $K_p = 0$, $K_i = 10$, and $K_d = 0$ appear to work well with the simple system; only two functions of the PID, consisting of the proportional and integral, are determining the controller output.

Code Listings

Listing 4-1. Arduino Code for PID Temperature Control

```
/********************************************************
 * PID Basic Example with the chamber temperature monitored
 * by a K-type thermocouple and an AD595 in deg.C. TC output
 * averaged for noise reduction CO output is in PWM format.
 * PID controller input on AO, CO output on PWM pin 3
 ********************************************************/

#include <PID_v1.h>

#define PIN_INPUT 0
#define PIN_OUTPUT 3

//Define Variables we'll be connecting to
double Setpoint, Input, Output;

//Specify the links and initial tuning parameters
double Kp=96, Ki=1.75, Kd=0.44;
PID myPID(&Input, &Output, &Setpoint, Kp, Ki, Kd, DIRECT);
//
double index = 0;
int avrgVlu = 0;

void setup()
{
  //initialize the variables we're linked to
  int raw = analogRead(PIN_INPUT);
```

```
    //Serial.println(raw);
    float Vout = raw*(5.0/1023.95);
    float temp = (Vout)/0.010;    // for AD595 10mV/deg C with
                                  K type thrmcpl
    Input = temp;
    Setpoint = 175;

    //turn the PID on
    myPID.SetMode(AUTOMATIC);
    // initialize the serialport
    Serial.begin(9600);
}

void loop()
{
    for (index = 1; index <= 100; index ++) {  // average added
                                               to lessen noise

        int raw = analogRead(PIN_INPUT);
        avrgVlu = avrgVlu + raw;
    }
    int raw = avrgVlu / 100;
    float Vout = raw *(5.0/1023.95);
    float temp = (Vout)/0.010;    // for AD595 10mV/deg C with K
                                  type thrmcpl
    Input = temp;
    myPID.Compute();
    analogWrite(PIN_OUTPUT, Output);
    Serial.print(Output);    // diagnostic or dual value plotting
    Serial.print(",");
    Serial.println(temp);
    raw = 0;
    avrgVlu = 0;
}
```

Listing 4-2. DAQFactory Sequence Code for Plotting of Multiple
Values from the Serial Port

```
// Parse multiple values from the serial port in the order in
   which they are sent
// Seqnc auto polls CommPrt_N in use for streamed Ardy data in
   comma delimited format
// Ordering data ensures same data plotted to same trace
   between sessions
// Ensure null protocol has been selected in protocol window
   and that correct data is streaming into SP
// Data on the SP must be a carriage return/newline-separated
   stream of n comma-delimited values
// Create n channels to hold the data for plotting, Ardy_1,
   Ardy_2 etc.
// To parse out the data use a loop to find the cr/nl delimiters,
   convert to numbers and Parse(datain,position #,",")
// into data1, data2 etc values and then use channel.
   addValue(datan) to assign numerical values to the channels.
//
// clear the buffer
device.Comm11.Purge()            // clear old data lines
device.Comm11.ReadUntil(13)     // clear any partial line reads
//
while(1)
   try
      // parse the first data point for plotting
      private string datain = device.Comm11.ReadUntil(13)
      //?datain                 // diagnostic
      private data1 = StrToDouble(Parse(datain,0,","))
      ardyValu_1.AddValue(data1)
      private data2 = StrToDouble(Parse(datain,1,","))
```

```
ardyValu_2.addValue(data2)
catch()
delay(0.5)
endcatch
endwhile
```

Listing 4-3. Arduino Code for PID control of LED–LDR Optical
Brightness Loop

```
#include <PID_v1.h>
const int photores = A0;    // LDR input pin
const int pot = A1;         // Potentiometer input pin
const int led = 5;          // LED output pin
double lightLevel;          // Indirectly store the light level
// Tuning parameters
float Kp = 0;               // Proportional gain
float Ki = 10;              // Integral gain
float Kd = 0;               // Differential gain
// Record the set point as well as the controller input and
    output
double Setpoint, Input, Output;
// Create a controller that is linked to the specified Input,
    Ouput and Setpoint
PID myPID(&Input, &Output, &Setpoint, Kp, Ki, Kd, DIRECT);
const int sampleRate = 1;        // Time interval of the PID
                                    control
const long serialPing = 500;     // How often data is recieved
                                    from the Arduino
unsigned long now = 0;           // Store the time that has
                                    elapsed
unsigned long lastMessage = 0;   // The last time that data was
                                    recieved
```

```
void setup()
 {
 lightLevel = analogRead(photores);        // Read the set point
 // Arduino has an analogueRead() resolution of 0-1023 and an
    analogueWrite() resolution of 0-255
 Input = map(lightLevel, 0, 1023, 0, 255);     // Scale the input
 Setpoint = map(analogRead(pot), 0, 1023, 0, 255);  // Scale the
                                                     set point

 Serial.begin(9600);                     // Initialize serial
                                         communications at 9600 bps

 myPID.SetMode(AUTOMATIC);               // Turn on the PID control
 myPID.SetSampleTime(sampleRate);        // Assign the sample rate
                                         of the control

 //Serial.println("Begin");              // Let the user know that
                                         the set up s complete

 lastMessage = millis();                 // Serial data will be
                                         received relative to
                                         this first point

 }

void loop()
 {
 Setpoint = map(analogRead(pot), 0, 1023, 0, 255);  // Continue
 to read and scale the set point
 lightLevel = analogRead(photores);      // Read the light level
 Input = map(lightLevel, 0, 1023, 0, 255);     // Scale the input
                                                to the PID

 myPID.Compute();                        // Calculates the PID output
                                         at a specified sample time

 analogWrite(led, Output);               // Power the LED
 now = millis();                         // Keep track of the elapsed
                                         time
```

```
if(now - lastMessage > serialPing)        // If enough time has
                                             passed send data
{
//Serial.print("Setpoint = ");
Serial.print(Setpoint);
Serial.print(",");
Serial.print(Input);
Serial.print(",");
Serial.println(Output);
//Serial.print("\n");
// The tuning parameters can be retrieved by the Arduino from
   the serial monitor: 0,0.5,0 set Ki to 0.5.
// Commas are ignored by the Serial.parseFloat() command
if (Serial.available() > 0)
{
for (int x = 0; x < 4; x++)
{
switch(x)
{
case 0:
Kp = Serial.parseFloat();
break;
case 1:
Ki = Serial.parseFloat();
break;
case 2:
Kd = Serial.parseFloat();
break;
case 3:
```

```
for (int y = Serial.available(); y == 0; y--)
{
Serial.read();
}
break;
}
}
Serial.print(" Kp,Ki,Kd = ");   // Display the new parameters
Serial.print(Kp);
Serial.print(",");
Serial.print(Ki);
Serial.print(",");
Serial.print(Kd);
myPID.SetTunings(Kp, Ki, Kd);   // Set the tuning of the PID loop
}
lastMessage = now;              // Reference the next serial
                                   communication to this point

  }
}
```

Summary

- PID control algorithm theory, theoretical process
  response to perturbations, and the theoretical methods
  that can be used to initialize the implementation of a
  process-control loop are reviewed.

- A PID heated chamber temperature control
  implementation shows the process working and
  demonstrates the limitations of microprocessor
  implementation of the process-control algorithm.

– An educational, compact, inexpensive, optical desktop apparatus is assembled and connected to a strip-chart recording system to record the PID control-loop response to perturbations in a controlled light beam intensity.

– In Chapter 5, programs able to plot streamed data as a function of time in the format traditionally known as strip-chart recording are developed.

CHAPTER 5

Realtime Data Plotting and Visualization

Numerous experimental measurement techniques depend upon the monitoring of a sensor response as time progresses. Usually an investigator is interested in a change in response; achieving a maximum or minimum signal value; or, in the case of spectroscopic, chromatographic, or electrochemical voltammetry systems, examining the actual shape of the recorded trace.

Although the essence of this chapter is the recording of a sensor response as a function of time, numerous informative data recordings need not be time based, but rather may be recorded as a function of parameters such as frequency, wavelength, temperature, applied pressure, or voltage.

Supervisory control and data acquisition (SCADA) systems such as DAQFactory have been rigorously developed for commercial application to run on Windows operating systems in order to accommodate the large industrial and commercial need for process control. Commercial SCADA programs such as Azeotech DAQFactory and Factory Express are able to offer two-dimensional plotting facilities for *x* versus *y* or to display continuous tracings based upon time-stamped data acquisition.

Arduino and the Raspberry Pi have evolved informally in the open source format to fill the constantly changing needs for education, experimental designs, or science-based investigations that may require

© Richard J. Smythe 2021
R. J. Smythe, *Advanced Arduino Techniques in Science*,
https://doi.org/10.1007/978-1-4842-6784-4_5

the rapid prototyping of special- or general-purpose hardware–software combinations. While standardization is virtually an industrial–commercial necessity, it is difficult to realize or implement in a constantly changing "open source" environment where novel technological advances often outweigh legacy compatibility.

The Arduino microcontroller IDE is available in both PC- and RPi-hosted formats. The serial ports on the PC-hosted Arduino are compatible with Microsoft Windows and the DAQFactory program. The RPi-hosted Arduino is compatible with the Linux serial ports and the Python programming language.

The Python realtime data display and recording programs presented in this chapter have been collected from various online and textbook sources then specifically modified to display and record typical Python-derived data or data obtained from interfaced Arduino microcontrollers using the Linux USB-based serial port data-transmission protocols.

Although several of the plotting programs presented are derived from previously published works, the primary intent of this section is to allow the investigator using the Linux-based RPi to develop a simple Python-based, customized plotting facility able to accommodate data from the experimental investigation at hand.

Recalling that a graphic visualization of data can take essentially two forms, consisting of a static or a dynamic display, we should be able to envision that a dynamic display can be created by rapidly displaying a series of slightly differing static images.

Intuitively, the key to minimizing the processing time required to up-date or change the individual static graphic images being displayed is to change only the data that differs between sequential static displays. In order to create a responsive visual display depicting a stream of data coming from a sensor, the individual data points can be stored in an array, and the individual elements of the array can then be positioned sequentially in the screen displays being used to create the dynamic input/sensor-response tracing.

As discussed in previous chapters of this book, graphical displays consume a large amount of computing resources. Complex computing systems often have separate graphics display hardware with very fast dedicated software that is not part of the simpler RPi–Arduino systems.

With limited computing resources available, the graphics displays on the RPi must be relatively simple and optimized for the task at hand. A Python-based graphical strip-chart recorder (SCR) display is literally orders of magnitude slower than the Arduino's ability to process and stream out data on the serial port.

Figure 5-1 is a screen capture of the recording created when the shaft of a 10 kΩ potentiometer connected between 5V and ground is turned, with the wiper voltage wired to the Arduino A0 analog to digital converter (ADC) input. The recording program written in Python is the Matplotlib animation example code: strip_chart_demo.py. The published code, written to emulate an oscilloscope-type response, has been modified to accept data streamed out to the serial port by the Arduino's ADC. Listing 5-1 (Arduino) and Listing 5-2 (RPi) are able to produce the recording shown in Figure 5-1. (All code listings are provided at the end of the chapter.)

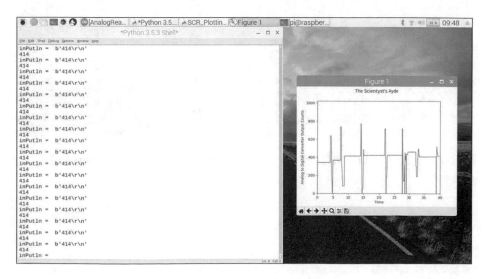

Figure 5-1. *Python plot of Arduino ADC output*

The Matplotlib program operates by displaying recorded input tracings in timed-width frames. The width of the frames is adjustable, and the correlation between the displayed time units and the actual time of the recording must be determined by the experimenter.

If an actual time base is required for an experiment, the console display can be used to record the current time as the experimental trace for the investigation at hand is displayed. The time-stamped data on the console display can be archived on an SD card if required.

Figure 5-2 depicts a dual-trace display of the temperature and pressure outputs from an RPi Sense HAT board. Listing 5-3 has been written in Python 3 and is based upon the tutorial series presented by P. McWhorter P. Eng.[1]

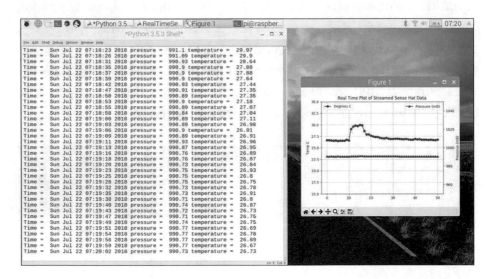

***Figure 5-2.** Python plot of Sense HAT temperature and pressure sensors*

---

[1]http://www.toptechboy.com/tutorial/python-with-arduino-lesson-10-installing-drawnow-to-allow-live-plotting-with-matplotlib/

The two Python-based graphical display programs presented are relatively easy to use and understand. Both programs have been well documented, are well tested, and are adaptable to the different types of sensor-monitoring applications presented in this book.

Listing 5-1. Arduino Code for Transmitting the 0–1023 ADC Values to the Serial Port

```
/*
  AnalogReadSerial
  Reads an analog input on pin 0, prints the result to the
  serial monitor.
  Attach the center pin of a potentiometer to pin A0, and the
  outside pins to +5V and ground.
 */

// the setup routine runs once when you press reset:
void setup() {
  // initialize serial communication at 9600 bits per second:
  Serial.begin(9600);
}

// the loop routine runs over and over again forever:
void loop() {
  // read the input on analog pin 0:
  int sensorValue = analogRead(A0);
  // print out the value read:
  Serial.println(sensorValue);
  delay(500);        // delay in between reads for stability
}
```

Listing 5-2. Python Windowed Strip-Chart Recorder with Variable-Width Digit Logic for Serial Port Data Plotting

```python
# RPi Python Strip-Chart Recorder of Arduino Output
# SCR Plotting of serial data from Arduino output over serial
  port
# Arduino serial output must be numerical values only and
  delivered at a rate.
# slow enough for the SCR pgm to plot. i.e., delays of > 250 ms
import matplotlib
import numpy as np
from matplotlib.lines import Line2D
import matplotlib.pyplot as plt
import matplotlib.animation as animation
import time
import serial
#
#
#
class Scope:
    def __init__(self, ax, maxt=40, dt=0.02):
        """maxt time width of display"""
        self.ax = ax
        self.dt = dt
        self.maxt = maxt
        self.tdata = [0]
        self.ydata = [0]
        self.line = Line2D(self.tdata, self.ydata)
        self.ax.add_line(self.line)
        self.ax.set_ylim(0, 1023)  # y axis scale
        self.ax.set_xlim(0, self.maxt)
```

```python
    def update(self, y):
        lastt = self.tdata[-1]
        if lastt > self.tdata[0] + self.maxt: # reset the arrays
            self.tdata = [self.tdata[-1]]
            self.ydata = [self.ydata[-1]]
            self.ax.set_xlim(self.tdata[0], self.tdata[0] +
            self.maxt)
            self.ax.figure.canvas.draw()
        t = self.tdata[-1] + self.dt
        self.tdata.append(t)
        self.ydata.append(y)
        self.line.set_data(self.tdata, self.ydata)
        return self.line,
#
ser = serial.Serial("/dev/ttyACM0", 9600)
#
def rd_data():
    while True:
        inPutln = ser.readline()
        print("inPutln = ", inPutln)
        nbr_dgts = len(inPutln)
        if (nbr_dgts > 6 or nbr_dgts < 3): # skip noise or
        corrupted data
            continue
        if (nbr_dgts == 3):     # there is only 1 digit
            line = int(str(inPutln)[slice(2,3)])
        if (nbr_dgts == 4):     # there are 2 digits
            line = int(str(inPutln)[slice(2,4)])
        if (nbr_dgts == 5):     # there are 3 digits
            line = int(str(inPutln)[slice(2,5)])
        if (nbr_dgts == 6):     # there are 4 digits
```

```
            line = int(str(inPutln)[slice(2,6)]) # convert
            arduino serial output stream
        # to a Python string, parse out the numerical symbols
            and convert to a value
        print(line)
        yield (line)

fig = plt.figure()
fig.suptitle("The Scientyst's Ayde", fontsize = 12)
ax = fig.add_subplot(111)
ax.set_xlabel("Time")
ax.set_ylabel("Analog to Digital Converter Output Counts")
scope = Scope(ax)

# uses rd_data() as a generator to produce data for the update
  func, the Arduino ADC
# value is read by the plotting code in 20 or so minute windows
  for the
# animated
# screen display. Software overhead limits response speed of
  display.
ani = animation.FuncAnimation(fig, scope.update, rd_data,
interval=50,
blit=False)

plt.show()
```

Listing 5-3. Sense HAT Temperature and Pressure Data Plotting and
Console Display for Archiving

```
# Realtime plotting of temperature and pressure from the
  SenseHat board
import numpy  # Import numpy for array manipulation functions
```

```python
import matplotlib.pyplot as plt #import matplotlib library
from drawnow import * # animation of plotting library
from sense_hat import SenseHat  # sense hat library
import time    # time stamping data
#
#
sense = SenseHat()    # instance of the detector board and sensors
sense.clear()         # clear the board
#
#
tempF= []              # list array for temperature data
pressure=[]            # list array for pressure data
#
plt.ion()              #invoke matplotlib interactive mode to
                       plot live data
cnt=0                  # initialize plotter window width counter

def makeFig(): #Create a function to make the plotting window.
    plt.ylim(15,35)                    #Set y min and max values
    plt.title('Real Time Plot of Streamed Sense Hat Data')
    #Plot title
    plt.grid(True)                #Turn on grid lines of plotter
    plt.ylabel('Temp C')                            #Set ylabel
    plt.plot(tempF, 'ro-', label='Degrees C')   #plot the
                                                temperature in
                                                red dots

    plt.legend(loc='upper left')                #plot the legend
    plt2=plt.twinx()                            #Create a
                                                second y axis
```

```
    plt.ylim(950,1050)              #Set limits of second y axis-
                                    adjust values as required
    plt2.plot(pressure, 'b^-', label='Pressure (mB)') #plot
    pressure data
    plt2.set_ylabel('Pressrue (mB)')        #label second y axis
    plt2.ticklabel_format(useOffset=False)  #Force matplotlib
                                            to NOT autoscale
                                            y axis
    plt2.legend(loc='upper right')          #plot the legend

while True:
        localtime = time.asctime(time.localtime(time.time()))
        # time of measurement
        pressSH = sense.get_pressure()      # collect pressure
                                            data
        press = round(pressSH,(2))          # round decimal to
                                            reasonable value

        #
        temperature = sense.get_temperature()
        temp = round(temperature,(2))
        print("Time = ", localtime, "pressure = ", press,
        "temperature = ", temp) # time stamped data log or record
        tempF.append(temp)              #Build tempF array by
                                        appending temp readings
        pressure.append(press)          #Build pressure array by
                                        appending P readings
        drawnow(makeFig)                #Call drawnow to update
                                        our live graph
        plt.pause(.000001)              #Pause Briefly. Important
                                        to keep drawnow from
                                        crashing
```

```
cnt=cnt+1                # increment window width
                         counter
if(cnt>50):              # at 50 or more points, delete
                         the first one from the array
    tempF.pop(0)         #This allows us to just see
                         the last 50 data points
    pressure.pop(0)
```

Summary

– Information in experimental data can be contained
  in the actual numerical values generated by the
  experiment, in the trace provided by plotting the
  value as a function of time, or in the shape of a two-
  dimensional x–y plot of the data.

– Programs for plotting one or two streams of sensor data
  as a function of time are presented and their limitations
  described.

– Chapter 6 describes the concepts of frequency and
  presents methods and simple equipment for measuring
  the cycles that determine frequency.

171

CHAPTER 6

Frequency Measurement

Repetitive actions as encountered in the fading or flashing of LED intensity, the square-wave electrical signals for digital-logic clocks, electromagnetic waves, alternating current electricity, rotating motors, mechanical vibrations, sound waves, and pendulum or even planetary motions are recurring events in completely different contexts. However, all have a common feature in that there is a time period over which their individual cyclic actions repeat. A repeating event such as the vibration of a musical instrument string may take place thousands of times a second, while the Moon orbits the Earth on a monthly basis. Frequency is a measure of the number of times an event occurs in a unit of measurement. The units of measurement can take several forms and involve such diverse entities as time, spatial orientation, biochemical composition, or genetics and traits of populations.

Sensors, physical computing, and data processing are often used to monitor the electrical signals generated by sensors monitoring a repeating physio–chemical event that results in a repetitive electrical-signal variation.

© Richard J. Smythe 2021
R. J. Smythe, *Advanced Arduino Techniques in Science*,
https://doi.org/10.1007/978-1-4842-6784-4_6

As noted in the studies of Galileo concerning pendulum oscillation, the time required for a cyclic process to repeat is termed the *period. Frequency* is the inverse of the period and is noted as

$$f = 1 \, / \, T$$

where *f* is the frequency and *T* is the period of the repeating event. When a frequency is described in terms of the number of repetitions or cycles of the event that occur in a time of one second, the unit of frequency is cycles per second (cps), also known as hertz and written as Hz in honor of Prof. H. Hertz, who discovered radio waves in the 1880s.

In biological, chemical, and certainly astronomical or geological investigations, many repetitive phenomena and reactions occur at time scales measured in minutes, hours, or significantly longer time spans that can be considered as the extreme low end of the frequency scale. Certain ranges of frequencies have been given names, such as the audio frequency range that is defined by the typical frequencies audible to humans and the ultrasonic range that is above the human hearing scale. Dogs, elephants, orcas, dolphins, and bats are all known to have hearing capabilities either above or below the frequency range sensed by humans.

Events that occur over much longer time scales have come to be described in terms of their period. Visible-light frequencies are in the 4 to 8 MHz range, while most animal migrations occur twice per annum.

In some investigations involving frequency, the period of a cyclic wave–like event can be referred to as the wavelength. In Figure 6-6 the full cycle caption defining one complete oscillation of the waveform is often termed the wavelength of the signal.

In keeping with the introductory nature of this book, the frequency ranges being considered for measurement are those accessible with the readily available materials and electronic components accumulated thus far in developing the previous exercises and measurement techniques.

A distinction exists between electrical signals that do not vary in intensity over time and can be classified as static DC signals and electrical signals that vary repetitively over a fixed interval of time. Cyclic signals can be measured with techniques that determine either the frequency or period of signal oscillation. This chapter describes the techniques for measuring electrical signals with respect to their frequency or their period.

High-frequency electrical signals over the megahertz (10^6 cycles per second) range require special equipment to measure and visualize. To minimize cost and complexity, the experimental portions of this chapter will be confined to the frequencies accessible with inexpensive, readily available, and well-documented signal generators. A simple signal generator can be assembled around any of the 555 timers as depicted in Figures 6-1 and 6-2. Websites and kits are available to make more complex sine-, triangle-, and square-wave signals from both the 555 timer and Arduino microcontrollers. An inexpensive function generator available from Elenco Electronics ($60 USD) as depicted in Figure 6-3 was used by the author to generate some of the data used in this chapter.

Microcontroller high-speed computational software clocked in the megacycle range is amenable to measuring kilo (kHz) and mega (MHz) cycle frequencies with code that monitors whether a digital pin is connected to a high- or low-logic source. However, when a signal frequency drops into the double-digit, single-digit, or fractional Hz range a different measuring technique must be used. For higher-frequency signals the counting of cycles per second is measured, while for lower-frequency signals the inverse concept of seconds per cycle or period may be required.

As noted in previous texts, when designing a process for measuring physio–chemical phenomena through the use of detectors or transducers, the characteristics of the electrical signal produced by the phenomenon–detector combination at hand must be reproducible before any form of quantitative data collection can be considered.

Experimental

An Arduino library can be used to create an experimental frequency-measurement system that can be read from any host computer. The FreqMeasure library is available from the Arduino organization (https://www.arduinolibraries.info/libraries/freq-measure). The library is provided in two formats: FreqMeasure, for measuring the frequency of signals in the 1/10 to 5 or 6 Hz range; and FreqCount, for measuring signal frequencies in the kilohertz range.

As demonstrated in previous sections of this book, the 555 timer can be configured to produce low-voltage electrical signals that can have periods varying from many minutes per cycle to the megahertz range. Figure 6-1 contains a circuit diagram for a variable low-frequency pulse generator with a Schmidt trigger, an active low-pass filter signal-conditioning circuit that can be powered from an independent 5V supply or that available from either an Arduino or an RPi.

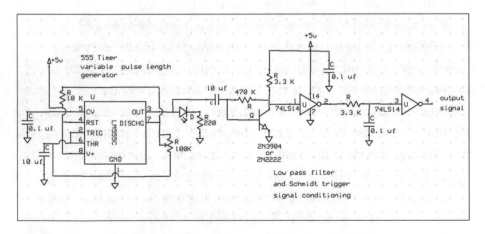

Figure 6-1. *Circuit diagram for a variable low-frequency pulse generator*

When the FreqMeasure library is downloaded and installed on the Arduino, there will be two entries in the Examples menu, as depicted in Figure 6-2. Each of the menu entries has two submenu selections, for a serial port or an LCD output.

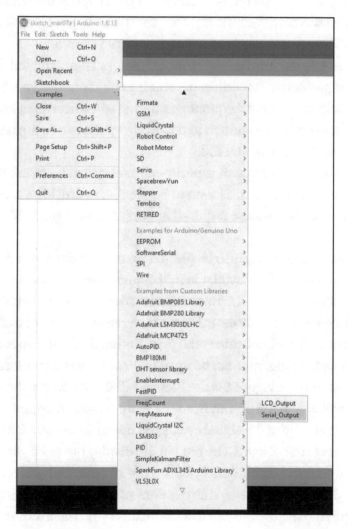

Figure 6-2. *The Arduino frequency measurement selections menu*

Two program options are available to the investigator, as can be seen in Figure 6-2. FreqMeasure is a program that measures the half-period of the signal cycle, while FreqCount measures cycles per second count in kHz.

In Figure 6-3, two signal generators are depicted, along with a Sparkfun Red Board Arduino–type microcontroller. A prototype of the circuit in Figure 6-1 is seen on a 2¼ x 3¼ in. (5 x 8 cm) breadboard along with an Elenco FG500 commercially manufactured signal source.

If a sensor signal from an experimental setup, kit-assembled, or breadboard prototype function generator is to be monitored by the microcontroller's resident frequency-counting software, the signal's amplitude must be large enough to positively measure as a digital logic 1 or 0 on the system at hand.

Oscillating signals from an experimental setup can be monitored as a stream of numerical values, as seen in Figure 6-4, to provide a measured numerical value that may be required as part of an electronic filter design process.

Frequency values may also be plotted to record a change in frequency with time. In both options available in the menu selections seen in Figure 6-2, the measurement output can be streamed to the serial port. Subject to the limitations inherent in the response times of the DAQFactory, RPi, and Arduino serial port plotter, the host computer's graphical display programs can be used to record the sensor frequency as a function of time. In Figure 6-5 the Elenco FG500 has been connected to a microcontroller, and the output from the FreqMeasure program measuring the half-period time of the signal cycles has been plotted as a DAQFactory strip-chart recorder display. The data in the display has been generated by setting the coarse dial on the FG500 to the 10 scale and rotating the fine dial to the degrees indicated in the captions of the display. The same type of display seen in Figure 6-5 can also be created with the Arduino plotter.

Examination of the two exemplar programs provided with the Arduino library reveals that the FreqMeasure program has a digital signal-processing default code that collects thirty values for averaging the data integrated into the code. Signal-noise reduction by the averaging of data requires time. If the signal being sampled has a large cycle time then the averaging of readings will multiply the already long sample measurement time by the number of data points collected. As a consequence of the multiplied time between data collection, the investigator may experience wait times of multiple seconds or minutes before data appears on the serial monitor.

The code in the examples can be adjusted by the investigator to control the rate at which data is streamed out to the serial port for single-value read-out or plotting.

Care must be exercised when using the FG500 as the square-wave output can rise to 8V and could possibly damage 5V or 3.3V detector circuitry. Sine and triangular wave outputs are variable from 0V to 3V peak to peak.

It is noted by the library author that the measuring programs are interrupt driven and hence should not be used with programs that employ interrupt timing on the microprocessor.

Observations

An assembled generator–signal conditioning system as depicted in Figure 6-1 and seen on the prototyping board was able to produce a signal variation of 0.70 Hz to 13.69 Hz at the extreme ends of rotation of the 100 kΩ potentiometer.

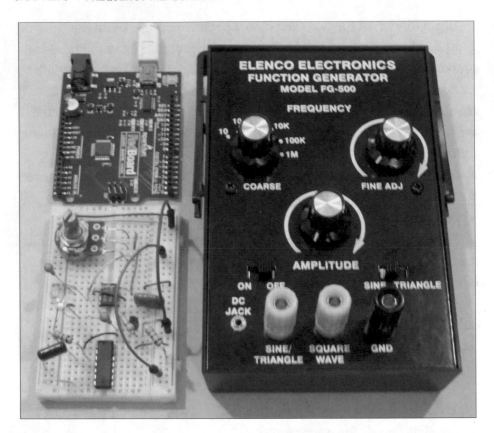

Figure 6-3. *A prototype signal generator with signal conditioning circuitry, FG500, and Red Board Arduino*

Figure 6-4 depicts the frequency-measurement data stream received by the serial port for the maximum output frequency of the 10 uF–100 kΩ RC combination for the 555 prototyped timer-signal generator.

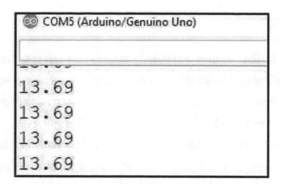

Figure 6-4. *Streamed serial port data from FreqMeasure program*

At the low-frequency end of the generator's variable scale, the 0.70 Hz measured data was timed at 30 LED flashes in 42 seconds or 30/42 = 0.71 Hz. A measured frequency of 1.40 Hz created 30 flashes in 21 seconds or 1.43 Hz, while a measured frequency of 7.3 Hz produced a data point every 4½ s. A stopwatch and the LED signal indicator are thus able to validate the low-frequency measurement system.

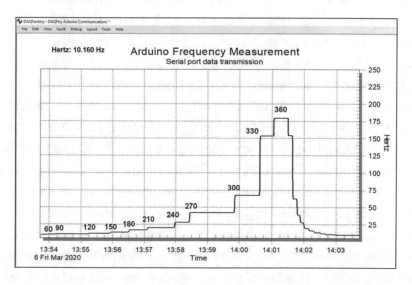

Figure 6-5. *Frequency values generated by fine adjust control rotation Elenco FG500*

Discussion

The URL found in the "Experimental" section directs the investigator to the Arduino libraries information site, which contains a link to the FreqMeasure creator's web page (`http://www.pjrc.com/teensy/td_libs_FreqMeasure.html`).

In Figure 6-6, a square wave as is produced by the 555 timer output has been captioned similar to the sine wave illustration found at the FreqMeasure website, indicating the cycle length and the half-period portions of the waveform used in the FreqCount and FreqMeasure libraries, respectively.

The cycle period and wavelength concepts are used in the study of the mechanics of waves and wave propagation. If required for further experimental design, the details regarding the relationship between the velocity of propagation, wavelength, and period can be found in most physics textbooks.

The FreqMeasure site provides extensive details on the construction and applications of the two software methodologies for determining the frequency of rapidly and slowly oscillating signals. For the testing and validating of experimental applications of either library function, generators can be inexpensively fabricated from 555 timers. Varying the RC timing components in the circuitry of Figure 6-1, and a large number of websites can provide circuits for single or multiple waveform outputs that can provide a fixed- or variable-frequency signal for experimental setup validation. Low-pass filters are optional and may not be necessary in low-noise experiments.

Kits and commercial function generators are available from most electronic supply facilities. Regardless of the source of the function generator, in order to achieve the correct determination of the frequency of the signal under study, the generator signal must be strong enough to be read by the logic circuitry of the microprocessor and be of a uniform oscillation period. Experimenting with the amplitude control on the FG500 while generating a sine wave with a 3V peak-to-peak maximum voltage caused a loss of counting capability in the FreqCount program at approximately half of the dial rotation. It is recommended that the function generator outputs be compatible with a TTL load of 5V.

Irregular waveforms as seen in Figure 4-8 of Chapter 4, "The PID Process Control Algorithm," will produce erroneous frequency determinations that DSP may not be able to overcome.

For relatively slowly oscillating signals, the FreqMeasure program can be used as demonstrated with the 0.7 to 13 Hz square-wave example created by the circuitry of Figure 6-1. When a signal of 0.64 Hz was measured with the FreqMeasure program, approximately 48 seconds elapsed between data points appearing on the serial monitor.

An Arduino microprocessor has a 16 MHz clock and is thus able to read signals with the FreqCount program into the MHz range capability of the FG500.

Figure 6-6 illustrates the two different timing measurements that are used to distinguish between the high- and low-frequency oscillations. For signals with a long cycle, the half-period measurement can result in large timespans between data appearing on the serial port. Higher-frequency signals are measured with the FreqCount program, which determines how many full cycles occur in a fixed timespan.

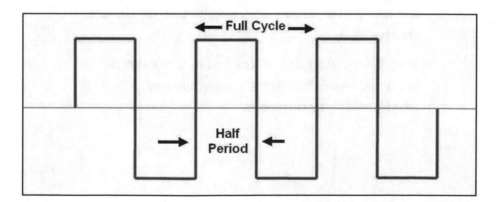

Figure 6-6. *A square waveform and frequency-measurement parameters*

A semi-quantitative graphical data recording was implemented with a DAQFactory plotter, the FreqMeasure program, and the FG500 signal generator. Figure 6-5 is the plotter response recorded when the FG500 coarse selector was set to the 100 scale and the fine adjust dial was set to the nominal degrees rotation caption on each step increment. By using the stepped increment the plotting illustrates the system's ability to quantitatively follow changes in the signal frequency. The virtually vertical traces between increments of the frequency change were validated by the apparent simultaneous movement of the display trace with the rotation of the fine adjust dial.

Summary

- Frequency is defined as the number of occurrences of a repeating event per unit of time.

- Electronic frequencies are often measured in terms of cycles per second, while natural and biological events are often expressed as units of time per event.

- Software libraries, filters, commercial signal generators, and low-cost experimenter-assembled signal sources are reviewed.

- In Chapter 7, the often overlooked inherent errors in experimental data and the importance of reproducibility are explored.

CHAPTER 7

Quality Assurance, Quality Control, and Error Analysis

This chapter will deal with the quality of the data produced by experimental measurements. To use data, it must be reproducible and validated. Experiments and experimental setups must be able to generate reproducible data that can also be reproduced by other investigators using the same experimental technique. Once data can be replicated it can be validated or tested for veracity or truthfulness. A simple technique for validating a weighing instrument is to weigh a well-known defined weight standard. A second method for validating data is to use a different measurement technique to confirm the original observation. A mercury-in-glass temperature determination could be verified by either a thermistor or a thermocouple reading.

Quality Assurance and Control

Repetitive measurement techniques such as weighing, measuring a temperature, or measuring relative humidity that are part of another experimental process should be subjected to a quality assurance, quality control procedure so the data generated by the experimental process

© Richard J. Smythe 2021
R. J. Smythe, *Advanced Arduino Techniques in Science*,
https://doi.org/10.1007/978-1-4842-6784-4_7

of which they are a part can be monitored and ultimately validated. The quality of repetitive measurements can be monitored through the application of statistical process control (SPC) in the form of control charting.

All measurements have errors in them, and when a large number of measurements of the same type are made, a large number of different values, all very similar to one another, will be obtained. The large number of values can be averaged to obtain the mean value. If the original large number of individual measurement values, of the common parameter, are organized into categories consisting of values equal to the mean, values one greater than the mean, values one less than the mean, values two greater than the mean, values two less than the mean, and so on, until a point is reached at which there are no values greater or less than ten values different than the mean, as is illustrated in Figure 7-1, we can construct a very well-known plot. If the number of occurrences for each value above and below the mean are collected and graphed, a curve as depicted in Figure 7-1 is realized.

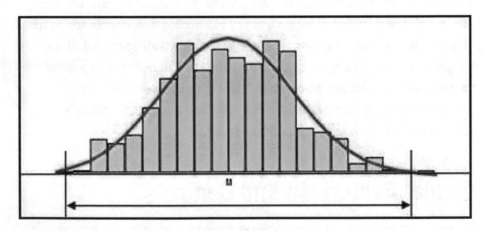

Figure 7-1. *The Gaussian distribution*

The shape of the plot in Figure 7-1 is a "normal" or "Gaussian" distribution. Averaging the large number of values calculates the mean value, M or $\underline{x}$. The standard deviation of the data set can then be calculated by well-known mathematical techniques. A standard deviation is a measure of the variation or dispersion of a set of data. The value is represented by σ. The mean and standard deviation are calculated with the two equations in the following section. In Figure 7-1, the arrow represents the points at which the probability of finding values in the data set represented by the given distribution curve in red that are 10 or more above or below the mean value of M is very small. The majority of values lie between + or – 3σ. Because the probability of there being a value of the known data set outside of the 3σ limit is very small, it is possible to set up a "3σ" control chart. Repetitive measurements of the same parameter value should all cluster around the mean value. The probability of the measured value at hand being more than twice or three times the standard deviation of the mean becomes increasing small, and hence if such a value occurs repetitively, then the system is said to be "out of control."

A statistical rule of thumb (Chebyshev's Theorem) states that 68 percent of the dataset will lie within one standard deviation of the mean, 95 percent within 2, and 99.7 percent within 3.

Control charts are dynamic graphic displays used to document how a process changes over time. Data values are plotted in a sequential time order about a central horizontal axis defining the median value of the data. Under normal conditions the data being plotted should be randomly scattered above, below, and occasionally on the median value or center line. To aid in visualizing a randomly distributed data set and detecting values not in conformance with the random distribution assumption, six additional lines parallel to the median axis at +/- 1σ, +/- 2σ, and +/- 3σ are added to the chart.

Figure 7-2 depicts a typical 3σ control chart.

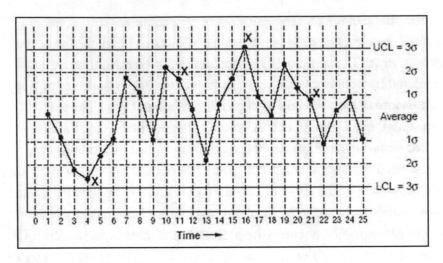

Figure 7-2. *A typical 3σ control chart*

On a 3σ control chart, the top and bottom lines are referred to as the upper and lower control limits that have been determined from validated historical data collected prior to the construction of the control chart.

Consecutive data points falling within the upper and lower control limits indicate that the data being generated are consistent and are referred to as being "in control." If data points are outside of the control limits, they are unpredictable, and hence the measurement system is "out of control."

There are a large number of problems that can be detected with control charts besides the "in or out" of control condition. Consecutive data points should not drift up or down in a predictable trend. The data points should be randomly distributed above and below the median axis. An experimenter encountering a deviation from the expected performance of the measurement system must find the source of the deviation and correct the method being used to collect or generate the data.

A typical application for a control chart can involve validating the performance of a weighing device before it is used in an actual weighing operation as part of a research investigation. Prior to a daily or "when needed" weighing operation, a reference standard whose weight value is well known is measured. The newly determined weight value is entered into the control-charting operation. If the newly entered value is acceptable, the device can be used for weighing operations. At the end of the experiment or at the end of the day, the reference weight is re-weighed and the fresh value entered into the control-chart program. If the end-of-experiment or end-of-day value is acceptable, then all the weight determination values conducted between the two "in control" determinations of the reference weight can be deemed valid.

Error Analysis

It has been realized for hundreds of years that even very carefully made measurements of the same parameter do not produce the same results. As is illustrated in Figure 7-1, multiple repetitions of a reliable measurement technique always produce a collection of numbers that conform to a bell-shaped pattern when the mean value and the individual numerical differences of the data set of numbers are calculated and plotted.

The mean or average of a set of observations is calculated by dividing the sum of the individual values by N, the number of entries in the data set. The mathematical notation for calculating the mean is:

$$\overline{x} = \frac{x_1 + x_2 + \ldots + x_k + \ldots + x_N}{N} = \frac{\sum\limits_{k=1}^{N} x_k}{N}$$

A common statistical notation representing a mean or average value is to place a small dash or "bar" over the variable representing the value obtained when the sum of all the values is divided by the number of values summed. The Σ notation ("sigma" notation) to the right is read as "the sum of the variables Xk for all k values from $k = 1$ to $k = N$.

As noted, the tendency of a set of numbers to conform to the pattern seen in Figure 7-1 was first noted by the mathematician Gauss and is called a Gaussian distribution. The pattern is also known as a "normal" distribution.

For the set of numbers observed during N repetitions of a measurement technique, a measure of the dispersion of the results about the mean value is called the standard deviation, and one method for determining the value is given by the following formula:

$$\sigma = \sqrt{\frac{\Sigma(\text{x-mean})^2}{\text{n}}}$$

In statistics, N or n is usually the number of data points in the set, and the squared term $(x - \text{mean})$ is the difference between each individual x value and the mean value of the set. The squaring operation converts all positive- and negative-difference values into positive numbers whose squared value is then summed as noted by the Σ notation. The summed value is then averaged by dividing by n—the number of data points prior to having the square root extracted of the averaged squares—to return a result value in the original scale. If a measurement is repeated many times, at least 68 percent of the measured values will fall in the range $+/- 1\sigma$ of the mean. (In statistical terms, the preceding formula is often stated as "the standard deviation is the square root of the variance." The variance is the quantity under the root sign. The statistics discussed thus far pertains to only a single set of data obtained from one experiment. If the data under consideration is part of a larger data set, the experimenter must consult a textbook on statistics to obtain the correct formulas for dealing with a subset of a larger population.)

A standard deviation can be thought of as the average difference between the data values and the mean or as the dispersion of the data around the mean. Experimental development programs are often focused on decreasing the value of the standard deviation in the results of a measurement system or in the variations of a product created by a process.

A small value of a standard deviation, however, does not ensure the accuracy of a set of measurements or determinations. Errors are divided into two categories termed *random* and *systematic*. Random errors are inherent in all measurements. Systematic errors have an identifiable cause.

Once an experiment has been able to reproduce a set of observations, the experimenter can then begin to determine the accuracy and precision of the determination by quantifying the possible errors in the results. Accuracy and precision are often envisioned in the form of the positioning of darts on a dart board. In Figure 7-3 the positioning of the darts shows good precision in the tight grouping of the clustered darts in both A and B. Although the grouping in A is good, the cluster of darts is too high, while the grouping in B is said to be more accurate.

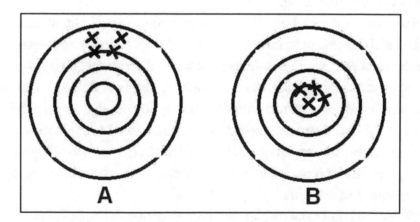

Figure 7-3. *A dart board analogy for precision and accuracy*

The scatter within each grouping is representative of the inherent random error that occurs within all measurements. The high grouping in A can be said to have a systematic error. There is no prescribed way to find systematic errors. All the possible sources of a systematic error must be considered or examined and small experiments conducted to see if the suspect sources are active. The ultimate goal of the process is to reduce systematic errors to values less than the random errors in the determination. To reduce the systematic error in A, a longer flight time for the darts could be implemented by having the player step back from the board.

Accuracy is most often assessed with reference standards. Standards are available for virtually any measurement, such as for weights, lengths, temperatures, chemical compositions, and as methods to ensure uniformity in procedures conducted at different locations and times. Standards are provided by organizations such as the Canadian Standards Association (CSA Can.), the National Institute for Standards and Technology (NIST USA), and the International Standards Organization (ISO UN) of the United Nations.

An often overlooked aspect of the reporting of experimental data is the use of significant figures. The accepted convention in reporting experimental errors is that only one uncertain digit should be used.

Calculations using numbers with differing levels of significant figures must always generate results with no more significant figures than the lowest found in the entries entered into mathematical formulations.

Many of the data variations to be expected in the values collected during experimental work can be conveniently demonstrated using digital multimeters and resistors.

Figure 7-4 shows the display from a Siglent SDM3055, 5½ digit, bench-top meter measuring the resistance of a 1 Ω 1% tolerance 12W precision resistor.

Figure 7-4. *Components for measuring data variation with resistors and a sensitive DMM*

A data-collection experiment was conducted with the SDM3055 using the three different resistance values seen in Figure 7-4. In a sequential, serial protocol, resistance measurements were made of the 1 Ω 1%, the 2 Ω 5%, and the 110 Ω 5% resistors. For each measurement made with the sensitive DMM, the display value was not recorded until the observed displayed values were stable for several seconds. The massive 12W and 5W resistors settled to final values in seconds while the 2W device required from three to five minutes to stabilize. Once a satisfactory set of ten values was obtained for each of the three resistors, the data was entered into a spreadsheet and the average and standard deviations were calculated. The data collected and calculations from the experiment are tabulated in Table 7-1.

Table 7-1. *Repetitive High-Sensitivity Resistance Measurements*

Resistor	Reading 1	Reading 2	Reading 3	Reading 4	Reading 5	Reading 6	Reading 7	Reading 8	Reading 9	Reading 10	Average	σ
1 Ω 1% 12 watt	1.083	1.075	1.075	1.074	1.070	1.069	1.081	1.078	1.077	1.072	1.0754	0.0045
2 Ω 5% 5 watt	2.060	2.052	2.056	2.053	2.055	2.058	2.059	2.059	2.058	2.062	2.0572	0.0032
110 Ω 5% 2 watt	108.867	108.867	108.865	108.866	108.851	108.866	108.873	108.858	108.858	108.859	108.8630	0.0064

From the table, it seems that the largest dispersion is in the device with the highest resistance value and smallest wattage rating. The smallest device also took the longest time for the display to stabilize. There are several hypotheses that may account for the observations derived from the reproducible data. The time to stability may be directly proportional to the physical size or thermal masses of the different-sized resistors, or it could be hypothesized that the three different resistor types have different resistive core materials that respond differently to electrical excitation.

In addition to the inherent random spreading seen in measurements of the same parameter by the same technique, a number of additional sources of variation are encountered in experimental work.

Different instruments measuring the same parameter will produce variations in the measured results. The repetitive manufacturing of devices with a nominal value or dimension produces variations in the individual unit values.

To illustrate some of the conventions used in reporting experimental data and demonstrating sources of error and variation, a second table of numerical values for the measured resistance of a set of resistors was collected. Ten element samples of 5% tolerance, 1/8 W resistors, spanning five orders of magnitude from 10 Ω to 100 kΩ were measured for their actual resistance with four different digital multimeters.

The 1 MΩ ten-element population differed from the bulk of the experimental subjects in that although each member was a nominal 1/8 W, 5% unit, the subjects were from two additional manufacturers.

The ten-element data sets were then tabulated in a spreadsheet program and the average or mean value and the standard deviation for the individual data sets were computed. The data sets and computed results are tabulated in Table 7-2.

Table 7-2. *Resistance Measurement Data Set*

Manufactured nominal resistance	10 Ω	2	3	4	5	6	7	8	9	10	Average	σ
Circuit-Test DMR-1000 (200 Ω scale)	10.4	10.4	10.4	10.4	10.4	10.4	10.4	10.4	10.5	10.4	10.41	0.03
Extech EX505 (200 Ω scale)	10.0	10.0	10.0	10.1	10.1	10.0	10.0	10.0	10.0	9.9	10.01	0.06
Velleman DVM890C (200 Ω scale)	10.4	10.5	10.5	10.6	10.6	10.6	10.5	10.5	10.5	10.5	10.52	0.06
Siglent SDM3055 (BTM autoscale)	10.088	10.068	10.044	10.087	10.05	10.066	10.068	10.095	10.125	9.996	10.0687	0.035
Manufactured nominal resistance	100 Ω											
Circuit-Test DMR-1000 (200 Ω scale)	101.0	99.1	100.3	100.8	101.5	100.4	100.3	99.6	101.9	98.7	100.36	1.01
Extech EX505 (200 Ω scale)	101.6	98.9	100.1	100.2	101.2	100.1	100.1	99.3	100.5	98.5	100.04	0.96
Velleman DVM890C (200 Ω scale)	101.0	99.2	100.4	100.7	101.6	100.5	100.4	99.7	101.0	98.8	100.33	0.86
Siglent SDM3055 (BTM autoscale)	100.942	99.052	100.173	100.622	101.409	100.327	100.172	99.566	100.831	98.665	100.1759	0.861
Manufactured nominal resistance	1,000 Ω (1 K Ω)											
Circuit-Test DMR-1000 (2K Ω scale)	1001	1007	997	999	999	1006	999	999	1003	1010	1002	4.3
Extech EX505 (2K Ω scale)	1.000	1.005	0.995	0.998	0.997	1.003	0.998	0.998	1.001	1.008	1.0003	0.004
Velleman DVM890C (2K Ω scale)	1.005	1.011	1.001	1.003	1.003	1.009	1.003	1.003	1.006	1.015	1.0059	0.004
Siglent SDM3055 (BTM autoscale)	1.00265	1.00882	0.99884	1.00122	1.00073	1.00731	1.00114	1.00122	1.00460	1.01199	1.003852	0.00423
Manufactured nominal resistance	10,000 Ω (10 K Ω)											
Circuit-Test DMR-1000 (20K Ω scale)	10.10	10.01	9.98	10.25	10.03	10.00	10.04	10.13	10.01	10.06	10.061	0.08
Extech EX505 (20K Ω scale)	10.12	10.02	10.00	10.26	10.04	10.00	10.04	10.15	10.10	10.07	10.080	0.08
Velleman DVM890C (20K Ω scale)	10.14	10.04	10.02	10.26	10.06	10.03	10.06	10.15	10.01	10.09	10.086	0.08
Siglent SDM3055 (BTM autoscale)	10.122	10.0355	10.0116	10.2789	10.0588	10.0288	10.0638	10.1618	10.0327	10.0873	10.08812	0.0814
Manufactured nominal resistance	100,000 Ω (100 K Ω)											
Circuit-Test DMR-1000 (200K Ω scale)	101.2	100.2	100.3	99.7	101.4	101.4	99.1	100.6	100.3	100.1	100.43	0.75
Extech EX505 (200K Ω scale)	101.1	100.2	100.3	99.8	101.3	101.3	99.2	100.6	100.0	100.0	100.38	0.69
Velleman DVM890C (200K Ω scale)	101.5	100.6	100.7	100.1	101.6	101.6	99.5	100.9	100.5	100.4	100.74	0.69
Siglent SDM3055 (BTM autoscale)	101.404	100.512	100.634	100.067	101.651	101.667	99.518	101.097	100.601	100.428	100.7579	0.698
Manufactured nominal resistance	1,000,000 Ω (1 M Ω)											
Circuit-Test DMR-1000 (2M Ω scale)	1001	990	1061	1016	1008	1014	1028	1018	1026	1013	1017.5	18.9
Extech EX505 (2M Ω scale)	0.997	0.985	1.054	1.013	1.002	1.010	1.028	1.013	1.023	1.010	1.0135	0.019
Velleman DVM890C (2M Ω scale)	1.005	0.993	1.063	1.021	1.010	1.018	1.036	1.023	1.030	1.017	1.0216	0.019
Siglent SDM3055 (BTM autoscale)	1.00487	0.99374	1.06347	1.02123	1.01070	1.01852	1.03661	1.02364	1.01240	1.01783	1.020301	0.01900

Four different meters were used to measure each of the ten-element resistor sets. The Circuit-Test is a low-cost, four-digit, basic volt, ohm, ampere meter for instrument and lab equipment servicing ($20 CDN). The Velleman DVM890C is a 3½-digit meter with numerous additional functions for capacitance, thermocouples, and other lab-oriented measurements ($50 CDN). The Extech Ex505 is an industrial-grade, autoscaling multimeter with a basic 0.5% accuracy and numerous additional measuring features ($150 USD). The Siglent SDM3055 displayed in Figure 7-4 is a research-grade benchtop meter with a 5½-digit display ($600 CDN). (½-digit notation describes a display in which the most significant digit of the display can be either a 1 or a 0. The remaining number of digits can display digital values from 0 to 9. A 3½-digit display can thus represent a maximum value of 1.999 and any value below that. All ½-digit meters with scale switches are indexed in multiples of two to accommodate the upper 1.999 display limit.)

Recall that digital multimeters are built around high input impedance ADCs that measure voltages. Different meters use different techniques to measure the voltage directly or through precision resistors for resistance and current determinations. ADCs are available in different operational formats with higher digital resolutions, and usually the more precise and accurate measurement circuitry is more expensive to implement.

As can be seen in the 10 Ω measurement data, the lowest standard deviations are seen because the sensitivity of the measurements being made may not be sufficient to see the natural inherent variation that exists in all measurements along with the variation in resistance due to manufacturing.

Note that by convention the number of significant figures recorded is increased by 1 when the average value is reported.

Examination of the data for the 1000 Ω specimens shows the standard deviation σ being returned in the same range or format as the population entries. The Circuit-Test meter uses a four-digit, whole-number display for values less than 9999, while the other meters change display format.

If a comparison chart is drawn up as in Table 7-3 relating the less-expensive hand-held instruments to the benchtop meter, it can be seen that the effects of instrument costs on accuracy are not necessarily correlated. Instruments must be selected to provide the optimum performance for the task at hand.

Table 7-3. *Low-Cost Meter Comparison to High-Resolution Benchtop Meter*

Mfg. Value	closest	2nd match	3 rd match
10 Ω	Extech	Circuit-Test	Vellman
100 Ω	Extech	Vellman	Circuit-Test
1 K Ω	Extech	Circuit-Test	Vellman
10 K Ω	Vellman	Extech	Circuit-Test
100 K Ω	Vellman	Circuit-Test	Extech
1 M Ω	Vellman	Exteck	Circui-Test

Calibration and Curve Fitting

In numerous presentations of tabulated data in this book, a line has been drawn on the plotted data along with an equation and a correlation coefficient. Most of the data has been used to create a straight line that can be used to easily interpolate or calculate values not actually measured in the initial or calibration procedure. The statistical technique used to calculate the straight lines is known as a least squares fit.

The least squares fit is defined as follows: "A method of determining the curve that best describes the relationship between expected and observed sets of data by minimizing the sums of the deviation between observed and expected values." In very simplified terms, the line is the best fit to the scatter in the data set. The R^2 term is called the correlation coefficient and is a measure of how well the equation fits the data. A perfect fit in which all the data points fall on the line would have a correlation coefficient of 1.

There are a number of curve-fitting statistical mathematical operations built into the spreadsheets available today. A textbook on statistical methods is best consulted before the experimenter unfamiliar with these methods applies them to a problem at hand.

Summary

- All replicated measurements made of any quantity have a naturally occurring inherent variability in their measured values that when analyzed statistically and plotted form a Gaussian or normal bell-shaped distribution.

- Three σ quality-control charts use the inherent variability to monitor the validity of the values generated by the measurement system at hand.

- Accuracy, precision, and random and systematic errors are discussed and demonstrated, with the results obtained from a series of resistance measurements.

- Systematic errors are demonstrated in Chapter 8 when the problems and limitations of using the USB for both power and transmission of sensitive experimental data are considered.

CHAPTER 8

Power and Noise from the USB

During the creation and development of this book, the USB has progressed, since its introduction in 1996, through three iterations, and was scheduled for a fourth revision in 2019. In essence, the USB connection is a concept expressed as a written standard that describes an electro-mechanical and software protocol system through which a host computer is automatically interfaced to peripheral devices when a standardized electrical cable is plugged into each unit.

In USB 2.0 cables there are four wires for electrical transmissions and power delivery. Digital information is transferred on a twisted pair of wires known as D+ and D- (color-coded as white and green, respectively). A nominal 5V, 400 mA power is carried on the cable's red wire, with the remaining black serving as a ground. (Occasionally, orange and white are powered with green and blue data lines.)

USB 3.0–compliant cables have an additional two insulated twisted-pair data lines in addition to the four-wire 2.0 specifications to aid in increasing the data-transfer capability of the newer specification.

Information in digital systems is carried by the high-frequency on–off binary nature of the encoding. The digital-based USB communication system is very dependable and not only connects and interfaces the host and peripheral devices but also transmits data, usually without error. However, audio and high-sensitivity electronic measurements have

© Richard J. Smythe 2021
R. J. Smythe, *Advanced Arduino Techniques in Science*,
https://doi.org/10.1007/978-1-4842-6784-4_8

been reported to be compromised by high-frequency noise on the USB connection.[1] An experimental noise-reduction filtering system and its effects are detailed in the UK website, and numerous USB audio noise-suppression devices and methods are available commercially. An in-depth white paper is available as a PDF from the Wurth Elektronik company entitled "ANP024 The USB Interface from EMC Point of View."[2] The thirteen-page paper fully describes the USB standard, hardware, electrical specifications, topology, and protocols for the system. The paper discusses in detail the electromagnetic compatibility (EMC) of the components and systems of the USB communications connections and details the techniques and components that can be used for controlling signals and noise on the link with various USB filters. A kit is available from the Wurth company for developing a USB EMC filter to suit a particular experimental application.

In an effort to minimize the USB noise level in the author's computer system, an iDefender 3.0 USB isolator and noise filter, manufactured by the iFi audio company, was purchased ($100 CDN) (ifi-audio.com) and installed, as seen in Figure 8-1 on the author's desktop computer.

---

[1]andybrown.me.uk/2015/07/24/usb-filtering

[2]https://www.we-online.com/web/en/electronic_components/produkte_pb/ application_notes/ANP024_USB_Interface_from_EMC_Point_of_View.php

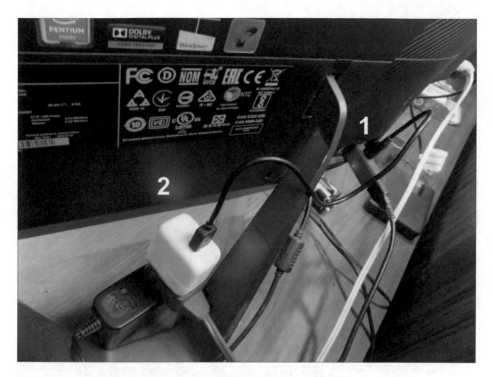

Figure 8-1. *The iDefender and a 5V auxiliary power supply installation on a desktop host computer USB port*

Item 1 in Figure 8-1 is the isolation device that is plugged directly into the host bus port. The glow on the bottom portion of the red case is from the pilot light for the auxiliary 5V supply that is powering the downstream devices on the bus. Item 2, the white rectangular box, is a 5V supply powering the positive and ground wires in the USB cable connected to the iDefender. The USB power lines in the cables connected to the iDefender are thus drawing current from the line or mains supply and are bypassing the host computer's internal supply and wiring buried inside the electromagnetic wave–filled environment within the host's grounded metal case.

System noise reduction can be increased through electromagnetic compatibility considerations that include high-quality shielded USB cables fitted with ferrite bead chokes and well-regulated external bus power sources. For host computers with multiple USB ports, test each one with a high-scale expansion strip chart recorder display to find the connection with the lowest level of spurious signals, spiking, and noise.

Typical Baseline Noise and Large Signal Distortions

Ringing is depicted in Figure 8-2 and can also be seen in the black trace of Figure 8-3, recorded during the development of high-sensitivity thermistor temperature measurement.

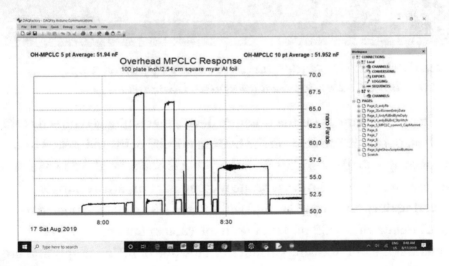

Figure 8-2. *Ringing at 8:30*

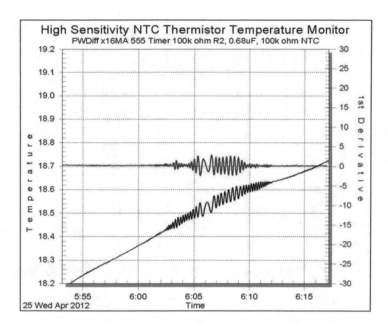

Figure 8-3. *Ringing at 6:05*

Figures 8-4 and 8-5 show spiking at different levels, high and levered, respectively.

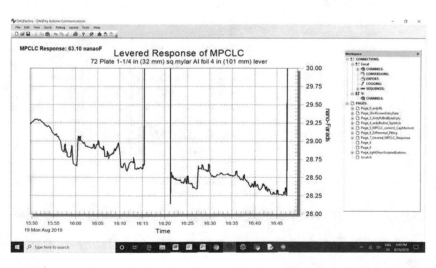

Figure 8-4. *Spiking during high-sensitivity differential signal noise band RC time-constant recording*

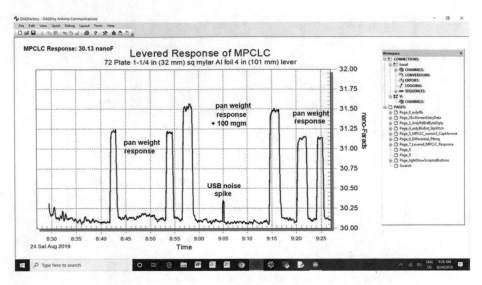

Figure 8-5. *Spiking during levered pan and weight-response recording with RC time-constant software*

Noise from differential signal sources is shown in Figures 8-6 and 8-7.

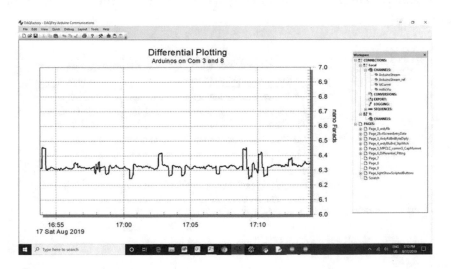

Figure 8-6. *Differential signal noise band from RC time-constant testing*

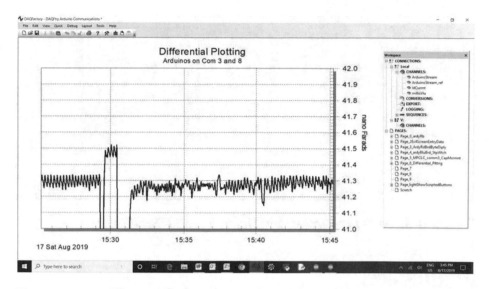

Figure 8-7. *Differential signal noise band from frequency variation*

Commercially Available Noise-Reduction Devices

USB audio devices are often found to have extraneous noise embedded in the audio being played. Background hum, clicks, and other noise elements are often reported as distortions that have been attributed to "ground loops" in the grounding circuitry and fluctuations in the nominal 5V power system (USB power is called VBUS). As depicted in Figure 8-1, iFi Audio (ifi-audio.com) manufactures a "plug-in" noise and power-line filter called the iDefender 3.0 that significantly reduces USB noise and provides a bypass, allowing an external 5V supply to power the downstream devices drawing power from the VBUS line. Figure 8-8 illustrates the observed baseline noise reduction provided by the isolation filter.

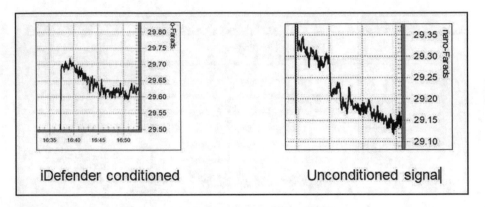

Figure 8-8. *Noise reduction by iDefender 3.0 USB filter*

Discussion

The USB connection is a two-way transmission system that is usually embedded in a noisy environment of high-frequency, high-intensity electromagnetic radiation within the host computer metal case. In the author's Windows system, the Device Manager USB entry indicates the presence of eleven super-speed hubs, regular hubs, composite devices, mass-storage devices, and root-hub controllers. Some of these USB devices are running continuously at kHz clock frequencies, and external peripherals such as keyboards, mice, thumb drives, external hard drives, and audio-visual displays create substantial activity on the bus.

Where possible, bus noise can be lowered by reducing or eliminating other devices on the bus being used to communicate with high-sensitivity testing equipment.

Audio-improvement discussion groups suggest the use of only one mains power outlet that may be connected to a power bar to supply all of the components in an audio system. The use of a single power outlet minimizes the possibility of a ground loop's developing.

Figure 8-8 indicates that the iFi iDefender 3.0 virtually halves the baseline noise seen on the author's capacitance measurement experiments. High-quality USB cables equipped with ferrite "beads," heavy braided-metal mesh EMI insulation and inner foil-wrapped wiring should be used for all high-sensitivity instrumentation.

Filters, quality cabling, ground-loop prevention, and the elimination of other devices on the bus in use can substantially reduce the noise on the USB to the point at which experiments at higher sensitivities can be carried out with reasonable reproducibility.

Summary

- Spiking and ringing are the two main interferences encountered by the author when using the USB for high-sensitivity experimental measurements.

- Ground loops, USB power, and high-frequency bus noise are suggested as the sources of the interference.

- Separate power supplies, commercial USB filters, and using only one mains outlet with a power bar are suggested as methods to lower the interference.

CHAPTER 9

Analytical Front Ends

In previous work dealing with the measurement of heat and temperature, the physical, performance, and monetary costs of the various readily available, inexpensive temperature sensors were reviewed and are pictured in Figure 9-1. Included in the photo is the original large, black, plastic square LM35 device, which is direct-reading, calibrated, and temperature-sensitive. Newer integrated circuit (IC) devices, including the TMP35, 36, and 37, are all available in the three-lead T3 (TO-92) packages, which are large and bulky in comparison to the microbead glass thermistors and thermocouples also depicted in Figure 9-1.

© Richard J. Smythe 2021
R. J. Smythe, *Advanced Arduino Techniques in Science,*
https://doi.org/10.1007/978-1-4842-6784-4_9

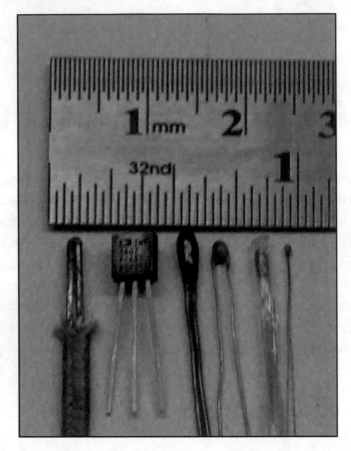

Figure 9-1. *Relative temperature-sensor sizes*

From the left in Figure 9-1 are the thermocouple, the TMP36, an epoxy-coated thermistor, a glass-coated thermistor, a second smaller glass-encased thermistor, and an EPCOS microbead, glass-coated thermistor. Although the three-terminal TO-92 IC temperature sensor is the largest of the common sensors, it is the least complex to integrate into experimental setups for use within the –55 to 125°C temperature range.

IC-based Sensors

The IC-based sensors are inexpensive; have a linear, calibrated, temperature voltage output over their specified range; are relatively sensitive; and are conveniently read with simple computer code. The LM35/TMP36 IC–type temperature sensors do not require a cold junction. Table 9-1 is a comparative tabulation of many of the thermal and electronic properties of the application-specific integrated circuit (ASIC) sensors.

Table 9-1. *Comparison of Solid-State Temperature Sensors*

Parameter/IC	LM35		TMP35		TMP36
Calibration	°C		°C		°C
Range °C	-55 to 150		10 to 125		-40 to 125
Supply Voltage	4 - 30		2.7 - 5		2.7 - 5
Response	10 mV/°C		10 mV/°C		10 mV/°C
Offset Voltage	0		0		0.5
Output at 25°C	250 mV		250 mV		750 mV
Accuracy °C	+/- 0.5		+/- 2		+/- 2
Linearity °C	+/- 0.25		+/- 0.5		+/- 0.5

LM35 is available from suppliers at $3 per piece, and the TMP36 is $2 (CDN).

In an experimental measurement of low quantities of heat exchange in which temperature differentials of less than a half or a quarter of a degree Celsius are generated, the investigator may use a thermistor or increase the sensitivity of a readily available IC-type temperature sensor with a microcontroller and an "analog front end" (AFE).

Very sensitive medical diagnostic equipment for measuring the electrical signals from nerves, hearts, and brains, along with physio-chemical instrumentation for potentiometric gas sensors and pH acid–base monitors, have used AFEs for many years. An AFE for use with much simpler, less expensive, microprocessor-based experimental measurement systems has been described in the February 2016 issue of *Nuts and Volts* magazine (NandVM) by Prof. E. Bogatin.[1]

Microcontrollers

A typical microcontroller is equipped with a 5V analog-to-digital converter (ADC) that in the case of an Arduino is a 10-bit converter able to resolve 5V/1024 or 4.883mV per analog-to-digital converter unit (ADU). If the sensor and ADC are powered by the less noisy 3.3V supply, then the conversion factor drops to 3.22mV/ADU. If the experiment at hand will only generate very small changes in temperature, the data sheets for the IC-based temperature sensors indicate that we will be dealing with low voltage-difference values. A distinct increase in system sensitivity could be realized if the small analog signal developed by the low-level operations were amplified to a value close to, but less than, the 5 or 3.3 volts maximum response available for the ADC in use. By using a pre-amplifier we can re-scale or move our low-level-voltage experimental signal that will activate only a small portion of the full ADC range to one that will activate a large portion of the converter's total span. If it is known that an experiment will only generate at a maximum, 1¼V differentials, then a pre-amplifier with a gain of 4 would allow our readout signal to use close to the full 1024-bit resolution of the converter. In theory, the resolution of our 5V sensor readout has been increased from 4.884mV to 1.22mV per ADU. If the less noisy 3.3V supply on the Arduino is used as an AFE power source then the increase in resolution is the same for the proportionally lower operating voltage range at 0.805mV/ADU.

---

[1]https://www.nutsvolts.com/magazine/article/february2016_
AnalogFrontEnds

Amplification of DC signals is usually effected with operational amplifiers. In addition to amplifying a low-voltage signal, the configuration of the op-amp can be used to adjust the output impedance for the sensor. It has been noted in the NandVM reference that the Arduino's Atmega328 IC manual indicates that the ADC input has a capacitance of 14 pF. Recalling the properties of capacitors, a capacitor requires a certain amount of time to charge up to its final voltage as determined by the circuit RC product. A current flowing through a resistor into a capacitor charges the capacitor until the voltage across the plates equals that of the charging signal. Once the capacitor on the ADC input has stabilized at the level generated by the sensor, the ADC can accurately convert the voltage into ADC units. It is recommended by the manufacturer of the Atmel 328 chip that the input resistor on the ADC input should be less than 10 kΩ so that the voltage on the capacitor of the input channel has stabilized before the conversion is begun.

Examination of the data sheets for the IC sensors indicates that the quiescent current for the devices is nominally 50 μA. If measured temperatures are such that the output voltage is in the range of 1¼ V then the output impedance is 1.25V/ 50 x 10^{-6} A or 25 kΩ, which is substantially higher than recommended for the Arduino CPU input pins.

Operational Amplifiers

Operational amplifiers (op-amp) are a host of integrated circuits based upon the idealized concept of the perfect, theoretical DC amplifier. An ideal op-amp has infinite open loop gain, infinite input impedance, zero output impedance, infinite bandwidth, and zero output voltage, with no voltage across the input terminals. The ideal op-amp has a pair of differential inputs termed the inverting and non-inverting inputs that invert or reproduce the voltage of the respective inputs at the device output.

Operational amplifiers are the descendants of analog computers once used to perform mathematical operations in many linear, non-linear, and frequency-dependent circuits. Integrated circuits such as the general-purpose μA709 introduced in 1965 and the μA741 first produced in 1968 and still in production today are reasonable approximations to the ideal DC amplifier concept.

In the application at hand, an analytical front end (AFE) is being assembled from a general-purpose operational amplifier and a special-purpose ASIC in which three general-purpose operational amplifiers have been fabricated onto a single chip in an arrangement known as an instrumentation amplifier.

In Figure 9-2 three op-amp circuit configurations are displayed as A, B, and C that help to illustrate the functions that make up an analog front end.

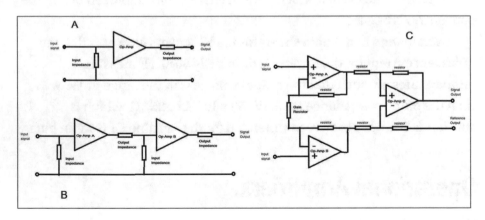

Figure 9-2. *Op-amp circuits used in a temperature sensor analog front end*

Circuit A illustrates the essential configuration of an op-amp. The op-amp device has a substantial input impedance between the inverting and non-inverting input terminals. When connected to a signal source some current must flow through the input terminals, and this signal voltage must drive the current through some form of resistance that can be represented as the input impedance. As is illustrated in circuit A, the input impedance is in parallel with the signal source. At the output terminals of the device there is a theoretical resistor in series with the current flow from the amplifier. As more current is drawn from the amplifier, the voltage will drop in proportion to the internal output impedance of the device.

Circuit B depicts an op-amp circuit in which two amplifiers have been "cascaded" so that the output from amplifier A can serve as the input for amplifier B. The main point to be observed is that the output impedance of amplifier A and the input impedance of amplifier B form a voltage divider. To optimize the signal transfer from the output of amplifier A to the input of amplifier B, the output impedance of A should be substantially smaller than the input impedance of amplifier B.

Circuit C is a block diagram of a three op-amp configuration termed an instrument amplifier (in-amp). Instrument amplifiers are available as a single-unit IC as dual inline packages (DIP) and as surface-mount technology (SMT)–format ASIC. In-amps are very high input impedance, dedicated, dual-differential input amplifier devices that buffer the voltage source with a pair of op-amp followers on the input circuitry. The gain of the device is controlled by a single externally mounted resistor that can vary the gain from unity into values in the thousands. (See "gain resistor" in Figure 9-2, circuit C, and consult the data sheet for the device in use.) Because in-amps are differential input devices, the output may or may not be isolated from the system ground. In the circuit of Figure 9-3, based upon reference 1, the analytical front end in-amp is referenced to the system ground and the separate reference output terminal of the AD623 must also be connected to the system ground.

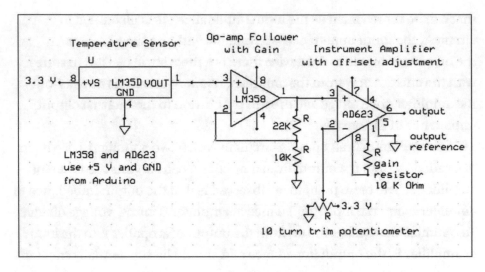

Figure 9-3. *The circuit for a high-sensitivity temperature measurement analog front end*

Within the AFE, the op-amp has amplified the DC signal from the sensor. An amplified millivolt signal from the pre-amp is applied to the positive input of the in-amp, and the inverting input of the in-amp is provided with an adjustable positive DC voltage from the multi-turn potentiometer. With an equal positive DC voltage applied to both of the inputs of the in-amp, its output is zero. If the sensor responds to a small temperature change in its surrounding environment, the pre-amp amplifies the sensor output that in turn increases the voltage on the in-amp non-inverting input. The inverting input is at a fixed voltage as determined by the potentiometer setting. Only the difference between the inputs is the portion of the signal that is amplified by the in-amp. The non-inverting input has been adjusted to match the quiescent value from the pre-amp so that the in-amp will only respond with an amplified output when the output from the pre-amp increases.

The in-amp provides the final amplification of the AFE by responding only to the change in the pre-amp output.

After the AFE has been assembled on either a prototyping or printed circuit board, the system must be configured properly in order to function. An IC temperature sensor typically produces a 10mV/°C voltage that at room temperature is approximately 250mV. An op-amp amplification of 3 or 4 brings the voltage up to approximately 0.75V or 1V. (Adjustments must be made in the microprocessor voltage to temperature-transfer function or calculation software to accommodate the temperature sensor in use; TMP36 has an offset while the 35 devices do not.)

As outlined, an instrumentation amplifier is used in the AFE to remove the bulk of the DC signal present in the op-amp output. Instrumentation amplifiers only amplify the voltage difference between the inverting and non-inverting inputs. Examination of the circuit in Figure 9-3 shows the inverting input connected to the wiper of a potentiometer able to supply up to 3.3V of DC signal to the instrumentation op-amp. The in-amp has a gain of ten, so with a meter connected across the in-amp inputs the wiper is adjusted until the voltage difference is as close to zero as possible. At room temperature with the author's circuit assembled on a prototyping breadboard, the minimum value obtainable was 10.3mV. When tested with a meter, the AFE output varied from 10mV to 3.7V with the application of finger heat to a TMP36.

As can be seen in Figure 9-4, when assembled, adjusted, and programmed with the theoretical voltage-to-temperature conversions, the three test points of the author's reproduced AFE generate different values in response to finger heat on the sensor.

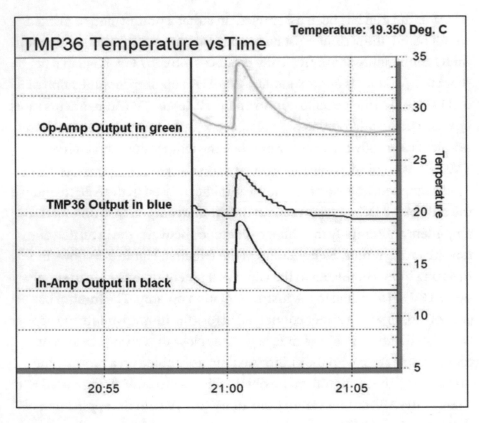

Figure 9-4. *Recorded temperature outputs for the stages of the analog front end*

Figure 9-4 is a graphic demonstration similar to that depicted in the NandVM reference given earlier in which the outputs from the three stages of the AFE to the application of finger heat on the sensor are qualitatively displayed. Building the AFE from two discrete ICs and resistors on an unshielded prototyping breadboard and using theoretical calculations to generate a temperature from the voltage seen at each test point in the AFE has produced the three different temperature measurements for the sensor output.

The true sensor temperature recording in blue displays the low resolution provided by the direct analog-to-digital conversion of the sensor data into a "stepped" digital format. The green trace is the temperature as

218

calculated by the ADC microcontroller–augmented output of the op-amp AFE section, and the black trace is the apparent final-stage temperature as calculated from the in-amp output.

In order to quantitatively demonstrate the operation of an AFE built for experimental determinations such as the higher-resolution monitoring of small temperature changes, a defined quantity of electrical heat energy sufficient to generate a 1°C change in a dry-well temperature was used to produce the traces depicted in Figure 9-5. (See Chapter 3, "High Heat and Temperature," Figure 3-3, "*A laminated aluminum plate dry well*").

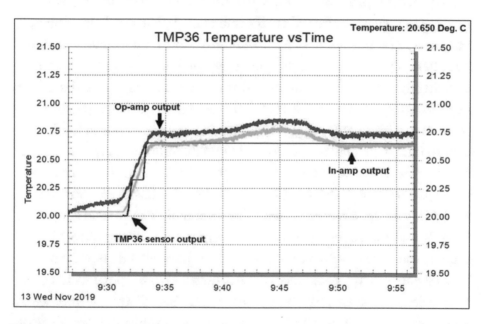

Figure 9-5. *A 1°C temperature differential normalized outputs for the elements of the analog front end*

In Figure 9-5, the analog voltage signal from a TMP36 sensor has been processed by the author's breadboard prototype analog front end throughout the 1°C temperature differential induced in an insulated dry well. All three stages of the AFE have been normalized by adjusting the microprocessor software voltage to temperature-transfer functions for each stage to output a value close to 20°C. It has been assumed and confirmed by the dry well's mercury-in-glass thermometer that the raw TMP readout is in accordance with the manufacturer's suggested theoretical calculation to generate a temperature value within the specifications detailed in Table 9-1. To normalize the pre-amp output, the temperature calculation based upon the observed voltage at the test point is divided by the op-amp gain before the temperature is calculated. As can be seen in Listing 9-1, an additional offset correction of approximately 50 was required to normalize the op-amp output to the desired 20°C value (all code listings provided at the end of the chapter). The op-amp gain resistors as seen in Figure 9-3 are 5% tolerance, 10 kΩ and 22 kΩ values, that provided a measured 3.12 gain factor. As noted, an instrumentation amplifier only measures the difference between the inverting and non-inverting inputs. If the in-amp inverting input voltage is adjusted to match the constant voltage output from the pre-amp then the in-amp has nothing to amplify. A 5% tolerance 10 kΩ gain resistor has been chosen for the in-amp final stage of the AFE. (An 11 kΩ 1% tolerance resistor is required to achieve a gain of 10 in the AD623 in-amp.) Examination of the code in Listing 9-1 will reveal that the in-amp output value has been normalized by dividing the observed voltage by approximately 30, the total gain of the AFE, and correcting the calculated temperature with an offset of approximately 20 to achieve the desired 20°C normalized recorder trace.

In Figure 9-5 the black trace of the Arduino ADC output consists of three voltage levels corresponding to two ADC "steps." The thermometer appeared to transit from 19¾ to 20¾°C, and the graphical record suggests that the temperature differential may not have been a full degree. Each ADC step is 3.22mV, and a full degree temperature change should have produced three 3.22mV steps in the 10mV/˚C response of the sensor. The op-amp output in blue and the in-amp output in green have been normalized and can be used with a scale expansion in the plotting program to gain significantly increased sensitivity if desired.

A second temperature-increase experiment was conducted at twice the heating time (i.e., five minutes) to produce a set of recordings that can be compared with the initial observations made in Figure 9-5. Figure 9-6 illustrates the normalized temperature values seen at the outputs of the AFE components.

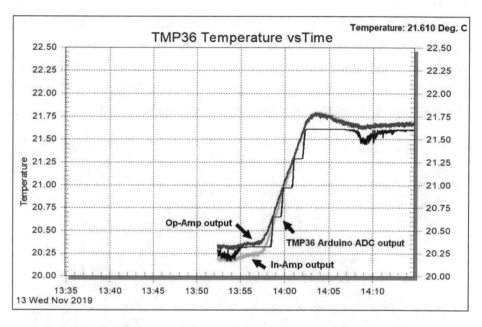

Figure 9-6. *A 2°C temperature differential normalized outputs for the elements of the analog front end*

Conducting a second thermal-difference experiment to generate twice the expected trace deflection essentially confirms the observations seen in the primary measurement. Although the mercury-in-glass thermometer appeared to measure a one- and two-degree difference from the incremental timed application of electrical energy, both graphical temperature deflection records are lower than expected.

If the mercury-in-glass thermometer is taken as the primary standard, then in both of the tests the stepped response is one and two units less than expected.

TMP36 and LM35 both have sensitivities of 10mV/°C, and a single-degree temperature change should produce a 10mV/3.22mV/ADC unit or 3.1 ADC steps.

A low voltage at the output of the sensor could be caused by excessive current draw by the preamp, and a voltage follower between the sensor and pre-amp may lessen the voltage drop. An experimental modification to the AFE circuitry in Figure 9-3 was made by wiring in a voltage follower with the unused op-amp in the LM358, as seen in Figure 9-7.

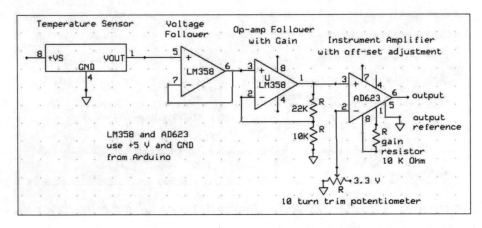

Figure 9-7. *The voltage follower–modified AFE circuit*

Figure 9-8 indicates an improvement in the circuit response that could be attributed to the insertion of the voltage follower into the pre-amp input.

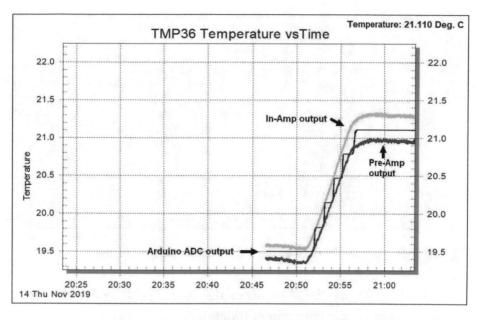

Figure 9-8. *A 2°C temperature differential with voltage follower*

A second prototype, high-sensitivity, analytical front end temperature-measurement circuit was assembled on an Adafruit Industries prototyping shield for the Arduino microcontrollers (P/N 2077 $15 USD for kit). A blank shield for assembling prototype circuits is depicted in Figure 1-2 of Chapter 1, "Arduino and Raspberry Pi." An Arduino shield platform was chosen in order for a compact device to result that could be fitted inside a grounded metal case with a small benchtop footprint. Figure 9-9 is a block diagram–schematic that was built around two 8-pin DIP sockets to hold the dual op-amp and in-amp ICs. A terminal board with wiring access holes to the interior of the enclosure was mounted on the front plate of the metal case in which rectangular cutouts for the Arduino USB, auxiliary power plug, and set-screw of the in-amp inverting input-voltage adjustment potentiometer were cut.

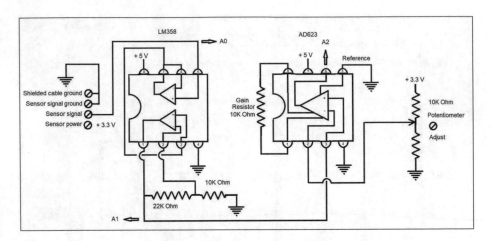

Figure 9-9. *AFE PCB or perfboard circuit configuration*

Figure 9-10 depicts the front face of the second prototype AFE during a low-temperature water ice testing validation.

Figure 9-10. *AFE low-temperature water ice validation*

As can be seen in Figure 9-10, the terminal board has connections for the cable-shielding ground (silver wire on the left), the signal ground (black wire), the signal wire (white wire), and the 3.3V power to bias the sensor. The "Pot. Adjust" label identifies the potentiometer wiper-adjusting screw slot used to balance the inputs of the instrumentation amplifier in the output stage of the AFE. (The potentiometer is held/glued in place by a short bar passing through the forward mounting hole in the device.) (The front face–mounted terminal board can also be used to add high-value capacitors to filter out excessive voltage spikes in electronically noisy environments.)

In Figure 9-11 the base of the metal case was covered with a thin layer of scrap polyethylene plastic perforated with four holes to hold the mounting bolts in position while the stand-offs, seen to the left and right of caption 1, were placed over the bolts to fix the blue Arduino board, item 1, in place and allow the green shield, item 2, to be press fitted into the main board.

Figure 9-11. *Arduino with AFE shield-mounted circuitry*

Item 3 is the multi-turn potentiometer used to balance the inputs of item 6, the AD623 instrument amplifier. Caption 4 is between the mounting bolts of the terminal board with the system ground tab on the right. Item 5 is the dual op-amp LM358. Both of the integrated circuits are mounted in 8-pin DIP sockets to avoid possible heat damage to the chips during initial assembly and facilitate IC replacement if necessary.

Connections between the sensor, pre-amp and in-amp outputs, and the Arduino ADC are made using the input headers of the shield at caption 7. A dual-channel terminal board, item 8, connects the inverting input of the in-amp to the wiper of the potentiometer and provides 3.3V power to the sensor-biasing terminal "P" on the front panel.

One of the major practical applications of the AFE is to augment the sensitivity of a temperature measurement. Immersed in a liquid or fluid, changes in temperature often accompany chemical reactions or changes of physical state in the fluid medium. In many sciences, samples requiring analysis or testing are of very limited size having been recovered from biological systems or as residues or remnants of materials involved in failures and hence must be processed with the maximum sensitivity available. An AFE allows the investigator to work with IC sensors compatible with smaller masses and the reduced temperature differentials generated within these scarce samples.

Working on a smaller scale is possible with the plastic sensors illustrated in Figure 9-1, and increasing the sensitivity of the IC devices provides an easily implemented temperature monitor. Equipping a small 25 to 30 ml plastic container with a stirring apparatus and a temperature sensor can create a miniature calorimeter with which to follow thermometric changes in liquid systems.

Figure 9-12 depicts a simple solution calorimeter or heat-monitoring system. Item 1 is an Arduino temperature monitor, fitted with an AFE to augment the sensitivity of the wooden dowel–mounted probe tipped with a TMP36 temperature sensor, captioned as item 6. To ensure homogeneity in the fluid medium under study, a stirring blade or agitator, item 7, for the miniature calorimeter has been assembled from a second Arduino at caption 2 and a small servo motor, item 4. Brushless DC and stepper motors have been used in previous work but for a low-mass heat monitor such as this calorimeter system, a small servo motor was chosen to power an agitating system. Very small and inexpensive servo motors such as the Tower Pro Micro Servo 9G units are available online and from hobby shops ($5 CDN). The lightweight, powerful gear-reduction miniature servo motors are sold with screw-mounted four-, two-, and single-arm "horns" or "bellcranks." By mounting the motor on its side so the horn/bellcrank moves in a vertical oscillation of 7/16 in., or 11 mm, a variable agitation action can be realized. Agitator speeds can be adjusted by altering the delay(n) millisecond values in the testNuChar() functions of Listing 9-2. A 15 ms delay produces approximately 1 stroke in 2 seconds, a 10 ms delay creates approximately a stroke per second, while a 5 ms delay oscillates at a little less than two strokes every second.

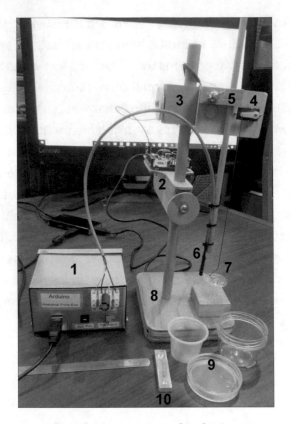

Figure 9-12. *A simple solution-agitated calorimeter*

Items 2 and 3 are wooden blocks drilled vertically to accept the ½ in. (12 mm) dowelling of the lab stand, item 8. The drilled mounting blocks are held in place with #10-32 machine screws (⅛ in. diameter, 32 threads per inch (tpi), 3 mm diameter, 32 threads per 2.45 cm). The machine screws are parallel to the lengthwise, horizontal center line of the blocks that run through 32 tpi nuts cemented to the flat ends of the mounting blocks to tighten against the lab-stand shaft. As can be seen in Figure 9-12, the machine-screw heads have been cemented to 1½ in. (38 mm) diameter, ⅛ in. (3 mm) thick disks of plywood to allow finger adjustments of the block positions.

Figure 9-13 provides a close-up view of the servo motor mounting, horn/bellcrank push-rod configuration, and adjustable temperature sensor-probe mounting. Item 1 in Figure 9-13 identifies a group of plastic film shims that are used to maintain a vertical alignment of the temperature probe and pushrod with respect to the lab stand. Caption 2 marks the clamp positioning the ¼ in. (6 mm) dowel to which the TMP36 IC sensor wiring has been clamped with small cable ties. Captions 3 and 4 mark the servo motor and the horn pushrod assembly that drive the agitator disk in the calorimeter vessel.

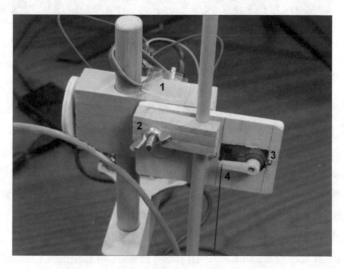

Figure 9-13. *The adjustable mountings of the servo motor and independent temperature sensor probe*

Figure 9-14 provides a detailed view of the Arduino used to control and power the vertical agitator servo motor. The alignment shims are labeled as item 1, item 2 is the backside of the servo motor, and item 3 is the mounting platform for the servo control microprocessor. Also visible in the figure are the details of the servo motor mounting and the mechanism for the independent adjusting of the temperature-sensing probe.

Figure 9-14. *Servo motor Arduino controller*

In Figure 9-15, a typical preparation for a calorimeter experiment is presented. A typical 50 ml vessel is indicated by caption 1, and a 25 ml container is seen at the lower-left corner of the lab-stand base. Item 2 is the agitator platform, shown in greater detail in Figures 9-16 and 9-17. To prepare for an experiment, the spacer block, item 4, is inserted beneath the vessel of choice, and the heights of the temperature sensor and oscillating plate are adjusted. The sensor must be completely immersed in the solution under test. The oscillating plate must not contact the bottom of the vessel nor the temperature sensor during its vertical travel.

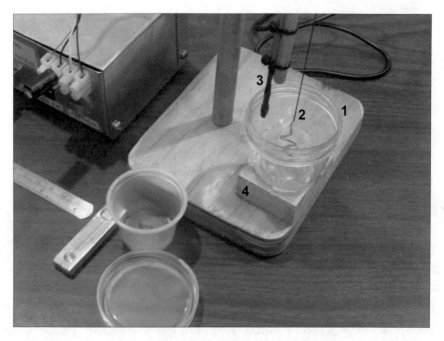

Figure 9-15. *A typical preparation for a calorimeter experiment*

Item 1 is a 50 ml volume test vessel, while a 25 ml vessel and a 0.113 cm³ aluminum-bar powder measure are seen in the lower left-hand field of view between the reference rule and the top of the larger vessel. (The larger measure's top depression was formed by drilling a ⅜ in. diameter cavity ⅜ in. deep into the ½ x ¼ in. (12 x 6 mm) aluminum-bar stock.)

A gentle fluid agitation device was created by cementing a perforated clear PET (polyethylene terephthalate) plastic disk to a wire "zigzag" platform bent into a piano wire. The angled bends form a flat base or surface on the push rod so the plane of the 1¼ in. (30 mm) disk was at right angles to the vertical oscillations of the servo motor. The details of the agitator plate are depicted in Figures 9-16 and 9-17.

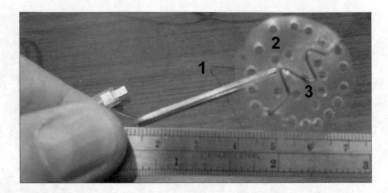

Figure 9-16. *A bottom view of the agitator plate*

Caption 1 identifies the right-angled ⅛ in. (3 mm) "crank" that engages the servo motor horn or bellcrank, which is 7¾ in. (19.5 cm) from the ⅛ in. hole perforated-disk base plate identified as item 2 in Figure 9-16. The pushrod was fabricated from 0.025 in. or 22 ga (0.64 mm) diameter piano wire. The pushrod was bent so the main long shaft of the rod was perpendicular to and concentric with the flat plane of the agitator disk and its supporting z-shaped bent-wire pattern identified as item 3 in Figure 9-16.

Figure 9-17 depicts the bottom end of the long pushrod shaft as item 1. The configuration of the supporting wire prior to passing through a hole located on an edge of the perforated-disk agitation plate, item 2, is shown.

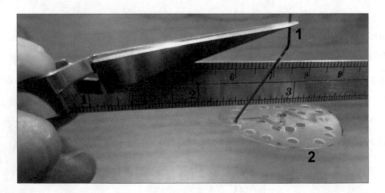

Figure 9-17. *Agitator plate side view*

Plywood to steel machine screw, spring steel to PET plastic plate, and wood cementing were all accomplished with cyanoacrylate adhesives that have yet to show any signs of deterioration after months of service. Cyanoacrylate glue was also used as a sealant around the base of the LM and TMP IC temperature sensors. The three lead devices were soldered to the red power, black sensor ground, and white signal, shielded, triple-wire 24 ga twisted conductor cables. Prior to soldering, short lengths of heat-shrink tubing were fitted over the plastic insulation of the three cable conductors, and after lead soldering the heat-shrink tubing was positioned over the solder joint abutting the base of the IC and shrunk. The three insulated connections were then coated with liquid plastic insulation to further protect and stiffen the electrical connections. Prior to testing the sensor in a solution media, the joint at the base of the IC and the plastic coating on the cable end were coated with several applications of cyanoacrylate glue to ensure a watertight connection.

Two Arduinos were eventually used by the author when single programs written to both measure the temperature and stir the solution produced random errors in the temperature readings.

Recall that the USB software enumerates the hardware on the bus and loads the appropriate driver software such as the COM ports as required. To set up the calorimeter the first Arduino is launched then activated to either measure or stir, and when its operation has been validated the GUI is minimized. A second instance of the Arduino IDE is then launched loaded with the appropriate code and assigned to a second COM port for controlling the second operation.

Listing 9-1 is the microprocessor code for monitoring and normalizing the three stages of the AFE. Listing 9-2 is the Arduino code for controlling the vertical oscillations of the servo motor, while Listing 9-3 is the DAQFactory sequence for receiving and plotting multiple serial port–transmitted data.

Calorimeter Testing, Validation, and Applications

To generate any reliable thermometric data using an IC with augmented temperature sensitivity, all reagents and test equipment must be at the same initial temperature. If experiments are to be conducted at room temperature, the investigator must ensure that the room temperature is constant and that the apparatus and reagents have reached thermal equilibrium with the immediate environment.

Stirring a fluid can add energy to the liquid system and create heat; thus, any stirring action must be gentle and controlled in order to not add measurable energy to the liquid. As can be seen in the following qualitative and semi-quantitative demonstrations, the strip-chart recording method of data collection for this type of measurement provides several advantages over the collection of time-stamped numerical value lists. A level stable baseline is easily recognized by the human eye and allows the investigator to conduct multiple sequential experiments, as depicted in Figures 9-18 to 9-21.

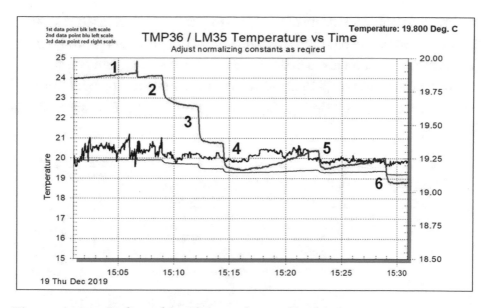

Figure 9-18. *Sodium bicarbonate heat of hydration*

In the following two figures the temperature decreases have been created by the dissolution of 0.113 cm³ (0.0069 in.³) of the nominal finely powdered salts in 50 ml quantities of water.

The trace at caption 1 represents the recorded temperature of the agitated water charge prior to the introduction of the sodium bicarbonate (NaHCO₃). The "spike" between captions 1 and 2 was caused by the author striking the IC probe with the powder scoop while dispensing the first portion of the salt. The five portions of salt powder show a reasonable reproducibility, with 3 showing the greatest heat uptake and 5 the least. Portions 2, 3, and 4 were measured as soon as the recorder trace appeared to resume a constant temperature. Portions 4 and 5 were allowed to run for greater lengths of time to illustrate that these measurements were actually being made under conditions that only initially approximated adiabatic conditions. (Under adiabatic conditions heat is not exchanged with the system environment.) To definitively measure the heats of dissolution, accurate weights and purity of reactants together with increased vessel insulation would be required to achieve substantially better reproducibility from which to extract more definitive data with statistical significance.

In Figures 9-18 and 9-19 the signals from all three test points from the AFE are recorded, while in Figures 9-20 and 9-21 only the final stage output is displayed.

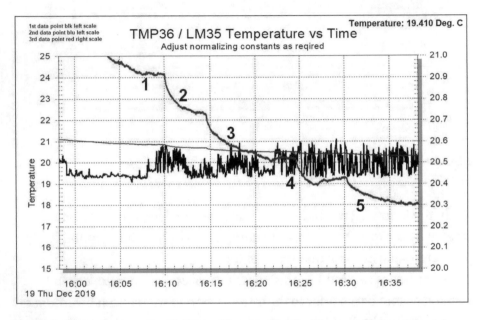

Figure 9-19. *Reproducibility of heat of hydration sodium chloride*

Figure 9-19 displays a similar pattern of reasonably reproducible endothermic heat uptakes by the dissolution of the various portions of sodium chloride powder (NaCl). Caption 1 again identifies a constant temperature in the 50 ml charge of water in the test vessel. Caption 2 identifies the observed temperature decrease in the water as the agitated two-phase system is converted into a homogeneous, single-phased solution.

Preliminary testing of the temperature change to be expected with the dissolution of common table sugar (sucrose $C_{12}H_{22}O_{11}$, a glucose fructose disaccharide) indicated that the 0.113 cm^3 powder scoop did not dispense enough material, even using several sequential portions, to produce a strong reproducible signal. To offset the expected low heat of solution a level teaspoon measure (4.93 ml) was used to increase the system response. An alternate method for increasing the signal response for these types of experiments is to decrease the mass of the water solvent to 25 ml.

In Figure 9-20 the left-hand temperature scale has been adjusted so the signal recordings for the IC and the preamp stages of the AFE are off-scale and do not clutter the final stage display. One of the advantages of the strip-chart recorder displays in experimental work can be seen in the constant "drift" from 17:15 at 21.25°C to 17:53 at 20.70°C. In spite of the drift, the heat-of-solution measurement can still be made at 17:31. The important information is contained in the temperature decrease recorded at 17:31 from 21.00°C to 20.85°C at 17:35. The initial heat uptake by the dissolution of the larger portion of solute generates an initial temperature decrease that causes the solution to behave initially as an adiabatic system. However, as the temperature drops by 0.15°C to an apparently constant value, the reproducible, virtually linear overall system heat loss to the environment is reestablished at 17:36.

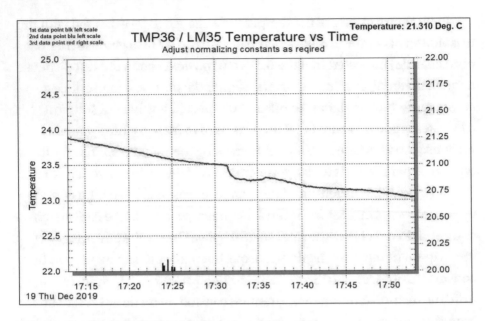

Figure 9-20. *Heat of hydration sucrose*

As noted in the previous text, the greatly augmented IC temperature sensitivity provided by a microcontroller AFE is especially useful for the chemical analysis methodology of titrations. Titration methods in which standardized solutions are used to determine the concentration of solution under test use many different visual or electrochemical methods to determine the titration reaction end or equivalence point. Many titration reactions can be followed by monitoring the solution temperature as the standardized solution is added to the solution under test. A simple, semi-quantitative emulation of a titration using innocuous, readily available reagents is presented in Figure 9-21.

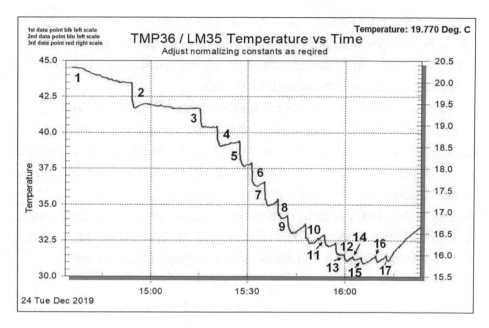

Figure 9-21. *Heat of reaction acetic acid and sodium bicarbonate*

Vinegar and baking soda are two foodstuff materials that can be used with the apparatus displayed in Figures 9-12 to 9-17 to generate a graphical recording of an emulated titration reaction.

Vinegar is a 5% v/v solution of acetic acid (CH_3COOH) in water, and food-grade baking soda is a relatively pure powder of sodium bicarbonate ($NaHCO_3$). Figure 9-21 was generated by monitoring the solution temperature of a 50 ml portion of vinegar as 0.113 cm^3 portions of sodium bicarbonate were added to the agitated solution. Powder additions for the first few increments should be dispensed carefully as carbon dioxide is generated in accordance with the following;

$$CH_3COOH + NaHCO_3 \rightarrow CH_3COONa + H_2O + CO_2\uparrow$$

The portion of the recording identified by caption 1 in Figure 9-21 is the downward temperature drift of the system. In general it can be seen that as the number of additions of powdered baking soda increases the solution cooling effect decreases. As the system temperature cools, the heat inflow after the addition of the powder causes the baseline to drift sharply upward. After the addition of 13 powder portions, the solution temperature stabilizes at approximately 15.8°C.

To convert the incremental powder addition of Figure 9-21 into a thermometric titration to determine the actual strength of the acetic acid in the vinegar, the solution temperature would be monitored as a function of the milliliters of standardized sodium bicarbonate solution added to the vinegar aliquot taken for testing. The end point for the titration would be located at the point where the temperature trace ceases to decrease and becomes a constant value. For further details, the researcher can consult the substantial literature that exists on the methods of thermometric titrations.

Code Listings

Listing 9-1. Arduino Code for Temperature Monitoring and Serial Port Data Transmission

```
// Low noise 3.3 Volt TMP36 - LM35 Temperature Sensing
// 3.3 Vlts used to bias sensor and re-define ADC range to 3.3 volts.
// Adjusted ADC units seen on A0, A1 and A2 monitoring TMP36/
   LM35, pre-amp and in-amp
// outputs of the AFE used to calc. sensor temp. offset
   constants and gains
// arbitrarily adjusted to calculate relatively the same temp
   values for each AFE stage.
// LM35 is 10mV/deg C and uses no offsets
//
int sensePin = A0;          // the sensor output monitor
int preampPin = A1;         // preamp output
```

```
int afePin = A2;            // AFE output
int sensorInput;            // variable for sensor input
int preampOutput;           // preamp output variable
int afeOutput;              // AFE output variable
double temp;                // variable for temperature in
                            //    degrees C.
float patemp;          // gain corrected preamp temperature
float afetemp;              // AFE relative temperature
double sumTobeAvrgd = 0;    // averaging sum
double avrgTemp;            // averaged temperature value
int cntrIndx = 0;           // counter index or number of
                            //    points to average
int numPtstoAvrg = 100;     // define number of points to
                            //    average
 //
void setup() {
  // setup code runs once:
  Serial.begin(9600);       // start serial port at 9600 baud
  //
  analogReference(EXTERNAL); // declare external reference for
                            //    inputs
}  // end of set-up
//
void loop() {
  // main code runs repeatedly:
  // loop to average the data
 for(cntrIndx = 0; cntrIndx < numPtstoAvrg; cntrIndx ++)
 {
  sensorInput = analogRead(A0);          // read ADC of sensor
  //Serial.println(sensorInput);         // diagnostic
                                         //    variable printout
```

```
 sumTobeAvrgd = sumTobeAvrgd + sensorInput;        // sum
} // end of sensor averaging loop
//Serial.println(sumTobeAvrgd);                     // diagnostic
                                                       variable
                                                       printout

sensorInput = sumTobeAvrgd / numPtstoAvrg;         // calculate
                                                      average

//Serial.println(sensorInput);
sumTobeAvrgd = 0;                                   // clear sum
//
// avrgTemp = (((float)sensorInput/(float)1023) * 3.30) *
100 - 50.5;    // TMP36
avrgTemp = (((float)sensorInput/(float)1024) * 3.30) * 100;
// LM35
//
preampOutput = analogRead(A1);              // read preamp output
//Serial.println(preampOutput);                    // diagnostic
//patemp = (((float)preampOutput / (float)1023 * 3.30 / 3.12)
* 100) - 53.3;                      // normalize TMP36 preamp
                                                output to temp
patemp = (((float)preampOutput / (float)1024 * 3.30 / 3.12) *
100);              // normalize LM35 preamp output to temp
//
//Serial.println(patemp, 4);          // diagnostic to ensure
                                            cast to floats in place
//
afeOutput = analogRead(A2);         // ADC value on A2 from AFE
afetemp = (((float)afeOutput / (float)1023 * 3.30 / 31.2) *
100) + 20.3;   // normalize in-amp output to temp as reqd
//
 Serial.print(avrgTemp);
 Serial.print(",");
```

```
Serial.print(patemp);
Serial.print(",");
Serial.println(afetemp, 4);
} // EoP
```

Listing 9-2. Arduino Code for Serial Port, Single-Character Control of Stirring/Agitation Servo Motor

```
// Servo Motor Control from Serial Monitor with single-
   character inputs.
// Do not forget to turn OFF the line endings during character
   transmission
// or the CR and NL will produce 2 extraneous empty character inputs.
// Uppercase S sent from the serial port starts the servo. Any other
// character sent from the serial port stops the servo. For
   long stop periods
// if servo "buzzing" disconnect power.
// oscillator freq: Delay(15) 1 stroke/2 sec, Delay(10) 1
   stroke/sec,
// Delay(5) 2 strokes/sec.
//
#include <Servo.h>          // the servo motor library
Servo myservo;              // create a servo motor instance
int pos = 0;                // the arm position variable in
                               degrees of rotation
char receivedChar;          // the string character variable
boolean newData = false;    // the logic flag variable
                               controlling input read repetition

void setup() {
    Serial.begin(9600);     // start the serial port
    myservo.attach(9);      // set the digital pin to control
                               the servo
```

```
    myservo.write(0);        // set arm to 0 degrees
}

void loop() {
    recvOneChar();           // function to receive 1 character
    showNewData();           // diagnostic function to display
                             //   the character
    testNuChar();            // function to test character and
                             //   act upon test result
}                            // End of program

void recvOneChar() {                    // function body to
                                        //   receive one character
    if (Serial.available() > 0) {       // test for character in
                                        //   buffer
        receivedChar = Serial.read();   // set character into
                                        //   variable
        newData = true;                 // loop() repetetion
                                        //   prevention flag

    }  // E of if
}          // E of fnction
void showNewData() {                    // function to display data
                                        //   character received
    if (newData == true) {              // if statement to limit
                                        //   reading to a single byte
        Serial.print("Control character invoked - ");
        // character display for error diagnostic
        Serial.println(receivedChar);               // display
        newData = false;                // flag set to stop
                                        //   repetetion in loop()

    }     // E of if
}          // E of function
```

```
void testNuChar() {                      // function to perform token
                                         associated actions
  if (receivedChar == 'S') {             // start servo oscillations
    for (pos = 0; pos <= 60; pos += 1) { // goes from 0
                                         degrees to 60
                                         degrees in steps
                                         of 1 degree
      myservo.write(pos);                // tell servo to go
                                         to position in
                                         variable 'pos'
      delay(10);                         // delay time
                                         before return
                                         stroke 15 to 5ms

    }
    for (pos = 60; pos >= 0; pos -= 1) { // goes from
                                         60 degrees to
                                         0 degrees
      myservo.write(pos);                // tell servo to go
                                         to position in
                                         variable 'pos'

      delay(10);                         // delay time
                                         before return
                                         stroke 15 to 5ms
    }                                    // E of Return for loop
  }                                      // E of function if
}                                        // E of function
```

Listing 9-3. DAQFactory Sequence for Plotting of Multiple Data Streams from the Serial Port

```
// Parse Multiple Values from Serial Port in the order in
    which they are sent.
// Sequence auto polls Com3 for streamed comma-delimited
   Arduino data.
// the order in which the data stream is to be parsed for the
   1st, 2nd etc data points.
// Ordering the data plotting ensures the same variable is
   always assigned to the same trace.
// ensure the null protocol has been selected in the protocol window
// and that the correct data is streaming into the DAQFactory serial
// port. Data on the SP must be a carriage return/newline-
   separated stream of n comma-delimited values.
// Create n channels to hold the data for plotting ardyValu_1,
   ardyValu_2 etc.
// To parse out the data use a loop to find the cr/nl delimiters
   convert to numbers and Parse(datin,position #, ",").
// into data1, data2 etc values and then use channel.
   addValue(datan) to assign numerical values to the channels.
//
// clear the buffer
device.Com3.Purge()             // clear old data lines
device.Com3.ReadUntil(13)       // clear any partial line reads
//
while(1)
   try
      //parse first data point for plotting
      private string datain = device.Com3.ReadUntil(13)
      //?datain
         private data1 = StrToDouble(Parse(datain,0,","))
```

```
        ardyValu_1.AddValue(data1)
        private data2 = StrToDouble(Parse(datain,1,","))
        ardyValu_2.addValue(data2)
        private data3 = StrToDouble(Parse(datain,2,","))
        ardyValu_3.addValue(data3)
    catch()
     delay(0.5)
    endcatch
endwhile
```

Summary

-   An AFE can be built from readily available, inexpensive
    op-amps to overcome the digital limitations to
    experimental measurement sensitivity imposed by
    microprocessor ADCs.

-   Using a printed circuit board and a protective metal
    case, an AFE can increase temperature resolution to be
    used with aqueous thermal analysis projects.

-   In Chapter 10, a technique to decrease the noise in a
    stream of sensor data is introduced and demonstrated.

CHAPTER 10

The Kalman Filter

Kalman filters reportedly came to prominence in the early years of the space program as a result of their success in definitively tracking space exploration vehicles. Kalman filters are mathematical processes first applied to extract vehicular courses or trajectories from noise-filled, measured radio-telemetry navigational data. Navigational data involves numerous degrees of freedom, such as roll, pitch, and yaw combined with forward, sideways, and vertical motions. Following a vehicle motion involves simultaneous application of the Kalman filter to each spatial dimension. Simultaneous, multiple filtering requires the application of advanced high-speed matrix algebra that goes beyond the introductory nature of this work. Kalman filtering is often taught by the application of mathematics to models of motion in a single dimension in which the uncertainty in position as a function of time is significantly reduced. The mathematical modeling of an error in a one-dimensional position as a function of time is equivalent to that of errors in a time-based sensor data stream.[1] (See Prof. M. van Biezen presenting the first six lectures of "The Kalman Filter" for an excellent qualitative and quantitative demonstration of the filter theory and practical single-dimension application to the smoothing of a temperature sensor data stream.)

---

[1] http://ilectureonline.com/

© Richard J. Smythe 2021
R. J. Smythe, *Advanced Arduino Techniques in Science*,
https://doi.org/10.1007/978-1-4842-6784-4_10

Kalman filtering can be used to significantly reduce or smooth the noise present in the output of a sensor data stream in which the errors in measurement form a Gaussian or normal distribution about the true value of the parameter being monitored.

The Single-Dimension Kalman Filter Process

As noted, in a Kalman filter smoothing of a single-dimension data stream, it is assumed that the errors in the data stream are of a Gaussian or normal distribution. (See Chapter 7, "Data Errors, Quality Control: Quality Assurance with Statistical Process Control.") A Gaussian distribution is completely defined by its mean value and the variance; hence, the error distributions in the previous, present, and future data points of a data stream are well defined and amenable to processing with the Kalman filter.

In very simplified terms, a Kalman filter can be considered as an iterative mathematical process in which the past data is used to estimate a correction to be applied to the present data in order to predict a more accurate estimate of a future, true value in a data stream. A Kalman filter uses three functions to continuously refine the value of a data stream by determining three parameters called the Kalman Gain, then using the error in the estimate and the error in the measurement to converge on a better estimate of the true value of the streamed data. A Kalman filter converges very quickly on a final output variable value and only uses a few points of data from the recent past to achieve the convergence.

Figure 10-1 records the output voltage taken from the wiper lead of a 10 kΩ potentiometer biased between 5V and ground. Listing 10-1 (provided at the end of the chapter) applies a Kalman filter to the streamed wiper voltage value that is depicted in the spiking orange trace. The code for the Arduino library can be found at `github.com/denyssene/SimpleKalmanFilter`.

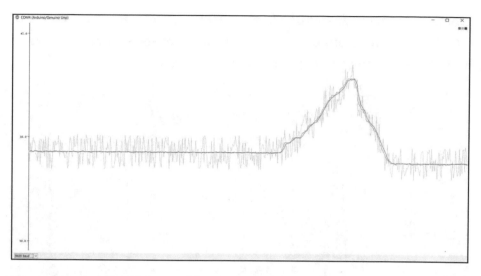

Figure 10-1. *The Kalman filter values from a wiper lead voltage from a 5V biased potentiometer*

Close examination of the expanded-scale recorder tracing of the noise-filled voltage signal from the potentiometer wiper displays the raw signal in orange, the correction in red, and the estimate or calculated value in blue (Figure 10-2).

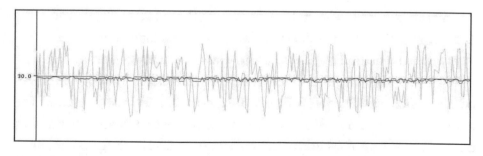

Figure 10-2. *An expanded-scale view of Figure 10-1*

Application of the Kalman filter to the data stream produced by a TMP36 or LM35 ambient temperature sensor and the addition of a sixty-four-point smoothing allows the experimentalist to use the scale

251

expansion of the DAQFactory plotting facility to vastly increase the sensitivity of temperature measurement with these simple, easy-to-use sensors. See Listing 10-2 at the end of the chapter.

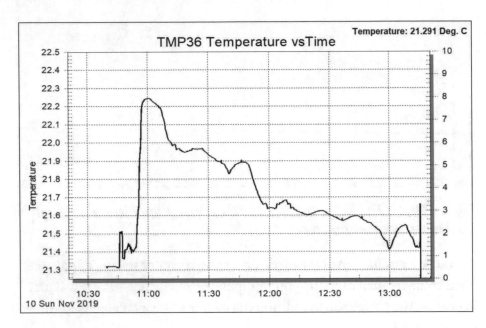

Figure 10-3. *A 1°C graphic recording calibration*

As can be seen in Figure 10-3, with an FSD of 21.25 to 22.50°C or 1.25°C, a nominal 1°C temperature jump in an insulated aluminum dry well, as measured by a mercury-in-glass thermometer, produced a 0.84°C recorder-tracing deflection from 10:50 to 11:00. (For dry-well configuration, see Chapter 3, Figure 3-3, *High Heat and Temperature*.) The cooling curve from 11:00 to 13:00 is marked by the temperature variations caused by the on/off cycling of the building's central heating system. As with other time-based recorded data streams, the tendency for heat to flow and the limitations of insulation to retard that flow are graphically illustrated by the periodic temperature fluctuations in the aluminum mass.

In Figure 10-4, the limitations of scale expansion are seen in the trace portions marked with the arrows.

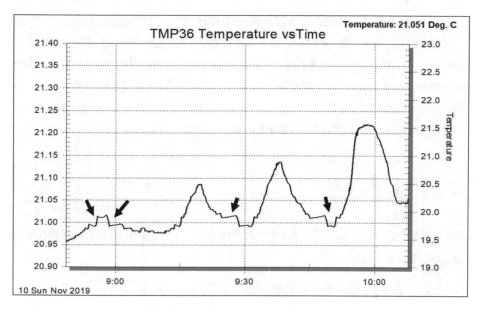

Figure 10-4. *An Arduino limitation on scale expansion*

Although the Kalman filter and signal averaging can greatly reduce the baseline noise in a data stream, there are electronic limitations imposed by the analog to digital converter (ADC) on the amount of scale expansion that can be used to increase signal sensitivity.

In Figure 10-4, certain areas of the trace containing "square steps" are marked with black arrows. The square portions of the trace are in reality the limit of resolution possible with a 10-bit ADC on the Arduino. The stream of data coming from the Arduino is the series of numerical values that have been created when the analog voltage from the sensor passes through the analog-to-digital converter on the microcontroller. At high sensitivities, low temperature differentials are being read, and as the sensitivity is increased to display smaller and smaller temperature differentials eventually the unit-value steps of the ADC are resolved.

The Kalman filter and signal-smoothing statistical packages from the DAQFactory plotting software are able to increase the resolution of the temperature differentials to the point at which the individual digital transitions become visible and limit any further scale expansion.

Sensitivity can be increased in many data-acquisition applications by inserting an analog front end between the sensor and the data-acquisition system in the form of an ASIC, such as the LMP9100, 9150, or 91200 AFE chips from Texas Instruments, or as a circuit built from common components as described in Chapter 9.

Code Listings

Listing 10-1. Arduino Code for a Single-Dimension Kalman Filter of Temperature Data

```
#include <SimpleKalmanFilter.h>
/*
 This sample code demonstrates how to use the
 SimpleKalmanFilter object.
 A TMP36 temperature sensor is used to generate a temperature-
 value data point for the reference real value.
 Random noise will be in the signal data stream, and the
 estimated value obtained from
 the SimpleKalmanFilter should match the real reference value.

 SimpleKalmanFilter(e_mea, e_est, q);
 e_mea: Measurement Uncertainty
 e_est: Estimation of Uncertainty
 q: Process Noise
 */
 //
SimpleKalmanFilter simpleKalmanFilter(2, 2, 0.01);
```

```
// Serial output refresh time
const long SERIAL_REFRESH_TIME = 100;
long refresh_time;

void setup() {
  Serial.begin(9600);
  analogReference(EXTERNAL); // the low noise 3.3 volt reference
                             is used not the noisy 5 volt
}

void loop() {

  // read a reference value from A0 and calculate temperature
     in real_value variable
  float real_value = analogRead(A0);
  real_value = ((float) real_value / (float) 1024) * 3.32;
  // convert to voltage
  real_value = (real_value * 100) - 50;
  // calculate IC off-set

  // add noise to the reference value if required and use as
  the measured value variable
 float measured_value = real_value; // for artificial noise ->  +
                                    random(-100,100)/100.0;

  // calculate the estimated value with Kalman Filter
  float estimated_value = simpleKalmanFilter.
  updateEstimate(measured_value);
  // send to Serial output every 100ms
  // use the Serial Plotter for graphic visualization
  if (millis() > refresh_time) {
    //Serial.println(real_value,4);        // single value for
                                           DAQFtry plotting

    //Serial.print(",");                   // IDE serial plotter
```

```
//Serial.print(measured_value,4);      // IDE serial plotter
//Serial.print(",");                   // IDE serial plotter
Serial.println(estimated_value,4);     // IDE/DAQFtry serial
                                           plotter
//Serial.println();                    // IDE serial plotter

refresh_time = millis() + SERIAL_REFRESH_TIME;
  }

}
```

Listing 10-2. DAQFactory Sequence Code for Plotting a Data
Stream on Com3

```
// This sequence auto polls Com3 for streamed Arduino data
// ensure the null protocol has been selected in the protocol window
// and that the correct data is streaming into the DAQFactory
   serial
// port
// clear the buffer
device.Com3.Purge()
while(1)
   try
      private string datain = device.Com3.ReadUntil(13)
      private data = strToDouble(datain)
      ArduinoStream_ref.addValue(data)
   catch()
      delay(0.1)
   endcatch
endwhile
```

Summary

- Kalman filters originally implemented in three dimensions to track and position space vehicles from noisy telemetry data have found use in reducing the noise in single-dimension data streams from experiments.

- A Kalman filter iteratively uses three parameters called the Kalman gain, the error in the estimate, and the error in the measurement to converge on a more accurate estimate of the true value of the streamed data.

An Arduino microprocessor using a Kalman filter library provides a voltage-based data stream for microprocessor plotting and a temperature-based data stream for a DAQFactory plotting of single-dimension sensor data streams.

APPENDIX 1

List of Abbreviations

A/D	analog-to-digital
ADC	analog-to-digital converter
AGM	absorbed glass mat; a form of lead acid battery
AMR	anisotropic magnetoresistance
API	application programming interface
ASCII	American Standard Code for Information Interchange
ASIC	Application-specific integrated circuits
AO	analog output
AWG	American wire gauge
BCD	binary-coded decimal
BJT	a base junction transistor, either an NPN or a PNP
BLDC	brushless direct current; a type of DC-powered motor
BMS	battery management system
BoB	breakout board; adapter to use SMT IC with a prototyping board
C4D	capacitively coupled contactless conductivity detection
C and C++	a compact efficient programming language and a variation for Windows applications
CCC	constant current charging

(*continued*)

© Richard J. Smythe 2021
R. J. Smythe, *Advanced Arduino Techniques in Science*,
https://doi.org/10.1007/978-1-4842-6784-4

cGLP	current good laboratory practice; a QA/QC protocol
CLR	current-limiting resistor
CMOS	complementary metal oxide semiconductor
CNTRL	control key
COM	serial communication port
cps	cycles per second
CPU	central or computer processing unit; a term used to describe the main processor chip
CPVC	chlorinated polyvinyl chloride
CR	carriage return in printer control code
CSA	Canadian Standards Association
CSM	current shunt monitor; an ASIC for current measurement
CSS	chip slave select in four-line SPI data transmission protocol
CSV	Comma-separated values; a common file data storage format
CV	computer vision
DHCP	dynamic host configuration protocol
DI/O	digital input–output
DIP	dual inline plastic IC package description
D/L	download
DMM	digital multimeter
DPM	digital panel meter
DSP	digital signal processing
DUT	device under test
DVM	digital voltmeter

(continued)

EEPROM	electronic erasable programmable read-only memory
emf	electromotive force
EMI	electromagnetic interference
EPS	electric potential sensors
ERH	equilibrium relative humidity
ESD	electrostatic discharge
FFT	fast Fourier transform or flicker fusion threshold
FOV	field of view
FID	flame ionization detector
FSD	full-screen display or full-scale displacement
GND	ground
GPIO	general-purpose input–output
GPR	Ground-penetrating radar
GPS	global positioning system
GPU	graphics processing unit
GUI	graphical user interface
HAT	hardware added on top; RPi add-on boards
HDMI	high-definition multimedia interface
HMI	human machine interface
HTML	hypertext markup language
HTTP	hypertext transfer protocol
HTTPS	secure hypertext transfer protocol
I^2C or I2C	Inter-integrated circuit data transmission protocol
ICAP	inductively coupled argon plasma; also ICP, a spectroscopic source

(continued)

ICFT	input-capture feature of the timer (Atmega 328)
IDE	integrated development environment
IEPE	integrated electronics piezo-electric; vibration sensors
IMS	ion mobility spectroscopy; plasma chromatography
IMU	inertial measurement unit
INS	inertial navigation systems
INU	inertial navigation unit
I/O or IO	input–output
IP	internet protocol
IR	infrared
ISR	interrupt service routine (programming code)
ISRC	internal stray resistance and capacitance on a circuit board or IC chip
ITO	indium tin oxide
LAN	a local area network of computers
LCD	liquid crystal display
LDR	Light-dependent resistor
LED	light-emitting diode
LF	line feed in printer control code
LFP	lithium iron phosphate; a lithium ion battery chemistry
LiMH	lithium metal hydride; a type of rechargeable battery and chemistry
LSB	least significant bit
MA	a moving average; a form of DSP
MAC	media access control
mAh	milliampere hours; sometimes as mAhr

(continued)

mcd	millicandela; a measure of light intensity
MEMS	micro-electro mechanical systems
MHz	megaHertz; or a frequency of millions of cycles per second
MISO	master in, slave out; four-line SPI data transmission protocol
MOSFET	metal oxide semiconductor field effect transistor
MOS	metal oxide semiconductor
MOSI	master out, slave in; four-line SPI data transmission protocol
MPCLC	multiple-plate capacitor load cell
MPPT	maximum power point transfer
MSB	most significant bit
N.C.	normally closed; relay or switch normal configuration; often NC
NiMH	nickel metal hydride; a rechargeable battery chemistry
NIST	National Institute of Standards and Technology
NMR	nuclear magnetic resonance; a form of spectroscopy and the basis for medical imaging
N.O.	normally open; relay or switch normal configuration; often NO
NPN	a base junction transistor consisting of a P type of semiconductor between two N types
NTC	negative temperature coefficient; a term used with thermistors
OCV	open circuit voltage
OH-MPCLC	over had multiple plate capacitor load cell
O/S	operating system
PC	personal computer; IBM/Microsoft Windows OS
PCB	printed circuit board

(continued)

PDIP	plastic dual inline package
PE	polyethylene; a plastic
PGA	programmable gain amplifier
PID	photo ionization detector; or proportional, integral, derivative; a control algorithm
PIN	an intrinsic PN junction used in high-sensitivity photo diodes; a thick, light-sensitive layer
PIR	passive infrared; an infrared sensor
PLC	programmable logic controller
PM	permanent magnet
PNP	a base junction transistor consisting of an N type of semiconductor between two P types
PV	photovoltaic
PVC	polyvinyl chloride; a plastic
PVDF	polyvinylidene difluoride; an inert plastic polymer
PWD	pulse width difference
PWM	pulse width modulation
PZT	lead zirconium titanate
RMB-PUM	right mouse button pop-up menu
RC	resistor-capacitor electronic circuit time constant elements; or radio controlled
RE	rare earth
REM	rare earth magnet
rf	radio frequency
RFI	radio-frequency interference

(continued)

RGB	red, green, and blue—the three basic colors used in LED displays
RH	relative humidity
rms	root mean square—a measurement form used with AC or sinusoidal power signals
RPi	Raspberry Pi
RPM	revolutions per minute—a measure of rotation speed
RTC	realtime clock
RTD	resistance temperature device
RTV	room temperature vulcanization—a term used to describe a silicone sealant/adhesive
SAR	successive approximation register—a type of ADC
SBC	Single-board computer
SC	specific conductivity
SCADA	supervisory control and data acquisition
SCC	short-circuit current
SCL(K)	the clock line designation in four-line SPI data transmission protocol
SCR	Silicon-controlled rectifier or strip-chart recorder
SD	secure data; a plugin digital data storage media/card
SDA	I^2C serial protocol for slave data
SHE	standard hydrogen electrode
SLI	starting lighting ignition; a form of lead acid battery
SOIC-8	small outline integrated circuit 8-pin SMT defined package format
SIP	single inline package; an IC with only a single row of power–I/O pins

(*continued*)

SMBUS	system management bus; a simple one-wire serial communications protocol
SMT	surface-mount technology
SoC	state of charge or system on a chip
SPAD	single photon avalanche diode
SPC	statistical process control
SPI	serial peripheral interface
SRAM	static random-access memory
SS	slave select
SSR	solid-state relay
TCR	temperature coefficient of resistance
TEC	thermoelectric conversion or converter
TEG	thermoelectric generator
TIA	trans-impedance amplifier
TIG	tungsten inert gas; a form of welding
ToF	time of flight; a form of distance measurement or mass spectrometry
tpi	threads per inch
TTL	transistor–transistor logic
UART	universal asynchronous receiver; transmitter serial data transmission protocol or IC
UAV	unmanned aerial vehicle
ui /UI	user interface
URL	universal resource locator; an internet address
USB	universal serial bus
UTC	universal time coordinates

(continued)

VCO	voltage-controlled oscillator
Vdd	voltage drain, usually the positive supply
VLS	visual light systems; a communications technique
VOM	volt ohm meter
VRSLA	valve-regulated sealed lead acid; a form of battery
Vss	voltage source supply, usually ground potential
VVC	variable value component; a GUI screen numerical display of DAQFactory software

APPENDIX 2

List of Suppliers

Chapter 6	74LS14	`https://www.onsemi.com/pub/Collateral/SN74LS14-D.pdf`
Chapter 8	iDefender	`https://ifi-audio.com/products/idefender3-0/`
Chapter 9	LM358	`http://www.ti.com/lit/ds/symlink/lm2904-n.pdf`
	AD623	`https://www.analog.com/media/en/technical-documentation/data-sheets/AD623.pdf`
	Tower Pro Micro Servo 9G	`http://www.towerpro.com.tw/product/sg90-7/`

© Richard J. Smythe 2021
R. J. Smythe, *Advanced Arduino Techniques in Science,*
https://doi.org/10.1007/978-1-4842-6784-4

Index

A

Analog-to-digital conversion (ADC), 11, 212

Analog-to-digital converter unit (ADU), 212

Analytical front ends (AFE)
  amplification, 213
  calorimeter testing
    acetic acid (CH_3COOH), 238, 239
    adiabatic conditions, 235
    advantages, 237
    hydration sodium chloride, 236
    hydration sucrose, 237, 238
    liquid system, 234
    preliminary testing, 237
    sodium bicarbonate ($NaHCO_3$), 235, 238, 239
    sodium chloride (NaCl), 236
    thermometric titration, 240
    vinegar/baking soda, 239
  IC-based sensors, 211, 212
  microcontroller, 212, 213
  op-amp (*see* Operational amplifiers (op-amp))
  relative temperature-sensor sizes, 209, 210
  serial port data transmission, 240–247
  solid-state temperature sensors, 211
  temperature monitoring, 240–247
  validation/applications, 234

Application-specific integrated circuit (ASIC), 211, 214, 215, 254

Arduino
  code modification, 28
  IDE software program, 2
  input–output capabilities, 2
  interrupts/timing applications
    chronological order, 23
    external events, 21
    fractions, 20
    input switch bounce detection, 24
    interrupts, 22–24
    millis() and micros(), 21
    photogates, 23–25
    software functions, 20
  library manager selection window, 15

© Richard J. Smythe 2021
R. J. Smythe, *Advanced Arduino Techniques in Science*,
https://doi.org/10.1007/978-1-4842-6784-4

Arduino (*cont.*)
    low-cost option, 14
    matplotlib plotting programs
        binary systems, 16
        K thermocouple, 17
        len() function, 17
        Python code, 17
        readline() statement, 20
        ReadSerialPortandSliceData
            utility, 19
        ReadSerialPort utility, 18
        symbolic relationships, 16
        transmission protocols, 16
        ValueError, 20
    meaning, 1
    mechanical
        connections, 4
    numerical symbols, 26, 27
    online forums, 14
    pin interrupt code, 29, 30
    prototyping breadboard, 5
    serial plotter selection, 15
    shields, 4
    Uno specifications, 2, 3
    utility program, 26

B

Brazing, 113–116

C

Calibration procedure, 197
Curve-fitting, 198

D

Display window, 39

E

Electromagnetic compatibility
    (EMC), 200, 202
Error analysis
    accuracy, 192
    comparison chart, 196
    dart board analogy, 191
    data-collection experiment, 193
    data sets, 195
    digital multimeters, 196
    Gaussian distribution, 190
    mathematical notation, 189
    measuring data variation,
        192, 193, 196
    random errors, 191
    repetitive manufacture, 194
    squaring operation, 190
    standard deviation, 191
    statistical notation, 189
Experimental work, 73, *See also* High
        temperatures and high heats
    AC/DC electrical energy, 111
    dry well calibration, 84–86
    K-type thermocouple, 81
    observations
        adjustable test, 106
        MOSFET power-control, 104
        nichrome wire, 104, 105
        PID algorithm, 106

spiral-wound heater
   filament, 104
thermocouple monitor,
   103–106
triac signal effect, 105
powering heading elements
   DC power-controller
      circuit, 90
   isolated components, 92
   K-type monitor, 93
   lab testing, 93
   microcontroller operates, 92
   MOSFET switch, 89
   open-air testing, 91
   sensing system, 91
   serial monitor output, 91
   thermocouple, 89
   triac device, 93
   zero-crossing, 92
refractory insulations, 99–104
resistance-wire heating
      elements
   apparatus design process, 85
   close-coiled filament, 88
   convenient refractory, 88
   cores/molds, 88
   heater-element
      parameters, 86
   heating elements, 87
   isolation, 88
   metal wire resistance, 86
   nichrome resistance
      wire, 85
   requirement, 87

temperature coefficient, 86
   voltage/current, 85
SSR (*see* Solid-state relay (SSR))
temperature measurement,
   81, 82

F

Final control element (FCE), 137
Frequency measurement
   astronomical/geological
      investigations, 174
   control rotation, 181
   cycle period/wavelength
      concepts, 182
   cyclic wave, 174
   electrical signals, 173
   experimental system
      FreqMeasure library, 176
      FreqMeasure program, 178
      kilo hertz, 176
      oscillating signals, 178
      pulse generator, 176
      selections menu, 177
      signal generators, 178
      signal-noise reduction, 179
   hertz, 174, 175
   irregular waveforms, 183
   kits/commercial function, 182
   musical instrument string, 173
   observations, 179–181
   recurring events, 173
   signal conditioning circuitry, 180
   square wave, 182, 183

Frequency measurement (*cont.*)
   streamed serial port data, 181
   timing measurements, 183
Fuel gases, 72, 113–114, 116

G

Gaussian distribution, 186, 190
General purpose input–output
      (GPIO), 11–14
Graphical user interface (GUI),
      34–36, 39, 42, 46, 51–54,
      56, 60

H

Hardware added on top
      (HAT), 10, 11
High-definition multimedia
      interface (HDMI), 8
High temperatures and high heats
   brazing, 115
   failures
      overheated insulation, 110
      oxidized zincs, 109
      thermocouple wires, 107
   fuel gases, 114, 115
   gas heating, 116
   safety consideration
      absorbing/emitting
         radiation, 80
      constant elevated
         temperature, 75
      construction, 73

   electrical energy, 74
   electrical power/sensor
      signals, 76
   energy transfer rate, 79
   filament-type resistance, 75
   galvanized steel, 72
   heating elements/power
      control SSR, 78
   heat input, 79
   measurement/power
      control, 80
   muffle/retort furnace, 73
   nichrome heating-wire
      elements, 74
   numerous salts melting, 77
   physical/electrical
      properties, 76
   power control systems, 74
   steps, 72
   thermal conductivity, 79
   thermo-electric
      properties, 77
   TIG welding electrodes, 80
   wood-burning fireplaces, 72
   zinc coating, 72
source code, 117–125

I, J

Integrated development
      environment (IDE), 2,
      14–16, 35, 162, 233
Interrupt service routine (ISR),
      22, 24, 93

K

Kalman filters
  expanded-scale view, 251
  graphic recording calibration, 252
  mathematical process, 250
  meaning, 249
  scale expansion, 253
  sensitivity, 254
  single-dimension process, 250
  source code, 254–256
  square steps, 253
  wiper lead voltage, 251
K-type thermocouple, 81

L

Light-dependent resistors (LDR),
    12, 13, 149, 150
Local area networks (LAN), 8

M

Microcontroller, 3, 35, 89, 90,
    146–150, 175, 212–213

N

Noise/power system
  electromagnetic
      compatibility, 202
  EMC filter, 200
  high-frequency, 199, 200
  iDefender/5V auxiliary
      installation, 201

reduction devices, 205
signal distortions, 202–205
transmission system, 206
USB 2.0 cables, 199
Non-contacting induction
    heating, 71

O

Operational amplifiers (op-amp)
  adjustable mountings, 229
  agitator plate, 231, 232
  amplifier, 215
  analog voltage signal, 219
  calorimeter experiment, 230, 231
  circuit configurations, 214
  connections, 226
  cyanoacrylate glue, 233
  DC amplifier concept, 214
  DC voltage, 216
  drilled mounting blocks, 228
  graphic demonstration, 218
  high-sensitivity temperature
      measurement, 216
  instrument amplifiers,
      215, 217, 220
  low voltage, 222, 223
  measurement circuit, 223
  microprocessor, 219, 233
  normalized outputs, 219
  normalized temperature
      values, 221
  perfboard circuit
      configuration, 223, 224

Operational amplifiers (op-amp)
(*cont.*)
   prototyping/printed circuit
      board, 217
   recorded temperature
      outputs, 218
   servo motor Arduino
      controller, 230
   shield-mounted circuitry, 225
   solution-agitated
      calorimeter, 228
   substantial input
      impedance, 214
   true sensor temperature, 218
   USB software enumerates, 233
   water ice testing validation, 224
   wooden dowel/mounted
      probe, 226

P

Process control algorithm
   theory
      derivative term, 137, 138
      features, 135
      flow chart, 134
      integral term, 137
      investigation process, 133
      mathematical function, 138
      proportional term, 136
      set point process, 135
      theoretical mathematical
       equation, 135
      time-based format, 136

tuning/practical applications
   control inputs, 139
   controlled process, 139
   doubling process, 143
   in-service undamped
     response, 143
   microcontroller
     program, 143
   oscillation amplitude, 139
   overdamped system, 139
   proportional type, 144
   recorded system, 144
   satisfactory process
     control, 141
   steady-state
     system, 141, 142
   system dynamics, 145
   theoretical system, 140
Proportional, integral, and
   derivative (PID)
   optical brightness
     beam-blocking
      perturbations, 150
     circuit diagram, 148
     control demonstration, 149
     noise examination, 151
   process control algorithm
     (*see* Process control
     algorithm)
   temperature control, 152–158
   thermal control, 145–147
Pulse-width modulation (PWM),
   22, 35, 50, 74, 75, 84, 89–91,
   94, 149, 150

Q

Quality assurance and control
  consecutive data points, 188
  Gaussian distribution, 186
  measurements, 186
  repetitive measurement
      techniques, 185
  standard deviation, 187
  3σ control chart, 187, 188
  weighing device, 188

R

Radio frequency interference
      (RFI), 93
Raspberry Pi
  analog-to-digital conversions, 11
  Arduino, 14–16
  GPIO, 11, 12
  hardware boards, 11
  HAT sense board emulator
      screen, 10
  inherent limitations, 11
  light-dependent resistors, 12
  MCP3008 IC chip, 13
  meaning, 5
  model 3, 7
  pixel file manager, 10
  pixel menus, 9
  SCADA systems, 36
  SPI protocol, 12
  terminal program/file manager, 8
  various models, 6

Real time data plotting and
      visualization
  ADC output, 163
  computing resources, 163
  dual-trace display, 164
  investigation, 162
  processing time, 162
  SCADA systems, 161
  sensor-monitoring
      applications, 165
  standardization, 162
  strip-chart recorder, 166–168
  temperature/pressure,
      164, 168, 170
Refractory insulations
  blanking plate, 102
  firebrick, 100
  free-flowing insulations, 100
  heat transfer, 100
  insulation/chamber design, 98
  non-metallic materials, 99
  outlets/building suppliers, 101
  pot furnace, 102, 103
  semicircular heater
      elements, 101
  testing chamber, 102

S

SCADA, *see* Supervisory control
      and data acquisition
      (SCADA)
Serial peripheral interface
      (SPI), 12, 13

Single-board computer
(SBC), 1, 5, 6, 8
Solid-state relay (SSR)
elevated
temperatures, 97
finer wire heating
elements, 96, 97
heating elements, 95
heavy/fine-gauge heating
wires, 95
inorganic synthesis/organic
analysis, 95
microprocessor
control, 94
PID process-control
algorithm, 94
pot/tube furnace, 95
temperature-control
mode, 96
time proportioning, 94
zero-crossing point, 93
Statistical process control (SPC),
186, 250
Strip-chart recorder (SCR), 63, 65,
66, 68, 69, 163
Supervisory control and data
acquisition (SCADA), 33
button experimental devices,
45–49
event-driven systems, 45
experiment/process-control
system, 34
frame displays, 36–38

graphical data displays
circuit configuration, 60
digitization/serial
transmission, 61
illumination recording, 65
LDR, 64, 66
oscilloscopes, 59
Python's strip-chart
recorder, 60
realtime displays, 59
SCR display, 63, 66, 68, 69
strip chart recording code,
62, 63
types, 59
open source systems, 33
pulse-width modulation, 35
radio buttons controls
code-modification
operations, 56
GUI panel code, 56–58
selection panel, 53, 54
Tkinter modules, 54–56
realtime display
Arduino output data
stream, 43
analog-to-digital
converter, 44
character string, 44
serial port, 41
source code data display, 39
Tkinter documentation, 38
USB serial connection, 38
widget output, 42

RPi systems, 36
significant
  concern, 34
sliding-scale implementation,
  49–53
static sub-window, 38
unit operations, 33, 36

Surface-mount technology
  (SMT), 81, 215

T, U, V, W, X, Y, Z

Tkinter documentation, 38
Tungsten total inert gas (TIG), 80

Printed in the United States
by Baker & Taylor Publisher Services